ANTHROPOLOGY UNBOUND

ANTHROPOLOGY UNBOUND

A FIELD GUIDE TO THE 21ST CENTURY

E. Paul Durrenberger & Suzan Erem

Paradigm Publishers

Boulder • London

green press INITIATIVE

Paradigm Publishers is committed to preserving ancient forests and natural resources. We elected to print *Anthropology Unbound* on 30% post consumer recycled paper, processed chlorine free. As a result, for this printing, we have saved:

12 Trees (40' tall and 6-8" diameter)
5,227 Gallons of Wastewater
2,102 Kilowatt Hours of Electricity
576 Pounds of Solid Waste
1,132 Pounds of Greenhouse Gases

Paradigm Publishers made this paper choice because our printer, Thomson-Shore, Inc., is a member of Green Press Initiative, a nonprofit program dedicated to supporting authors, publishers, and suppliers in their efforts to reduce their use of fiber obtained from endangered forests.

For more information, visit www.greenpressinitiative.org

Copyright © 2007 by Paradigm Publishers

Published in the United States by Paradigm Publishers, 3360 Mitchell Lane, Suite E, Boulder, Colorado 80301 USA.

Paradigm Publishers is the trade name of Birkenkamp & Company, LLC, Dean Birkenkamp, President and Publisher.

Library of Congress Cataloging-in-Publication Data

Durrenberger, E. Paul, 1943–
   Anthropology unbound : A field guide to the 21st century / E. Paul Durrenberger & Suzan Erem.
      p. cm.
   Includes bibliographical references.
   ISBN-13: 978-1-59451-261-2 (hc)
   ISBN-10: 1-59451-261-2 (hc)
   1. Cultural relativism.   2. Anthropology—Philosophy.   3. State, The.   I. Erem, Suzan.   II. Title.
   GN345.5.D87 2006
   306—dc22

                                                                    2006014532

Printed and bound in the United States of America on acid-free paper that meets the standards of the American National Standard for Permanence of Paper for Printed Library Materials.

Designed and Typeset in AGaramond by Straight Creek Bookmakers.

11 10 09 08 07   1 2 3 4 5

CONTENTS

ACKNOWLEDGMENTS

We could start at Olduvai with the first of our ancestors who started to walk on two feet. But that's a long list. This isn't just a joke, it's also an important fact—none of us knows anything by ourselves. We are all in this together. We know our cultures the way we know our languages. And when we learn special parts of our cultures, like anthropology, the same still holds. So Paul thanks all of his teachers and all of his fellow students from undergraduate and graduate school—even though it's a pretty long list.

There are some other anthropologists Paul needs to thank in addition. First are those who have written textbooks that he's read or used to teach, especially three who are now among the ancestors. He has used their ideas so much that they have come to seem like his own. These are:

Roger M. Keesing, *Cultural Anthropology: A Contemporary Perspective* (New York: CBS College Publishing, 1981). But that book was based on an earlier one, published in 1971 by Holt, Rinehart and Winston entitled *New Perspectives in Cultural Anthropology*. That one was in turn based on a 1958 book by Roger M. Keesing's dad, Felix M. Keesing entitled *Cultural Anthropology: The Science of Custom*, also from Holt, Rinehart and Winston.

Charles F. Hockett, *Man's Place in Nature* (New York: McGraw Hill, 1973).

Marvin Harris, *Culture, Man, and Nature: An Introduction to General Anthropology* (New York: Thomas Y. Crowell Company, 1971).

Another is Walter Goldschmidt who is thankfully still with us. His early work on industrial agriculture has been an inspiration as has been his recent (2006) book on human evolution and the human condition, *The Bridge to Humanity: How Affect Hunger Trumps the Selfish Gene* (New York: Oxford University Press).

One of the things these books share is that they are sustained and coherent arguments, empirically supported theoretical statements. When you read them, you know what these anthropologists are saying and why they are saying it. They don't try to tell you everything there is to know about anthropology and they weren't put together by committees to try to make everyone happy.

We've returned to that tradition with this book, but many of our friends and colleagues shared their ideas about what such a text book should be and do.

We especially thank Kendall M. Thu, Karaleah Reichart, and Josiah Heyman who read earlier drafts of this work and helped us write a better book. We owe a special debt to Gísli Pálsson who has contributed much to the substance of this book through his years of friendship and collaboration.

A number of other anthropologists read our proposal and outline and gave us their ideas and support early in the process, when we were just thinking about such a daunting undertaking as yet another introductory anthropology textbook. These include: Edith Turner, Catherine Wanner, Myrdene Anderson, Sandy Smith-Nonini, Robert Muckle, Tom King, Lloyd Miller, Richard Feinberg, Alan Benjamin, Alan Sandstrom, Ann Hill, Barbara Dilly, Beverly Ann Davenport, Christian Zlolniski, Cynthia Miki Strathmann, David Griffith, Ana Pitchon, Garry Chick, Jim Acheson, John Steinberg, Joyce Lucke, Larry Kuzner, Lois Stanford and Peter Richardson.

Suzan knows it's the anthropologists who make this book what it is, and thanks all of those listed here and others she talked to about the project for their support and their enthusiasm for an affordable, accessible textbook. She also thanks Paul for his keen sense of when to fight over an edit and when to agree to one. Few spouses have the good fortune of the writing partnership we share.

We also thank the editor of Paradigm Publishers, Dean Birkenkamp, who encouraged us to take on this project when we complained to him the lack of affordable comprehensive anthropology textbooks and who supported our approach to the topic.

USER'S GUIDE FOR INSTRUCTORS

We started thinking about this book because we were angry about the outrageous prices of textbooks for introductory courses. To us, that's an issue of class, one of the focal points of this book. It's more important to our daily lives than most of us think, it's a good example of our culture misleading us, and it's an excellent example of a political system manufacturing cultural concepts—all good material for today's anthropology.

But we also wrote it because so many introductory anthropology texts are just bad books. They look like committees have cobbled them together over long periods of time with a bit of this and a bit of that and everyone's favorite examples. Simply put, they are bland. They kill the excitement we feel for anthropology.

One colleague pointed out that a textbook is a means to an end. Students need a source of material they can review so they can understand what is going on in the course and to help them with the exams. Our colleague went on to say that he endeavors to address the world from the students' points of view but then to "pull the cultural rug out from under them," by respectfully challenging their assumptions about how the human world operates. That first exposure to the power of the concept of cultural relativity can be an epiphany. It may be unsettling, and it challenges students' senses of reality. To some, it's exciting as it opens a whole new world of concepts and experiences. To others, it is a threat because it rocks their sense of self and reality and looses all of the pests of Pandora's box upon them in the form of unsettling questions and doubts.

This becomes an opportunity to help students rebuild their worldviews by teaching them what anthropology *knows*:

- how science is different from other worldviews;
- how systems work and how to analyze them;
- that everyone today is connected in a global political economy;

- how and why people in different systems develop different world-views;
- the relationships among how people think, what they do, and the results of their actions.

Teaching what anthropology *is* gets us into the same groove that most of the introductory books are in now, and the last thing we need is another expensive, slickly illustrated compendium of assorted exotica in full-color native regalia with a catalogue of names, theories, and approaches combined with banks of questions to use on exams and quizzes, a Web site, an instructor's manual, and its own CD. We're not going to pummel you with every possible ethnographic example from around the world, either. Making their heads spin isn't going to help students learn. We offer many examples, but we choose a handful to refer to throughout the book so that by the end, you and your students can feel somewhat familiar with the Icelanders, Lisu, Shan, American union members, and others.

At the risk of sounding old-fashioned, cheap, or cynical, we believe those bells and whistles are just a means of jacking up prices to increase profits for publishing conglomerates. A textbook should be a guide to teaching and learning, not "Anthropology-in-a-Box" that contains everything you'll ever need to teach an anthropology course. Any intro book that promises that is selling you and your students short. This book gives you a framework for a semester of discussion, exams, questions, and answers. We know you are the best one to do the rest with your experience and your knowledge. So you can use this book to help you pass that on to your students.

We know that you have to give the students grades and that they have to do something to earn them, but our students are not children who need traditional textbooks to walk them through every answer that they must memorize for the test. We provide enough structure for exams but allow for more creative thinking as well.

Today's anthropology students are either young adults, just learning how to apply what they know to what they are learning, or older students who have even more to bring to the discussion but who may also bring with them more entrenched ideas of how the world works. They want to know how their learning relates to their lives. Given the opportunity, all students can be proactive in their educations. We can't teach anyone anything, but we *can* show them how to educate themselves. Our job is to facilitate our students' learning. This book, combined with your experience and knowledge, will allow students to *learn*.

We wrote this book:

For instructors—

- to provide exam materials and provocative questions for class discussion and essays;
- to give you a simple, affordable guide to current anthropology that speaks the language of your students;
- to show what anthropology knows when students open their minds to the new world order and start asking, "What can we do about this?"

For students (because we know you're reading this guide for instructors)—

- to provide material that you can refer to in preparing for exams and other exercises to get your grade in this course;
- to explain what anthropology knows in a way ordinary people can understand without assuming that you're an idiot;
- to give you a means to understanding the world you live in and your place in it.

Intro

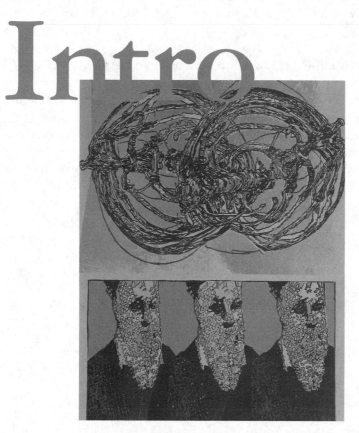

"Presume Something Happens."
Art courtesy of Roxanne Sexaur.
Used with permission

INTRODUCTION, OR HOW TO READ THIS BOOK

This is a book about anthropology—the study of people and their cultures. It will give you an idea of what anthropology has learned, how anthropologists think things through, the kinds of evidence we use, and the explanations we have worked out.

We're going to start that here by explaining how to read this book. First, why should you read it?

The best reason is because you want to learn what anthropology can tell you, what it knows. If that's why you picked it up, great, read on. But lots of folks will probably be reading it because a professor assigned it for a class. That's fine, too. Professors assign some of the world's best books for students to read in classes. You learned the drill for classes a long time before you got here. People have been teaching you since about the time you could walk about how to go to classes and take exams and sit still in a chair for an hour or two and how to pretend to be listening while your mind is off somewhere else.

How much of that was information you could use for anything? Not much. Except you could use it for getting out of that class and moving on to the next one and so on until you got here. But what's the point of it all? Only a tiny part of all that knowledge teaches you how to fix computers, run a business, or help sick people in hospitals. What is all the rest of it for?

Let's see what an anthropologist would do with this question. We want to figure out what the role of schools is in our society and why we have them. To do that, we have to be able to imagine something different—for instance, a society in which you learn everything you need to know just by growing up and people never see the inside of a school. That's the kind of vision anthropologists have; that's the kind of questions we ask.

So, why do we go to school? An anthropologist named Jean Lave (1988) observed that kids who don't do well in school could do very complex computations to figure out a number of bowling scores at the same time. How could they do that and *not* do well in math in school? She also noticed that people who *have* been to school don't use mathematics the way they were taught. When they are shopping and trying to figure out what jar of peanut butter to buy, people don't figure out the cost per ounce for the big jar and the little one and then select the best buy even though that's what we were all taught to do.

What we really do, she found out by observing lots of people, is compute by ratios. The big jar is about twice as much as the small one and costs less than twice as much. So it's the best buy.

Lave asked, if people aren't in school to learn the math they actually use, what are schools worth? In terms of the things we actually do, she came to the same conclusion many of you probably have come to. Not much.

So why do we have them? Why do we pay for them? Why do we hire teachers to teach if nobody is doing what they teach?

Lave's answer is that in the old days people knew their place. There were aristocrats and commoners. Everyone knew aristocrats were better than commoners, and everyone knew how to get along in that system. But in democracies nobody is supposed to be any better than anybody else. If that's so, how are we going to decide who gets the good jobs and who gets the bad ones? On the basis of merit.

Merit is something you earn. Nobody gives it to you. You aren't born with it. The problem was, how do you assign merit if everyone is going to be equal? One answer is to use school performance.

So, Lave argues, schools are the way of assigning merit to individuals in democratic systems. Many of you know exactly where you stood in your high school graduating class. You probably feel pretty good about that if you were somewhere toward the top. And if you were toward the bottom, chances are, you didn't go to the next level of school. If you did, all the better for you. Why would we say that? Isn't that rewarding someone for underperforming? For being less than meritorious? Could be, if you think that how people do in school is really a measure of their worth. But Lave's point is that it is not. It isn't even a good measure of how good they are at math, something that's supposed to be the strong suit of schools, that's supposed to be something you can only learn in school.

Is this wrong? Is it good?

One of the things anthropology teaches, and one of the things we'll talk about a lot in this book, is that we don't make judgments like that. To understand, we cannot judge. Our job is to understand and explain, not to judge. More on that later.

We're not asking whether that's good or bad; we just want to understand it. If you understand what's going on, you may be able to do something about it. We'll come back to that one later, too.

Here's another thing about anthropology. We all agree that the world is very complex. But instead of saying, "All things being equal," anthropologists say, "Let's understand the complexity of it."

Reality is complex, and it isn't going anywhere special; it's just there in all of its horrible and beautiful complexity. We have to figure out how to get along with that. Our different cultures give us different ways of doing that so that we don't all have to start from scratch. We learn from watching our parents. It doesn't matter much what they tell us. It matters what they do.

If your parents tell you that they love each other, but all you ever see them do is fight, you don't believe what they tell you. It isn't true to your experience. If they tell you that money isn't everything but spend all their time working and worrying about money, you don't believe it because it's not true to your experience. But you also learn what you're supposed to say.

The same for school. If your math teacher tells you to compare values by figuring out the per unit price and comparing them, you can do it, but you also know that's not what you do when you're shopping. People are good at learning by doing. And we're good at learning what we're *supposed* to know and say. Walter Goldschmidt (2006) even says that's the most important and basic thing about being human. It's bred into us as a species by natural selection.

That's why you're going to read this book and learn how to use it to help you get a good grade in your anthropology course. But we're going to try to make it close to your experience, too, so that you don't have to make that same leap as you do when you say the "right answers" to questions about love, money, and math.

But that comes with a price. The price is that you're going to have to give up some cherished ideas or at least suspend them for a while. If you want to understand your experience, you have to go beyond the easy answers your culture provides for you. That's what anthropology is all about.

There's a method for doing that. It's scientific method. It's a method for bringing what we say closer and closer in line with what we experience. When we think we know what we're talking about, we have to check it against experience. We also have to give up the idea that we're the smartest and most observant people on the planet. We have to agree that anyone else could see the same things we see—that's what we call *reliability*. And we have to make sense to other people—that's what we call *validity*. Scientific method is a way of keeping what we say connected to what everyone can experience.

There are a lot of connections going on here, but there's a way to keep track of these connections. Like all of the things we mentioned, this is a matter of putting simple things together until they seem complex, or the other way around—breaking complex things down into simple relationships so that we can check them one by one. We can do this with words and with pictures. So far we've been doing it with words, talking about culture. Let's take something more concrete and develop some pictures to go with the words.

Eric Schlosser (2002) is not an anthropologist. He's a journalist who wrote a book called *Fast Food Nation.* It's not an **ethnography** (we're going to highlight every vocabulary word we think you'll need to understand the concepts that come later; you'll find them in the back of the book in a glossary), which is what anthropologists call it when they live with a people and observe everything they do and say, but Schlosser compiled a lot of information about relationships that have gone into forming our culture. Paul's students like the book, so you might want to have a look at it some time.

Schlosser wants to understand all facets of fast food. He starts out talking about cars and the American love of our cars. What do cars have to do with fast food? Some restaurant owners in California made the first innovations in fast food to mass-produce hot meals for people in the same way that factories mass-produce cars, but they might have stayed in California if there wasn't more and more demand for fast food.

Automobile companies bought up the interurban and urban railroad systems and destroyed them so that people would have to either drive or ride the buses the car companies made. When mass transit was destroyed, people bought cars. Demand for fast food came as people drove more, and the interstate highway system intensified that trend. The interstate system started out as a defense project to link the United States after World War II, but it became a way for people to drive longer and longer distances. When more people had cars and there were more highways to drive on, people moved into suburbs, and developers built what we now call sprawl.

Why fast food? Because of cars. More interstate highways, more cars, and more sprawl. Cars make sprawl possible, and sprawl means people have to have cars because there's no alternative mass transit. We can make a map of these relationships (see figure I-1). Figure I-1 on the next page means more cars, more fast food; more interstate highways, more fast food. More interstate highways, more sprawl. More interstate highways, more cars; more cars, more interstate highways. More sprawl, more cars; more cars, more sprawl. More sprawl, more fast food.

Take some time to study the diagram, because you'll see a lot more of them in this book, and they get hairier as we go along. Here are some things to look out for in these diagrams. How many boxes are there? Here there are four. What are the boxes? Here, they are "fast food," "interstate highways," "sprawl," and "cars." Next, how may arrows are there? Here there are eight.

We expect that, like it or not, next time you get into a car, you will see things just a little differently. Maybe you will start asking yourself and

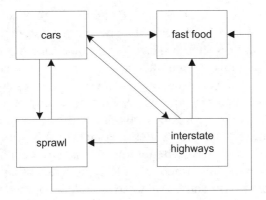

Figure I-1 U.S. fast food system.

others questions. For instance, where is the mass transit system where you live? If there is one, how well does it work? Why is every place connected with highways? This book will help you figure out what some of those questions are and how to answer them.

We think this sort of thinking contributes to democracy by helping people be more aware of the conditions of their own lives. We've been driving down interstates when we got hungry. We've been in a hurry to get home after a long trip. We've pulled over at a fast food joint and got burgers and fries. We've both read Schlosser and lots of other things that tell us that fast food isn't the healthiest choice. We've read lots about different corporations, and we've experienced some of that. We know about congestion and sprawl and global warming, and there we were being part of the problem. We were eating unhealthy food, contributing to a corporation that treats its workers unjustly and to an agricultural system that's unsustainable, and spewing hydrocarbons into the atmosphere as we did it.

Pretty reprehensible folks, aren't we? That's why we're not going to try to preach to anyone. To get where we were going ... well, you've been there. And we were hungry. We felt like we didn't have much choice. And we like burgers and fries. We don't advocate taking it as far as Morgan Spurlock, the guy who made the movie *Super Size Me*. He wanted to find out what would happen if he ate nothing but McDonald's food for a month. It's not pretty. Part of his test was that he had to eat everything on the menu at least once. So he had lots of choices.

Sooner or later anthropologists come to that question of choice. When do people have real choices and when do they not? We have a fancy word for that: **agency**. That word means different things in different contexts, but here it means how often you have real choices you can make.

This may be a required course. Your agency is nil. You have to take it. But maybe it's required only for certain programs of study. Nursing. Once you decide to take nursing, you have to take anthropology. But you could have decided on business, and then it wouldn't be required. If you are in a business program, you probably take anthropology as an elective. You can choose it or not. It's your choice. Finally, nobody said you had to go to college. You could have gone to work full-time in a fast food joint instead of part-time as a student. But someone probably told you that if you went to college, you'd have a better job and make more money later, so it would be worth the investment of time and money. What if you lived in a society that said you don't have to go to college, or med school, or law school, and we'll pay you just as much as someone who did? What does that do to your choices? Or what if they said, if you want to go to college, we'll pay the tuition and buy your books?

So agency depends on your point of view, on where you are in a system and what choices that system offers you. It also depends on your past choices, like the choice to go to college. But the choices that are available depend on the choices other people have made. Like the fact that somebody set up the college you're attending. In democratic societies, people are supposed to have a lot of agency, people are supposed to be able to make lots of choices about the significant things in their lives.

But now, let's go back to how to read the kinds of diagrams you are going to come across in this book. Some more vocabulary. We can call *fast food* in our diagram a **dependent variable**. Dependent variables hang on, or depend on, every other variable in the system. It is the thing we want to explain. Every other thing in the system is also a variable. A **variable** is something that can be more or less—it varies. So there can be more cars or fewer cars; more miles of highway or fewer; more or less sprawl. Each of these variables is an **independent variable** because each one causes or has something to do with the amount of fast food, the dependent variable.

Most real-world relationships aren't simple. For instance, more cars mean more highways, and more highways *also* mean more cars. These two are **interdependent**, like *cars* and *sprawl*. When an increase in one variable means an increase in another, and *that* increase means an increase in the first one, we have a circle, or a loop, as we call it. The more of the first, the more of the second; the more of the second, the more of the first. This is what we call a **self-intensifying loop** or process. It keeps growing with nothing that we know of to stop it.

All such processes grow or increase. Not only do they increase, but the rate of increase increases. So they are exponential. Instead of being straight-line processes that grow at the same rate, they grow faster and faster.

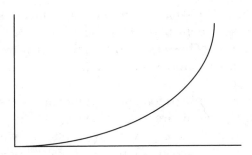

Figure I-2 Exponential curve

This chart (figure I-2) is an **exponential** curve of growth. You've probably noticed that there's no limit here. That's one observation about exponential systems. But the other observation is that, unlike a mathematical equation, in real life there is always some limit. No such curve of growth is **sustainable**. That means that any time we see a system that contains self-intensifying loops, we are looking at a system that's more or less doomed to destruction.

The classic example is yeast. A few yeast cells multiply, and there are more. But each one multiplies at the same rate, so the rate of growth of the whole population is exponential. Yeast consumes sugar and produces alcohol as waste. So pretty soon our liquid is teeming with reproducing yeast cells, each one producing alcohol and consuming sugar, until the level of alcohol becomes toxic and they all die. Then we take over and drink what they left us. Good for us. Bad for the yeast.

So, to get these diagrams, you'll need to remember the ideas of dependent variable—the thing we're trying to understand or explain; independent variables—the things in the system that influence the dependent variable; interdependent variables—variables that influence each other; self-intensifying loop—a circular relationship between two or more variables that keeps increasing each variable; and exponential curve of growth—a process whose rate of increase increases.

One more important idea about these systems is indirect relationships. *Sprawl* doesn't directly determine *highways*, but more sprawl means more cars, and more cars means more highways, so the relationship is indirect, through *cars.*

Schlosser goes on to show how sprawl means increased land prices around cities, and that means increased land and inheritance taxes that contribute to the decline of farms; how the interstate highway system makes possible industrial food preparation far away from the sites of consumption, and how that contributes to industrial food production and the destruction of local markets and economic linkages. So nowadays slaughter houses don't depend on the pigs from an independent farmer. Family farmers are out of business, and corporations own their farmland, pigs, and slaughtering factories now. The family farms that are left are contracted to big corporations that dictate every term.

At the other end, industrial food preparation means deskilling of jobs like cooking, and that means firms can use cheap and untrained labor; and that means low incomes, especially for teenagers who work in fast-food places; and low income contributes to people being depressed and dropping out of school; and that contributes to poverty and crime. Meanwhile, the cheap labor means more profits for the corporations and high pay for corporate officers. Those two things, the high profit rate and high pay for corporate officers, mean that corporations have money to contribute to political candidates who agree to support their view of the world and push legislation that favors the whole process, so the firms and their officers get involved in politics and use their influence to keep the minimum wage low so that the corporations will have access to cheap labor.

There are laws that are supposed to regulate job safety. The Occupational Safety and Health Administration (OSHA) is supposed to enforce the laws. It depends on Congress for funding. If it has no funds, it can't enforce the laws. Schlosser documents how corporate involvement in politics has made OSHA's job next to impossible.

Schlosser also shows how corporate politics gets firms subsidies and loans from the government, a kind of welfare for corporations.

There are also effects on our culture. Many people think that corporations are business, that business is not involved in government, and that government is not involved in business. That's wrong, but it suits corporations and politicians if people think that, so they invest money in creating those ideas and pounding them into us from all directions.

Here anthropologists borrow an idea from political science. **Hegemony** means when one country rules or controls others. So, we could say the Soviet Union used to have hegemony over Ukraine and Kazakhstan. Anthropologists use the same word when one group has power over another, especially by controlling the way they think. So we can say that in the United States, corporations are hegemonic, meaning that they have a lot of power to control peoples' culture and everyday thinking patterns by telling us what's natural, normal, and just something we have to accept.

If you want to, you can put all of these relationships in a diagram, starting with the part that we provided earlier with cars, highways, sprawl, and fast food. If you read Schlossser's book, you can add in meat packing, costs to local governments, immigration, turnover rates, drug use, union busting, insurance rates, and insurance fraud as well as subsidies to households, cultural hegemony, and the spread of disease.

Does that make the fast food industry good or bad? It wasn't that good for Morgan Spurlock, the *Super Size Me* guy, but he could quit. But it's not up to anthropologists to judge, just to understand. Maybe it wasn't that good for Spurlock, but it might have been good for some of the people who worked in McDonald's. When anthropologist Katherine Newman (1993) did the ethnography of fast-food workers in New York's Harlem, she found that the jobs were pretty good, given everything else going on around them. Fast-food joints gave them an alternative to their family lives that weren't always that good, a group of people to be with, a constructive way to structure their time that wasn't gang banging or something dangerous and against the law, some income, and these workers actually did better in school than kids without jobs.

Good for beer and wine drinkers is bad for yeast. Good for corporate officers may be bad for their workers; good for workers may be bad for corporate officers; good for politicians may be bad for their constituents. Schlosser documents a number of such relationships. From inside the system, we can say what's good for whom. Within a system, we can make judgments. We are citizens of democracies. We can ask what kinds of things make them more or less democratic. If we value democracy, the things that make our societies more democratic are good.

Aside from questions of good and bad, though, we can ask questions about sustainability. Spurlock's diet wasn't sustainable. His doctor said he would have died. Wherever there are self-intensifying loops, the system is not sustainable. At the same time, we have to point out that sustainable systems may look a lot like life in the Stone Age. And that wasn't sustainable in the long run because nobody lives that way anymore. The remaining hunters and foragers who in some ways resemble it are parts of larger systems. The fierce hunters of the Amazon sell their game, buy shotguns and ammunition, and use factory-made machetes. The burning of forests to clear them for pasture for cattle even determines the kind and number of animals that live in the forests for them to hunt. So these hunters are as much parts of the global system as anyone else.

Anthropology shows us what kinds of creatures we are, where we came from, and how we got to be the way we are. To us, almost nothing is left to "human nature." That's where we start this book. That'll get you right into the systems way of thinking we've been talking about here. Most folks have some stories about where they came from and how they got to be the way they are. We call these *origin stories*. So we're going to tell you the origin story that anthropologists have worked out. But before we go there, we're going to show you an example of another origin story so you'll be able to recognize this kind of story whenever you hear one.

Summary—How to Use This Book

Keep track of things like definitions and relationships. Work through all of the diagrams. Take the time to read the text and then study the diagrams. You can test yourself by reproducing the diagram. If you can do that, you understand the process. If you can't, it's a good idea to go back and try again.

Rocket scientists aren't smarter than you; they just did the work to understand the systems and relationships that have to do with rockets. This isn't rocket science. It's a whole lot more complex than that. That doesn't mean you have to be a genius to understand it. You just have to keep your eyes and your mind open.

If you do that, you will come to see yourself and your society and your culture in a different way. You will start to ask hard questions when you read the newspaper or hear the news. And you will have a way of beginning to answer some of those questions.

Do those things, and you become a better citizen. If lots of people do those things, we have a better society. In a democracy, that's a good thing.

PROLOGUE: IN THE
BEGINNING

In the beginning, there was the nothing; but to the south of nothing, everything was fire, and to the north, everything was ice. A giant formed where the warmth from the south caused water to drip from the ice. The giant lived on the milk that flowed in four rivers from a cow that lived by licking the salty ice. As she licked, a man appeared in the ice.

The son of the man married the daughter of a giant, and they had three sons. The first son was named Odin. These three killed the first giant, and his blood drowned the other giants except one, who got onto a hollowed log boat with his wife. The three then took the giant's remains to the middle of the emptiness and made the world from the parts. They made the sea from his blood; land from his flesh; mountains from his bones; rocks and pebbles from his teeth and jaws; and the sky from his skull. They put the sky over the earth and called the corners East, West, North, and South. They used sparks blowing from the fire in the south to make stars, planets, the sun, and the moon.

From the eyebrows of the giant they built a fortress around the world to protect them from the hostile giants. They called that place Middleworld and threw the giant's brains into the sky to make clouds.

There were two trees on the shore. Odin gave them spirit and life, and his brothers gave them understanding, movement, speech, sight, and hearing. All people come from those two, and the brothers gave them Middleworld to live in and built a fortress for themselves in the middle of it. They called it Godworld, and all the gods and their families live there. The gods are the children of Odin and his wife. Their first son was Thor. There is a wolf named Fenrir, who is half-god and half-giant. He is so destructive, the gods chain him up. The gods and giants and people keep on until the end.

The end is called Ragnarok. It starts with three bad winters in a row when there is no power in the sun. There are battles, and brothers kill each other for greed. Brothers and sisters sleep together. It is an axe age, sword age, wind age, and wolf age. The wolf that has been chasing the sun catches and swallows it. Another wolf bites the moon. The stars disappear. The earth and mountains shake until the trees and mountains fall down. The wolf, Fenrir, will break loose. The serpent that surrounds the earth will try to come ashore, and the sea will crash against the land. Fenrir comes, mouth wide open, upper jaw against the sky, lower jaw on the earth, eyes blazing. The serpent blows poison over the sky and sea. The gods ride across the rainbow bridge to the world but the bridge breaks. They go to a plain where the wolf and serpent wait. All the giants join the side of the wolf and serpent.

Odin rides in a helmet of gold toward Fenrir, the wolf. Thor is beside him and fights the serpent. Each god fights a giant. Thor kills the serpent just before dying from the snake's poison. The wolf swallows Odin. Another god puts his foot on the lower jaw of the wolf and his hand on his upper jaw and rips him in half. The giants and gods kill each other, and fire covers the earth.

All of the gods and people are dead, and the earth is burned up.

This is the story we have from the Icelandic scholar Snorri Sturlason, who wrote it down in the thirteenth century as "The Deluding of Gylfi," the story of the Swedish king who goes to talk to the gods to find out how the world came to be as it is.

Back in 1975, Miles Richardson wrote:

> The myth teller, the epic poet, stood on the fringes of his society and told of the great struggle between gods and humans, how they fought and how they loved. The poet knew these experiences; he felt their heat and pull, but something within him drove him to the margins of society where he could see all that was happening.... What he saw moved him. Before him stood the great hero. Two-thirds god, the hero wanted to do everything, learn everything, and understand everything. Because of the god-part that was in him, he could not accept death and strove to conquer it; but because of the human-part, he failed. He was the tragic hero, magnificent in strength, splendid in appearance, courageous in heart, but with one fatal flaw: he was one-third man. The myth teller saw in the struggles of the hero the lot of man. Man's lot is that he question; but it is equally his lot that he receive no answer. (pp. 528–529)

Odin, father of all people and gods, trades his eye for the knowledge of runes, writing. Thor, his son, combats giants and tries to compete with them, but he cannot drink the whole ocean and loses his wrestling match with old age. Snorri Sturlason wrote down the stories, but the verses they are based on is from the *Poetic Edda,* which he also wrote down. Those verses are attributed to a woman who was a visionary.

It's one story of origins. Here, we are going to start at the beginning, too, with the story anthropologists tell about how we got to be what we are. It's a good story, even if we don't know the names of any of the people. There may be some wolves in the story, but no giants, and no gods, and nothing as awesome as the world serpent or Fenrir. We didn't learn the story from the gods but from searching the world for evidence to interpret by the methods of science.

It's not the only story of human origins. Many different cultures have such stories about the beginnings of people. Anthropologists try to understand all of these stories because they teach us a lot about the cultures of the people who make and tell them.

The scientific story may not be the most dramatic, but we keep working on it, keep getting new evidence, and keep refining it so we can better know what kinds of animals we are—animals that walk on two feet, animals with language, animals with culture—and how we got to be this way.

A lot of cultures also have stories about how the world will end. Anthropologists don't agree on how it all ends. Some used to say it would be in a nuclear holocaust. Nowadays some say we will go out with a whimper as we poison our environment. Most of us don't know and don't care to speculate on things that we cannot know. We're content to wait and see how it all turns out.

Someone asked Nasrudin Hodja, the central Asian wise man, when the world would end. He said that would be when he died. "When you die the world ends?" this person asked, amazed. "For me it does," the wise man replied.

So our story doesn't go all the way to the end, just up to now.

Discussion Questions

- What are some of the things this creation story tells us about the Norse people who made it and told it?
- Can you think of any other creation stories? What do they do for the people who make and tell them?
- Why is it important for anthropologists to know the scientific creation story?
- What's the difference between a scientific creation story and other ones?

One author gets down and dirty! Paul Durrenberger is in over his head in this fieldwork in Iceland. *Photo by Rita Shepard. Used with permission.*

CHAPTER 1

SCIENCE BASICS

Anthropology asks how cultures and societies work and how they got that way. It asks about the history of our species from the beginning until now. It asks what kind of animals we are, how we got this way, in what ways that affects our cultures, and—the other way around—in what ways our cultures affected the kind of animals we are. To answer these questions, anthropologists specialize in one of four subfields.

Biological anthropology focuses on the history of our species, how we came to be the kinds of animals we are, and the role of culture in the process—questions about our biological nature and its relationship to culture. **Archaeology** concentrates on gathering and interpreting material evidence we can use to understand the histories of our cultures. **Linguistic anthropology** asks about the nature of language and how it is related to culture. **Sociocultural anthropology** is about how contemporary cultures and societies work and how they got this way.

Biological anthropology overlaps with anatomy and biology; archaeology can overlap with history and classics; linguistic anthropology overlaps with linguistics; and sociocultural anthropology can overlap with economics, political science, religious studies, history, comparative literature, and other social sciences and humanities. So being a sociocultural anthropologist is a lot like being a professional undecided major.

We are concerned here with sociocultural anthropology. We're not so much concerned with what anthropology *is* as with what it *knows*—the results of the work of many anthropologists for the past hundred years and more. But to understand that, we need go into some basic assumptions.

Three things make sociocultural anthropology distinct from other social sciences or humanities:

- It is holistic.
- It is comparative.
- It is ethnographic.

5

Holism means seeing things as connected. Instead of looking at religion, literature, politics, economics, or history as separate spheres of life, anthropologists see them as connected. Anthropologists think in terms of systems. A **system** is a set of elements connected such that if you change one of them, you also change the others. So we might ask how changes in an economic system affect the political system and how both of these affect religion, how all of these affect literature, and how literature and religion affect economics. Something about the religion may affect how people understand their history, and how people understand their history might affect their political system.

Everything may be connected to everything else, but some of the connections are stronger and more important than others. While knowing that everything is connected may not help us understand the price of tea in China, as they say, knowing about systems of trade does.

Comparative means noticing and explaining similarities and differences among many different systems. For example, some social systems have institutional forms known as states, but others do not. Anthropologists ask what else goes along with states. To answer questions like this, we compare as many examples as we can to find out what other things always go with states and what things go with not having states.

Ethnographic means that we base our ideas of how any given system works on detailed local description. We don't rely on data sets from the Census Bureau or the Department of Planning. Ethnography means learning about the systems and people we want to understand by as close observation as we can manage. It often means living with the people, doing **fieldwork**.

There's a saying that to understand all is to forgive all. If you could really understand all the circumstances and reasons another person does things, it would all make sense to you, and you would see that you would do the same thing if you were that person. If you would do the same thing, you can't judge the other person. The flip side of this is that if you want to understand someone, you don't judge the person.

So understanding means getting into another person's skin. Ancient Aztec people took that farther than most of us would want to when they skinned their war captives and wore their skins in ceremonies. But we could understand the practice if we could get into their, well, systems of culture and society. To do that, we can't start off with the opinion that it's horrid to skin other people. That stops the questions and makes a conclusion before we start.

To do fieldwork means to suspend judgments and opinions and be open to understanding other ways of life. Anthropologists call this philosophical stance **cultural relativity**. We try to describe the points of view of the people we want to understand, and we do this by being there with the people in our fieldwork, doing ethnography.

The opposite of cultural relativity is **ethnocentrism**, thinking that your way of doing things is either the only way or the best way. All people think their way of seeing things is obvious and natural. For example, of course a person only marries one other person at a time. Or of course you pay money for a product you get at the store. That's one of the features of culture—ethnocentrism is built into it. But once we understand that, and we open our heads to the ways other people make sense of the world, we can try to be less ethnocentric and more relativistic in our thinking.

Melford Spiro, an anthropologist who studied people in Israel and Burma, defined three kinds of cultural relativism:

- Descriptive relativism
- Ethical relativism
- Epistemological relativism

Descriptive relativism means suspending your natural ethnocentrism so that you can describe another culture from the point of view of the people in it. It allows you to understand other cultures.

Ethical relativism is the idea that there are no absolute values of good and bad; ethical judgments depend on the culture. You judge an Aztec skinning a captive by Aztec standards, not by your own. This helps us understand other people because it teaches us not to judge them by different standards. That doesn't mean that we have to accept their standards, but it does mean we can't judge them.

There is a debate about where the line between accepting another system of values and not judging it should be. One subject of the debate is female genital mutilation that some African and Mediterranean cultures do. Some people say that calling it "mutilation" is already judging it and that we should be more descriptive and call it "female genital cutting" because it involves cutting the clitorises off of girls. Some people say it's part of these cultures, and it's not ours to judge whether they should do it or not. Others say no matter what the culture, this practice is hurting women because the cuts get infected. The response is to suggest doing it in sanitary clinics so that nobody gets hurt. The answer back is that women wouldn't choose to do this if the men didn't make them, so it's an issue of power. The answer back to *that* is that in fact, older women make them do it because it's their tradition.

Look closer to home. Women are paid about $0.77 for every dollar a man makes. If a woman does the same work, is equally qualified, and does the work equally well as a man, she gets paid less. Is this just part of our culture that we need to accept in order to understand the United States? Or is this something that we should change because we believe in equality? We could have the same discussion about apartheid in South Africa before it was changed or about racism in the United States.

Ethical relativity can be a problem if it neutralizes our sense of right and wrong. That may be a good thing insofar as it helps us suspend judgment; it may be a bad thing if it paralyzes us so that we can't make political judgments. We'll discuss that topic more in chapter 15.

Epistemology means how we know things. Different cultures define different ways of knowing things. Some may value mysticism; some may value science. The idea of **epistemological relativity** is that all ways of knowing things are equally true. People who believe in this believe that no one way of knowing is any more true than any other. In this view, we can never really know reality; we can only know reality as our different cultures show it to us, and all those different ways are equally true.

Anthropology needs descriptive relativity and ethical relativity to describe and understand different cultures, but if we took epistemological relativity seriously, we couldn't really be descriptively or ethically relativistic. Epistemological relativity doesn't help scientists; it only helps tell a story from an ethnocentric point of view. All cultures have the assumption that they are natural, obvious, and true. If we pick just one, then we can only understand things from that one point of view and never question if there are other ways of knowing the world. If we can't ask the question, we can't answer it. So, paradoxically epistemological relativity means no relativity at all.

Science provides an alternative. The idea of **science** is that we never accept anything as really true, just as what we *think* we know until we find out differently by checking it over and over again. The idea is to think of things we can check.

Science rests on two important principles: validity and reliability. **Validity** means that you're really measuring what you think you are measuring. Suppose you have an odometer for your bike. It's supposed to measure the distance you go. What it really counts is the number of times the front wheel turns around. If you put on a larger or smaller wheel, it will still count the number of revolutions, but it won't be a valid measure of distance.

Reliability means that everybody else who checks the same thing will get the same results. It doesn't matter how fast or how far you pedal, the odometer will measure the revolutions of the wheel and convert that to a measure of distance. That measurement will depend on the size of the wheel, not the person pedaling.

The problem is that science is just one way of knowing things, and not everybody uses it. Does that make science better than other ways of knowing?

Think of the origin stories. Shall we just pick one and stick with it because we are ethnocentric? Or shall we decide not to commit to any belief, decide to try to get the story that best takes account of all of the evidence we can find, and then keep checking that story with every kind of evidence we can find?

Anthropologists take the second route because we want to be able to understand other cultures and times and not be trapped in our own, just going around in circles with our own stories.

Some people asked Nasrudin whether he knew where the exact center of the Earth was. "Yes," the wise man said.

"Then tell us,"

"It's just under the left hind foot of my donkey."

"Are you sure?" they asked. "How can you be so sure?"

"If you doubt me," Nasrudin said, "measure it for yourselves."

Discussion Questions

- What makes science scientific?
- What makes science different from other epistemologies?
- What makes ethnography scientific?
- What is the difference between validity and reliability? Can you think of some other examples?
- Think of some reasons a statement might not be reliable or valid. For example, why is it difficult to get a reliable answer to why a particular piece of literature, poetry, or music is good? Why is it difficult to get a valid answer to which political party is best?
- Which is the best origin story? Why?

Suggested Reading

Appignanesi, Richard, Chris Garratt, Ziauddin Sardar, and Patrick Curry. *Introducing Postmodernism*. Cambridge: Totem Books, 2005.

Kuznar, Lawrence A. *Reclaiming a Scientific Anthropology*. Walnut Creek, CA: AltaMira, 1997.

Salzman, Philip Carl. *Understanding Culture: An Introduction to Anthropological Theory*. Prospect Heights, IL: Waveland, 2001.

Sidky, H. *Perspectives on Culture: A Critical Introduction to Theory in Cultural Anthropology*. Upper Saddle River, NJ: Pearson, 2004.

2

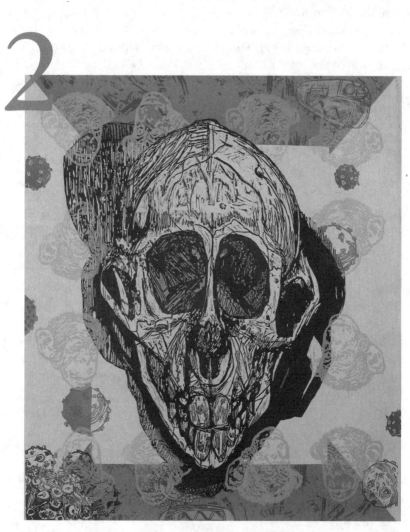

Anyone you know? "Unreliable Narrator," *courtesy of Roxanne Sexaur. Used with permission.*

CHAPTER 2

PEOPLE ARE PRIMATES

We are primates, by our loves and fears and hatreds, by the cock of our thumbs, and by the size of our big toes. Our thumbs have been modified to hold precision tools; our big toes have flattened to walk upon the ground; our loves and hatreds are shaped to the needs of human groups. But, above all, we are *Homo Sapiens*. Our primate ancestors took the path of learning, buffering themselves against the vagaries of their environment by the complexities of their society and their intelligence. We exchanged instinctive certainty for adaptive complexity, and in our myth bought knowledge at the price of innocence.

—*Alison Jolly (1972:357)*

Along with our cousins—chimpanzees, gorillas, monkeys, and gibbons—people are primates. One branch of biological anthropology devotes itself to the study of primates that are not human to better understand the similarities and differences among the kinds of primates. All primates share many features of creatures that are specialized for living in trees, even though some of us—like baboons and people—don't do that very much.

We can all grasp things. Primates typically can grasp things with both their feet and their hands. Most primates have **opposable thumbs**, as we do—they can grasp things between the tips of their thumbs and fingers. Unlike cats and dogs, we can hold things in one hand. But many primates also have opposable big toes. All primates have nails rather than claws.

We all have forelimbs that we can rotate, flex, and extend. Most primates have arms that are specialized for **locomotion**—moving around—and support. Most primates get around by swinging through trees. When they walk on the ground, they support themselves with their hands.

All of our primate eyes are at the fronts of our heads and have overlapping fields of vision so we all have good depth perception and distance judgment. If you have a dog or a cat, you know these animals sniff their food to identify it before they eat it. We primates pick up our food with our hands and look at it to identify it. So, when we eat, we use our abilities to grasp and see.

11

Dogs and cats have litters of babies, but primates have only a small number of offspring per birth. For their reproduction, most species depend on a few newborns surviving without much care for any of them after they are born or much intrauterine development. Maybe you've seen a film of newly hatched sea turtles rushing down the beach to get to the water. Clouds of birds dive down and eat lots of them. But a lot get into the water, where other predators eat most of them. The ones who survive may just be lucky enough to breed and survive and keep the species going.

Primates don't have many offspring, but they all have a relatively long time for development before they are born and when they are infants. Our young need a lot of postnatal care and protection. This long period of care allows infants to bond with their mothers. This bonding and the lengthy stage of dependency allow for a long period for learning.

Like humans, most primates have complex social behavior. The intense care and prolonged mother–child relationship results in highly social behavior such as **mutual grooming**—the practice of going through each other's fur looking for things that shouldn't be there and removing them—eating together (but not necessarily sharing food with each other), and well-developed visual and auditory systems of signaling about food, danger, and sexual state. In addition to mother–child relationships are female–female friendships, the clique of dominant males that reinforce one another's dominant status, juvenile peer groups, and the short-term breeding pair of a dominant male and a sexually receptive female, often after she's had sex with most of the other males.

One last thing that all of us primates have in common is our large brains and well-developed abilities to store information, generalize, remember things, and sort things by similarities and differences.

So, what makes us human? Let's start with this: Imagine how you would have to reengineer a gorilla skeleton so that the gorilla could be **bipedal**, walking on two feet all the time.

Gorillas and other apes use their feet for grasping and feeling as well as walking. We can't oppose our big toes. Our feet are restructured so that the weight goes first to our heels, then over a front-to-back and side-to-side arch to our toes. Then, leverage against the toes springs us off on the next step. We use our feet only for support and locomotion.

Other primates use their hands to swing through trees or for semierect motion on the ground, supporting their weight on their fists or knuckles. You may have thought of a roommate in these terms at some time—a real knuckle dragger. Bipedalism frees our hands and arms from locomotion. Only humans can walk long distances while carrying things in our hands. Other primate thumbs are short, but ours are long and muscular. Since we don't swing through trees, our long thumbs don't get in the way of getting around. They may even help if we're hitching a ride, but we didn't grow long thumbs because we needed to be able to hitchhike. We'll get to that in just a bit, but for the moment remember that there's no necessity in evolution. Just because a species "needs" something doesn't mean it is going to happen.

So you may have to walk, but we're in good shape for that. Our legs are the longest of all the primates relative to the length of our trunks. The large, strong muscles of our butts power our legs forward and back as we walk.

The gorilla's pelvis is a narrow tube with the legs attached at right angles at the rear. This transfers half of the weight of the gorilla's body to the rear legs. Because the center of gravity runs through our pelvis it is structured to be flat, broad, and strong to support everything above it and provide attachments for the muscles for locomotion and support.

The gorilla's spine is a simple arc, but ours has a lumbar curve to balance us and keep our center of gravity above our pelvis. Gorillas have powerful muscles to control their heads, which are attached to the ends of their spines. Our heads are balanced on the tops of our necks with only small muscles to hold them in place.

We use basic primate systems, but we've rearranged things a lot so that we can walk on two feet. As well-known anthropologist Walter Goldschmidt (2006:20) puts it, the bipedal posture disrupted our organs by hanging them from a vertical pole rather than from a horizontal rod.

There are some other, less obvious changes related to bipedalism. Most female mammals are sexually receptive only a few days before and after they ovulate when they're in heat. Other primate females let everyone else know they are ready to breed by using olfactory and visual signals, such as the colored swellings of the genital-anal area. But people have to complicate everything. Bipedalism rotates our genital-anal region down so nobody can see what's going on down there, even if we are naked. Females that were ready for sex any time, even if they weren't ovulating and could find cooperative males, had the best chances of getting pregnant and passing on those characteristics to their kids and on down to us. But this kind of sex life meant changes in hormones and social life.

So far, we have creatures with weak jaws, small teeth, and no claws who are always interested in sex. But we are different from other primates in two other important ways—we have language, and we have culture.

These similarities and differences developed through the process of **natural selection**. Charles Darwin knew about plant and animal selection. Breeders could select for certain characteristics by only breeding individuals that had what feature the breeders were looking for—a certain body shape or nose shape or color. After a few generations of selection, they have pure breeds, so that a male and female of the same breed will produce offspring of that breed. We still do that. It's artificial selection. But there are no breeders in nature, so how do members of species come to resemble each other and be different from other species? Darwin reasoned that it must be the same process that artificial selection uses but that it happens naturally. So he called it **natural selection**.

If you have some feature that lets more of your offspring survive and grow up to reproduce than those without it, then more and more individuals in later generations will come to share that feature. We say it is **adaptive**. If the characteristic doesn't help you have more offspring that survive and reproduce, then it becomes less and less common in later generations.

Remember, there is no necessity in evolution. Because a species needs a characteristic does not mean that it will magically appear to save the species. Some of those sea turtles we mentioned are endangered species. That doesn't mean they'll somehow be able to fend off the birds and fish that eat their young.

But if some individuals happen to lay more eggs and more of their offspring survive to reproduce, then that gets passed on down. Anything that helps to have more offspring is helpful to the species. But needs are not causes.

So why the big deal about bipedalism? Even limited walking freed our hands, and that allowed us to use tools. Those who could use them had an edge, an advantage, so they could have more kids. Because using tools did that, anything that went with using tools became more common. So being able to hold and use tools reinforced bipedalism (see figure 2-1).

Four million years ago we see the first bipedalism. Then, about a million and a half years ago, we see the first recognizable tools. But just being able to pick up and use stones and sticks, just using tools or simple shaping of stones was advantageous. Figure 2-2 illustrates this causal sequence. Individuals who could learn to use tools more easily had more complex and larger brains, so their brains gave them an advantage that reinforced tool use and tool use reinforced bipedalism.

Figure 2-1 Walking and tool use reinforce each other.

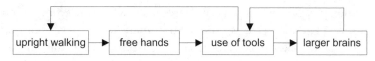

Figure 2-2 How brains are involved.

We see a system of several elements arranged so that if one of them changes, the others also change through the process of natural selection. If there is selection for walking—in other words, if it helps to reproduce the species—then there is selection for all of the reengineering that goes with walking, such as rotating and broadening the pelvis and restructuring the foot from grasping to walking. Broadening and rotating the pelvis narrows the birth canal. Now, if there is selection for a narrowed birth canal at the same time there is selection for larger brains, something's got to give. On the one hand, the birth canal is getting smaller; but on the other hand, the brains are getting bigger. The resolution was premature—by primate standards—birth. We are born before our brains become too big to exit through the narrowing opening of the birth canal. Moms who didn't have premature babies didn't survive the experience, and their babies didn't grow up to pass that characteristic on to the next generation.

Here's another step in natural selection: Those females whose infants were delivered prematurely had a better chance of reproducing more, but that created another problem because the premature infants weren't even developed enough to hang onto their mothers like other primate infants are. So the mothers had to carry the infants in their hands and spend even more time than ordinary primate moms taking care of their babies. Premature infants whose moms couldn't figure this out died, and those moms and infants did not contribute anything to the next generation.

Premature birth meant a long period of immaturity and development out-side the womb. That meant that the moms had to want to take care of their infants and that the infants would like being taken care of. Walter Goldschmidt (this guy published his last book at the age of ninety-two, so we figure he says something worth repeating) suggests that there are two parts to human evolution. One part has to do with the idea some call the "selfish gene." That is, you do whatever you need to in order to assure that you have offspring that survive and reproduce so that more of your species are like you. Think of turtle moms having more eggs that hatch so more of their babies get to the sea and more survive to breed and so on. Goldschmidt points out that all life forms work this way. It's what natural selection is, after all. It's what evolution is. The metaphor of the selfish gene appeals to some people, but genes can't really be selfish or unselfish. They are just there.

But when people come along, we introduce a whole different dimension to evolution. The part that is unique to humans is the part about taking care of and being taken care of, or nurturing. Goldschmidt calls this second part "affect hunger," the hunger we all have for love and affection. Our long period of learning depends on affect hunger. We want to please the grown-ups, so we try to learn what they are teaching us.

Our survival depends on pleasing the grown-ups. If we don't please them, they don't have to take care of us. It's pretty easy to see how natural selection would favor that. That doesn't mean that all moms and dads like their kids all the time, but it does mean that as a general thing, most moms and dads like their kids pretty much a lot of the time. And it means we all like being liked. That's enough to make a difference.

The larger and more complex brains gave infants greater abilities to learn during their long period of development. This, along with other changes in the brain, allowed them to learn the intricacies of language as well as social roles.

If a mother belonged to a group that cooperated in getting and providing food, she and her infant had a much better chance of surviving and reproducing than if she had to get all of her food by herself. Thus, cooperative food getting conferred a selective advantage. So did language and lower levels of aggression within the group. We can put these elements into our systems diagram of human evolution (figure 2-3).

Our system just got a lot more complicated. One of the reasons for the complexity is that there are more indirect relationships—for instance, between *upright walking* and *lower aggression*. Another is that there are multiple paths. You can follow the line by starting at the top left of

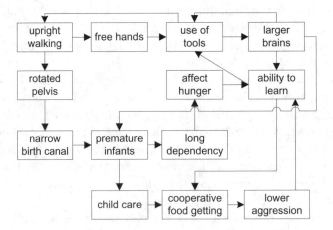

Figure 2-3 The consequences of the contradictions between walking upright and evolving larger brains.

the diagram moving to the right and down to *ability to learn* but also by going down from the top left box and then over to *long dependency* and back up or from *premature infants* down to *childcare,* across to *lower aggression* and back up. If following a series of arrows brings you back to the starting point, we call it a **loop**. This system is one self-intensifying loop. It defines a system that might have taken a long time to get going—between walking and tool making is two and a half million years. But it goes faster and faster when we put affect hunger and learning into the system. Take some time to study this system and understand how the diagram works, because they only get more elaborate from here on out.

The kind of animal that can cooperate with others in getting food and caring for infants is different from other primates. Most primates organize themselves into dominance hierarchies. One example is baboons. The large canine teeth of baboon males are a secondary sexual characteristic, like pubic hair and breasts, that develop with sexual maturity. Baboon males use their large canine teeth to scare others into being submissive and sometimes to fight to establish the order of dominance—who gives way to whom. When a female signals that she is in heat, the least dominant males breed with her first and the most dominant last, when she is most likely to conceive. Thus, the characteristic of large canine teeth is passed onto succeeding generations because it is the characteristic responsible for the fact that the dominant male impregnated the female that was in heat. This is another kind of natural selection, this time for aggression and the characteristics that go with it.

In primate groups with established dominance hierarchies, the weaker animals give way to stronger ones; females give way to males, and they share food only when stronger animals take it by force from weaker ones. When they threaten each other, they show their canine teeth. That's usually enough to cause the lower-ranking individual to back down. When a dominant animal threatens another, the one that's threatened can avert the eyes, crouch, whimper, look over a shoulder and grin, or walk backward. The signs of submission switch off the attack. The dominant individual may embrace the subordinate one, and everything is in order.

We're not like that. Stronger humans give food to weaker ones and don't take it from them. There is selection for cooperation and higher thresholds of rage and aggression. Humans don't get angry as fast as baboons. You can check this out by comparing what happens in some situations that typically evoke dominance displays and aggression in other primates. Sit in a bar or restaurant and watch what happens if a woman stares into the eyes of a man. Does he show his canine teeth at her and growl until she whimpers and picks up the check? Only on a date from hell.

Because cooperation in humans had a reproductive advantage, there was selection for it and for the biological structures compatible with cooperation.

Genetically determined biological mechanisms control aggression in other primates, but culture controls it in humans. We don't have any biological mechanisms to turn on rage as baboons do. The other side of that coin is that we don't have any biological mechanisms to turn rage and aggression off, either. There is nothing in primate life that is comparable to a person killing another person who is begging.

We are dangerous to ourselves because we have lost the genetic control of aggression. Victims of violence have no way to control aggressors by showing signs of submission. People can kill other people who have never offended or threatened them personally. In fact, if you're a general or even a private, you can't do as well if you're enraged than you can if you are cool, calm, and thinking things through as you act. Instinctual rage is not compatible with the mass killing of industrial warfare that proceeds according to careful plans and meticulous control of fast-moving machines.

What about hunting? Hunting may have been more or less important in this story. The earliest hominids in Africa were not big game hunters. They did scavenge other animals' kills and kill and eat small animals such as frogs. The first walking hominid comes in about four million years ago. These folks had larger brains and upright posture, but their facial bones were similar to those of the earlier *Australopithecus* that dates from about five million years ago. Their tools were about the same, too—**pebble tools**. A pebble tool is a large pebble with a **flake** or two knocked off to make a sharp edge. That can happen to pebbles rolling around in a river, so it's impossible to know whether any given broken rock was formed by a person or by nature unless you find it in a place where people were living.

It takes about two and a half million years for the next big innovation to come along. About a million and a half years ago, we find a new kind of tool—instead of just one or two flakes knocked off a pebble, these are symmetrical on both sides. People made these **hand axes** according to a plan they had in mind, something much more complex than just knocking a stone to get a sharp edge.

You can make pebble tools. Wear gloves, or you'll get your fingers all cut and bashed up. If you're right handed, hold a rock about the size of your fist in your left hand. Hold another rock the same size in your right hand. The rock in your left hand is a **core**; it's the one you're going to shape. Haul off with the stone in your right hand and bash the one in your left hand. Sooner or later you'll get the rock in your left hand to break. If a small piece breaks off, we call it a flake. The rock in your left hand we call a core. The rock in your right hand we call a **hammerstone**. Anyone can make pebble tools, but it takes some expertise to make an Acheullean hand axe.

Figure 2-4 Found in Europe and Africa, the handaxe probably served stone-age men and women in a variety of ways—cutting meat, scraping hides, chopping wood, digging holes, hammering wood, and even for defense. They vary in size—some are more than six inches in length. Acheullean handaxes from Saint-Acheul, France, date from 1,000,000 BCE to 100,000 BCE.

Knock a flake off a pebble we call a core, and you get a sharp edge. The people who made the hand axes shaped the core to be the same on both sides and threw away the flakes. The people who made the new tools, *Homo erectus,* walked on two feet out of Africa to eastern Asia.

Archaeologists find the remains of big game animals like deer, pigs, bison, horses, rhinos, bears, wolves, tigers, and saber-toothed cats with *Homo erectus,* but they think *Homo erectus* were mainly scavengers and that the big game wasn't that significant, especially when compared with catching smaller animals and eating plants. People couldn't eat by hunting alone, and most of our ancestors' food came from plants. In terms of evolutionary forces, we are in the last chapter of the story when this big

Figure 2-5 This is the linear view of human evolution. It didn't quite go like this straight line. It was a little more complicated.

game appears with human bones. Hunting could not make us killer apes. Walking is the key to our evolutionary history.

In the new environments, separated from each other, new species of people developed. We find *Homo heidelbergensis* in Ethiopia about six hundred thousand years ago with a brain on the small end of our own modern peoples' brains, still below our average. These people were in Europe by half a million years ago, and a thousand years after that, we find the first evidence of a couple of technological innovations—hearths for fires and simple structures to live in.

There was another innovation about two hundred thousand ago when *Homo neanderthalensis,* with brains as large as ours, began to make tools from the flakes in Europe and western Asia. From central Asia to the British Isles, these people made the same kinds of tools without much variation. They were scavengers and foragers, and they hunted only small animals. Meanwhile, *Homo sapiens,* people like us, sprang from the same African ancestor as the Neanderthals and *Homo heidelbergensis,* while *Homo erectus* were still going strong in Asia.

Modern people, *Homo sapiens,* showed up from Africa about a hundred thousand years ago in the eastern Mediterranean and shared the area with Neanderthals for some sixty thousand years. Both made the same kinds of stone tools.

About forty thousand years ago, our ancestors made another technological breakthrough when they figured out how to shape a core and then use an antler punch to detach long bladelike flakes. From those slivers of stone, those blades, they could shape any kind of tool they wanted. With this new method, people started making a lot of different kinds of tools.

Here's something to think about when folks talk about profit motives, patent rights, and intellectual property. What was the incentive for anyone to make any of these innovations? They didn't keep the advantages to themselves. Everyone benefited from them, kind of like the people who make open-source software. So why would they do it? That we can't say. But we know they did. That's why we're here. It's just not true that the market is the only motivation for innovation, or else we wouldn't be here.

All of our ancestors leading up to the Cro-Magnons did about the same things, if maybe a little better than the earlier ones. But with Cro-Magnon came a radical shift. Cro-Magnon did many different things that their ancestors never did. They began to paint on the walls of caves about thirty thousand years ago, made flutes of bone, marked bone tablets with what may have been lunar calendars, and made sculptures. By twenty-six thousand years ago, they were sewing with bone needles and baking clay in kilns.

The earliest modern humans produced the same tools and behaved the same way as Neanderthals for more than fifty thousand years. They

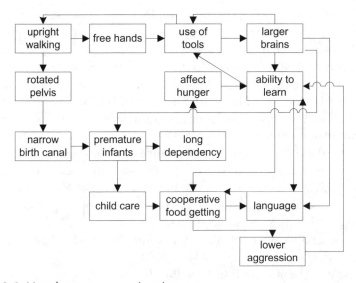

Figure 2-6 How language came into it.

had brains that were structurally like ours, but they did not use them the same way that Cro-Magnon did. What made the change?

Ian Tattersall (2004) suggests that language made the difference. The beginnings of language, a cultural innovation, unleashed the changes that are responsible for the first flourishing of symbolic behavior we see in Cro-Magnon with things like music and art. Thinking and talking both rely on using symbols. Now we can add language to our system and with it, learning takes off. We develop culture. Figure 2-6 is the same as figure 2-3, except that *language* makes a new self-intensifying loop with *cooperative food getting* and *ability to learn.*

The next big innovation came about ten or eleven thousand years ago when we started domesticating plants and animals. After that it was all over but the shouting.

Anthropologists continually work on the details of this story. Some look for fossil remains; some sift through the evidence from archaeological sites; some study other primates to better understand our similarities and differences; some untangle DNA for clues.

Discussion Questions

- Think of how your family is a system. If one person leaves or dies, how does that change what happens in the family?

- Describe and then draw an example of a self-intensifying loop in a system. How does removing one element of that system impact on the other elements of the system?
- Think again about the difference between the scientific origin story and the origin stories people make up to tell themselves. What's the role of evidence? What's the role of belief in each?
- Do you think it's possible for human beings to adapt biologically to polluted environments? Why or why not?
- Evolution is based on the importance of differences in members of the same species. Can you think of some differences in our species now that people of the future might look back on and, say, confer selective advantage? Consider overcrowding, poverty, global warming, immunities to diseases, hunger, physical strength, and endurance or other differences. What do you think the people of the future will be like?
- What role does the human ability to use and understand symbols play in the difference between a baboon getting into a fight and an air force pilot dropping a bomb on a city? What are some benign symbols? What are some dangerous ones?

Suggested Reading

Goldschmidt, Walter. *The Bridge to Humanity: How Affect Hunger Trumps the Selfish Gene.* New York: Oxford University Press, 2006.

3

Same ancestors—why are we so different? *Photo from iStockphoto, © Rasmus Rasmussen. Used with permission.*

CHAPTER 3

HUMAN VARIATION: RACE AND GENDER

Race

If all people living today evolved from the same ancestors, those first *Homo sapiens sapiens,* why are we so physically different today? There's a lot of talk about race and racism these days in America. What does race mean in terms of our evolutionary history?

It is true that the distribution of certain of our physical characteristics is not random—there are patterns. Think of these characteristics as being like elevation on a topographic map. If we connect all of the points of the same elevation, we define a **cline**. It's the same for weather maps—we can map barometric pressures by connecting all the pressures that are the same to each other. If we do that for human physical characteristics, we see that they do not form into neat bundles that go together. One cline may go one direction, and another a different direction.

For instance, the frequency of genes for dark skin gradually increases from Mediterranean Europe south along the Nile or across the Sahara with no sharp breaks, so the "peak" would be in central Africa. The frequency of the fold in the eye that many Europeans and Americans associate with Japanese and Chinese people, the *epicanthic fold,* gradually increases from west to east across Asia. Wavy hair increases in the opposite direction, toward Europe. You can see people from South Asia whose skin is very dark but who have very sharp facial features and straight hair.

These distributions are the results of two processes: gene flow and natural selection. In biological terms, species and races are about who breeds with whom. Two populations that cannot interbreed are two different species. A *race* is a large, geographically isolated population within a species that doesn't breed very much with other populations of the same species. If there are different environments or some other differences in

25

natural selection, then different species develop. So a race is a population on the way to being its own species.

One present-day example comes from a recent debate concerning the Endangered Species Act. There are many different kinds of squirrels in North America. One kind lives only on the national mall in Washington, D.C. It is a little different from other squirrel populations, and the streets and traffic around the mall keep these squirrels fairly isolated from other ones. So this kind may be evolving toward its own species. Some people worry about whether there are so few of these squirrels that they are in some sense endangered. We could be talking about legislators, but we're not. Those guys are isolated in a different place in Washington, and some wonder whether they'll ever evolve, but that's another story for a later chapter.

A common idea of race is that there are a specific number of "types" of people that are all more or less the same but different from other types. Americans typically think that they can tell the different types apart by skin color. Some might add type of hair, nose and lip shape, and stature. There are the archetypes of Europeans with pale skins, straight or wavy hair, body hair, narrow noses, and medium to tall stature; versus central Africans with dark brown or black skin, wiry hair, medium body hair, thick noses and lips, and medium to tall stature; and Asians with pale to light brown skin, straight black hair, brown eyes, epicanthic folds, short to medium statures, and no body hair. Somewhere we can find a perfect representation of each type.

The Cunard Steamship Company has a building in Liverpool, England. Over the front door is a sculpture of Neptune, the Roman god of the sea. Evenly spaced around the building at the same level are wonderfully sculpted heads of archetypes of each race on the planet. The Cunard collection of sculpture represents this idea of race.

The problem is that human characteristics don't fall into sufficiently neat packages to define races. Lots of people in Africa have thin lips and noses, wavy hair, and dark brown to black skin. Some South Africans have epicanthic folds, light brown to dark brown skin, and spiraled hair. So the actual distribution of people doesn't fit any of the archetypes of race.

In addition, archaeologists tell us that people have been in contact over very long distances ever since we started walking out of Africa. Where there's human contact, there's bound to be breeding. We're that kind of species and that's how we got here. In terms of our genetics, there is more variation within any category of people, or population, you can think of than there is between them. So the differences between any two people from any single category of people are greater than the differences between individuals of any two different categories.

How can we say that there are no racial differences when you can look around you and see that people are black, brown, pink, and all shades in between? There are differences, but they don't go together. Each difference follows a different cline. And it has always been that way. There is no time in the past when races were pure but different and somehow got mixed up. Let's look at one of the differences that Americans think is important. *Why* Americans think it is important is another question that we'll come to soon, but for the moment, let's think about skin color.

To understand skin color, you have to think about sunshine. This is one of those "blessing/curse" stories where something happens that people think is a great disaster until something else happens to prove that it was a blessing in disguise. Sunshine causes skin cancer. That's a curse, if your skin is white. Malignant melanoma is very deadly. The highest cancer rate is in light-skinned people who live in Australia. The rate quadruples for people who engage in outdoor sports, and it varies with the intensity of solar radiation from the equator north or south. In the United States, skin cancer is most frequent among urban whites in Texas—for instance, in Dallas and Fort Worth. It's less frequent where there's less sunshine—for instance, Detroit or Minneapolis. Men get it on the upper torso; women, on the legs. In Europe, Norwegians get it twenty times more than Spaniards.

So, if you have white skin and stay in the sun, odds are good you'll die of skin cancer. But there is protection from skin cancer. It comes from the melanin that makes our skins opaque to light, just as sunblock does, and protects our skins from ultraviolet radiation. That opacity is, incidentally, connected to color. The more the melanin, the more opaque the skin, the more protection from ultraviolet rays, the less the danger of cancer. Along with the opacity, the natural sunblock, comes darker skin. So if exposure to sunshine were as intense all over the globe as it is on the equator, we'd all be black. All the pale-skinned people would have died.

If we make a diagram of these relationships, it looks like figure 3-1. The plus sign above the arrow from *sunshine* to *skin cancer* means "the *more* the sunshine, the *more* the skin cancer." If sunshine increases, skin cancer increases. Likewise, if sunshine decreases, so does skin cancer. So, these two variables move in the same direction. That's what the plus sign means. The minus sign above the arrow from *melanin* to *skin cancer*

Figure 3-1 Effects of sunshine in equatorial areas.

means "the *more* the melanin, the *less* the skin cancer." It also means "the *less* the melanin, the *more* the skin cancer." It means that these two variables move in opposite directions—an increase in one means a decrease in the other. The plus sign over the arrow from *melanin* to *darkness of skin* means "the *more* the melanin, the *more* the darkness of the skin." It also means, "the less the melanin, the less the darkness of the skin." These two variables move in the same direction. Another way to say this is "the more the melanin, the darker the skin; the less the melanin, the paler the skin." What many people think of as "white" skin is actually pink because the skin is so transparent that we see the capillaries in the skin.

It's more complicated than that because sunshine is also a blessing. When skin is exposed to sunshine, it produces vitamin D that goes to our digestive system to help us absorb the calcium that is necessary for the growth and strength of our bones. Without it, people's bones become soft and deformed by rickets. Even if people with rickets could get along, women's birth canals would be so deformed that having a baby would kill the mother as well as the baby. So people who could use the sunshine to make vitamin D had a selective advantage in the north. The people with pale skins who could use the sunshine survived more and had more offspring. So paler skin meant more vitamin D, less bone deformation, and less melanin. Less melanin meant paler skin just as more melanin meant darker skin. Figure 3-2 shows this pattern. This means "more sunshine, more vitamin D; more vitamin D, less rickets; more rickets, less melanin; less melanin, less darkness of skin."

Both of these processes happened everywhere. Where there was lots of bright sunshine through the year, people who got skin cancer died; where there was less sunshine, people with rickets died. That left more people with darker skins toward the equator and more people with lighter skins toward the north.

If you can get vitamin D from somewhere besides the sun, then the pressure of rickets is off. People who live in the polar areas get vitamin D from marine fish, but these weren't available to people in Europe or Africa.

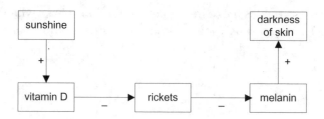

Figure 3-2 Effects of sunshine in northern areas.

So, there's a trade-off between rickets and skin cancer. The whole process looks like what is shown in figure 3.3.

We don't know what color our ancestors were, and it doesn't matter. Let's suppose that they were all black. If we started this system up just five thousand years ago, and the people with less melanin who could process vitamin D from sunshine had just 2 percent more children per generation, all of the people in those areas would have been pale by 0 A.D.

Some other things were going along with paleness. The best source of calcium for the northern people was milk. So along with paleness there was selective pressure for lactose tolerance—the ability to digest milk. Americans tend to talk about lactose intolerance as though it were some disorder. They even make medicines to fix it. In fact, tolerance for lactose is the strange thing. Most people are not lactose tolerant.

Now we are adding characteristics to our population. The more we do that, the less the characteristics form into neat bundles.

What can we say about race? Humans are a **polymorphic** species—*poly-* means "many," and *morph* means "form." So we are a species of many forms, with many partially isolated breeding populations, but we kept moving and mixing, never stopping in any one place permanently enough to develop different species. That explains the variation within groups and why it is greater than the variation among groups. We are a single species, a single breeding population.

So, if race isn't a biological reality, where did the idea come from? Part of it is from ethnocentrism. Part of it is from the idea that other people are different from us. This doesn't always have to do with skin color as it does in the United States. It can have to do with the way people speak. George Bernard Shaw wrote a play about that called *Pygmalion*. That play was later made into a movie with the same name and then into a musical called *My Fair Lady*. British people make the same kind of racist distinc-

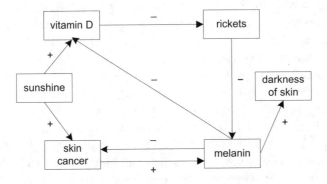

Figure 3-3 The evolution of human colors.

tions based on dialect or accent as Americans do based on skin color. In Britain, it has to do with class. We'll come back to that topic later, too.

The point is that people can emphasize any source of difference as a way to make categories of other people to treat well or badly. So where does this inclination to divide people into different categories come from?

Just like the origin stories, it's cultural. But it has to do with the culture of nation-states that developed in Europe in the sixteenth and seventeenth centuries and got consolidated into warring nations by the middle of the nineteenth century. Yes, this entire notion is pretty recent, historically speaking. There aren't any real borders among people, but the rulers of European-style states like to define certain territories and fight over them. The idea is that there is a homogeneous group of people all alike in their language and culture that gets along pretty well together. These people live inside the borders of the state and have a government that takes care of things for them and protects them from foreigners who may try to take over "our" country. Make people more afraid of foreigners than they are of their own rulers, and they won't look too closely at who is really doing them harm. Adolf Hitler's slogan was "One people, one government, one leader."

The basic idea is that there is a single people with a single language, government, territory, history, culture, music, and literature. Each nation claims to be the best one because this ideology of **nationalism** is a powerful source of ethnocentrism. If we project that ideology onto the whole species and assume that people come in linguistically and physically defined groups, we get the idea of race. In fact, early writers used *race* and *nation* to mean the same thing. Another thing that nations do is keep track of people so they can draft them for armies and tax them to pay for wars. When they start counting people, they make categories—occupations, regions, religions, races.

So racism, along with nationalism, belongs to the cultures of states. In the United States, the idea of biological races and biological racism is also connected to the European conquest of the Americas and the slave trade. The Europeans and their American descendants could use color as a handy marker for who was fair game to be captured and sold into slavery or kept in slavery. Then racism, the idea that people of one category are superior or inferior to those of a different one, could be used as a defense of slavery. After the Civil War, racism provided a rationale for political and economic repression. The history of that form of oppression is too complex to go into here, but if you haven't experienced some form of dominance because you're a woman instead of a man or because you're darker than someone else or because you have a different kind of name than someone else, then ask some people of a different gender, sexual preference, skin color, or surname system to tell you how that works.

The idea of race as a biological fact is itself a political weapon that some use to oppress others. Later on we're going to explain how some people can control the culture of others and discuss mind control, but for now just remember that if you're asking about the biology of race, you're asking the wrong the question. The real question is about the politics of race. It's quite possible to ask about human variation and how that works biologically, but to do that scientifically, we have to give up the assumptions of race, even the convenient assumptions of isolated human breeding populations that are like the squirrels in the National Mall in Washington, D.C. Otherwise, we're not doing science; we're justifying a pernicious political doctrine.

The Icelandic anthropologist Gísli Pálsson writes about an island mentality—that even anthropologists think about people as if they lived on little islands separated from other people. Biological anthropologists are trying to work out the history of our species by comparing the genetics of different groups. The problem is that if they assume such "islands" of population exist, they take their samples from the islands, and guess what? They prove there really are islands. They wind up proving their own assumption. This would be like assuming your bicycle odometer was accurate and using it to define the distance of one mile and never checking it against any other way of measuring the distance. Of course, your bike would always go exactly the distance the odometer said. You've proved your own assumption.

Another way to map genetic variation would be by dividing the world according to a grid or some other method of random sampling instead of looking for islands of populations.

Pálsson points out that the people who share features such as dark skin and hair texture, Melanesians and Africans, are as genetically different as it is possible to be. In terms of molecular markers, Europeans are closer to both Africans and Melanesians than Africans are to Melanesians. So what could a black race be? Some of the gene hunters, as Pálsson calls them, even try to define populations according to language. Most Americans are hyphenated Americans—Afro-Americans, Italian-Americans, and so forth. And most of them speak English. This example isn't that strange. Language is one of those things that nationalist ideologies made into islands along with genes. We're all mixed up and always have been.

But aren't there differences in performance? A greater proportion of black people than white people in the United States are poor. Isn't that because they are not as intelligent or as industrious as white people? Racists say so. But ability doesn't go with skin color; it goes with opportunity. Provide equal opportunity, and there will be equal performance. The United States does not provide equal opportunity. Black people don't have the same chances of going to good high schools that get kids into college as white people, and so on. Continue to deny equal opportunity on the basis of skin color or any other difference, and there will not be equal performance.

Here we have to shift gears for just a moment and mention that sometimes, as in this example, the racism is built into the system itself. It isn't a question of individuals being racist but of a whole system that's racist. You can have black Supreme Court justices and still have a racist system. To make a difference requires making a difference in the system, not in the people in it. You can change all of the people and keep the same system, and you'll get the same result.

Racism isn't just the prerogative of rulers. People who want to get along in the system can take up the practices and prejudices of the rulers. One example we recently came across is in Charleston, South Carolina. We were working on the story of a union of black longshoremen there. To understand what was going on, we had to understand about "race" relations in Charleston. We learned that people there aren't just white or black. There's a whole range in between. Historically, these started out as the offspring of matings of different kinds between white slave owners and slaves. The white owners often helped their brown children by setting them up in business. A brown elite thus grew up within the larger black community and acted as a link between the blacks and whites.

Even though the brown people suffered the same kind of racism as the black ones, they suffered less. They had many privileges in a system that ran on privilege, so they helped to keep the system going. They didn't want to change the system that was working well for them. They could deal with racism as long as they were getting along economically and had darker people to be superior to. During the civil rights movement of the 1960s, they advocated patience and reform rather than the big changes the civil rights movement promoted with its sit ins and demonstrations. The brown elite wanted to avoid any kind of confrontation with the white establishment.

The point is that racism and prejudice can cut in any direction. Sometimes when blacks are majorities and whites are minorities, black people can do unto others what has been done unto them—be racist toward whites in what some have called the oppression of the oppressed. Suzan saw some of this in her work with unions in Chicago. If racism and prejudice can cut in any direction, what is the solution? The solution is not to have any prejudice or any racism. Unfortunately, that's as easily done as having no more war.

Sometimes people get kicked out of their homelands and spread over the world. Sometimes the homelands get absorbed into bigger and more powerful states. Sometimes people dream of returning to their homeland to have their own state and do unto others what the others have done to them. Sometimes these folks get guns and tanks and airplanes and are dangerous to everyone around them and the rest of the world.

The lesson of anthropology is that there are no homelands except Africa. If we want to go back to our homelands, we have to start walking until we get to wherever our parents came from, then to where their parents came from, and farther and farther until we get to the great-great-great-whatever that was the first human in our ancestry to walk out of Africa. Then we keep on going until we get to Africa and we ... what? We stand on each other's shoulders? We duke it out for some place to sit down on the ground?

We are a species on the move. Every homeland has always been just a stepping-stone on our journey to wherever we are now. So we've always been moving and mingling, mixing and matching, and, above all, going on to the next place to do the next thing.

Gender

The differences of sex are greater in other primates than for us. The word for this is **sexual dimorphism**, or two forms by sex. Male baboons, for instance, are up to twice the size of females. But even in such highly dimorphic species, biology does not seem to be destiny.

The pattern we discussed in the last chapter with dominance hierarchies of breeding males and females is characteristic of savannah baboons that live in the grasslands. Remember, toward the end of her period of being in heat, the female forms a consort pair with the most dominant male so that he is more likely to get her pregnant and pass on his characteristics, such as large size and large canines that helped him to get and maintain his position in the hierarchy.

But we see a different picture in forest baboons. There are no dominance hierarchies. The older females lead the troop, and the males do not protect the troop as savannah baboon males do. So baboon sex roles seem to vary by habitat—different arrangements work in different conditions.

Gibbon males and females are about the same size and live in pairs in fixed territories that the males defend. They only copulate when the female isn't pregnant or nursing. But orangutan males are about twice the size of females, and the females occupy a stable area of forest, while the males range over large areas, do not protect females or young, or form pairs with females. So there doesn't seem to be any particular relationship in our primate relatives between sexual dimorphism and gender roles.

But in the chapter on evolution, wasn't there a big deal about women carrying the babies and foraging for food while the men were hunting and getting game to bring home? Maybe, but recent archaeological analyses suggest that most of that was scavenging big animals, not hunting them. But here is the most important point: We don't do that anymore. There is no connection between what was happening with the women in those early foraging and scavenging groups and the fact that women today are paid less for the same work than men.

If you think women should be treated differently from men, then we suggest you find some woman who will go with you and start foraging and scavenging. Keep her pregnant or nursing most of the time to slow her down. That means that you won't be having sex with her that often, but each time will count. Don't use any domestic animals or cars, don't live in a house, and surely don't use any money. If you get your family values from some scenario like this, we hope your woman leaves you high and dry because you sure don't deserve either her company or the food she's feeding you.

This part of the book is about gender, but we learn our gender roles from growing up in families where the older generations model them for us. To learn about gender roles, we have to stop and take a brief look at families. What is a family, anyway? Americans, like Europeans, tend to think in terms of a mom, a dad, and their kids living in a house with two cars and a dog named Spot and a cat named Puff. Most of the people of the world for most of the time we've been on this planet don't think that way.

Why? Because most people form into larger groupings called **lineages**. These come in two kinds—according to whether you can claim membership in them by virtue of the mom you have or the dad you have. Some are all the people descended from the same women; some all the people descended from the same man. Put that in Latin to make fancy academic words, and you have **matrilineal** (mother's line) and **patrilineal** (father's line).

These aren't mirror images of each other because the guys are in charge in both kinds. In a matrilineal lineage, it's the women's brothers who run the lineage. You'll learn more about this point later, but it doesn't hurt to bring it up here. Kinship is a key concept in anthropology.

Usually, family values means valuing the people of your lineage, not just your household. An early anthropologist, Bronislaw Malinowski, wanted to find out about the relationships between fathers and sons in the Trobriand Islands, where he did fieldwork. He'd been reading Sigmund Freud, who was writing about the Oedipus complex. That's the idea that as boys grow up they begin to compete with their own dads for the attention and then the control of their moms. Freud said as guys grow older, they want to kill their dads and possess their moms. That makes them feel guilty in all kinds of ways, and that guilt makes them give up any ideas of sex with their female relatives. The same sort of thing goes on with girls and their dads. Freud called that the Electra complex.

Malinowski wondered how that idea would work in a place with a different kind of family structure than Freud was seeing in Vienna. The Trobriand Islanders have matrilineal lineages. The most important adult male in any kid's life is his mom's brother, what Americans would call an uncle. Kids belong to the mom's family, not their dad's. The dad is just a sperm donor for the mom. The men of the mom's lineage, the mom's brothers, are responsible for raising the kids, for their family values. So, all of the closeness is between the children and their mother's side, and their uncles are the ones who raise the sons and model maleness for them. The uncles are in the roles of Viennese dads.

What about the Trobriand dads? They're involved with their sister's kids, the kids that belong to their families, their lineages, but to their "own" kids they are indulgent, like uncles in Europe. With a whole different kind of family structure, there wouldn't be any struggle between the dad and the son for the mom. It's not about moms and dads but about who has authority over the kids (Trobriand uncles and European dads) and who can be indulgent to them (Trobriand dads and European uncles). That is different in different systems.

So what does any of this have to do with gender roles?

One of the things that all people share is some kind of prohibition on having sex with certain relatives. We call that an **incest prohibition**. What's interesting is that different groups define the incest prohibition with respect to different relatives. Breeders who want to breed livestock or pets for certain characteristics look for males and females that share the thing the breeders are looking for. That's likely to be closely related individuals. So breeders encourage incest to bring out the traits they are looking for. The incest prohibition doesn't have anything to do with genetics or fears of inbreeding. Cleopatra, for instance, was the result of several generations of brother–sister matings. The Inca kings of Peru were so godly that no ordinary woman was good enough for them, so they had to mate with their sisters. You might say it's all relative.

The French anthropologist Claude Lévi-Strauss's answer to the puzzle was that the incest prohibition forces groups to have social relations with other groups so that they could help each other out when they needed it. That was the advantage of the incest prohibition.

The point is that the kind of kinship groups and the definitions of family are variable, and one of the things that goes along with those differences is differences in gender roles.

In the mid-1930s, Margaret Mead set out to explore the varieties of gender relations in her work in New Guinea. She found that Tchambuli women were dominant and the men, dependent; women, impersonal and managerial; and the men, irresponsible—the women seemed more like American males than American women in their behavior. Among Arapesh, nobody was very masculine by American judgments, and everyone was pretty equivalent in their cooperation and gentleness. She found Mundugumor of both genders to be aggressive even in making love. Her conclusion was that there is a wide variety of gender roles.

Some later anthropologists have criticized Mead's methods, but many others have found her conclusions sound. Whatever one's opinion of Mead's work, anthropologists agree that there is no necessary connection between biological characteristics and gender roles.

Nor is there any necessary single definition to marriage. Several men may be married to one woman at the same time. Several women may be married to one man at the same time; women and men may marry ghosts or trees or spirits; men may marry other men; women may marry other women.

Tibetan herders, at least before the Chinese took over, used all of these forms of marriage. The particular form depended on the livestock situation of the tent. Each child of the parents owned an equal share of the livestock, but the parents have two shares. So if there is a family with two sons and two daughters, each son and each daughter owns one-eighth of the herd. The father and mother each own one-fourth of the herd. Everything else hinges on the facts of herd ownership.

Two brothers might decide that they could do better by keeping their herds together. They know there cannot be two women in one tent unless the women are sisters or mother and daughter. So the older brother might offer to share his wife with the younger brother. So there's one woman and two husbands. The arrangement can be fragile because the woman may favor one husband over the other and kick one of them out with his herd, or the younger brother may want his own wife.

A family may have only one daughter, or maybe all the daughters except one have already married. The parents may bring in a son-in-law as a son. The only difference is that he is married to the daughter and that he can't set up a tent apart from the wife's parents' tent. If the father dies, the mother and daughter may share the same husband.

A wealthy married man may take a new wife and set her up with half of his share of the herd, but the two tents will stay together, even if the two wives are in separate tents. A man may marry several sisters, or a father and son may share a single wife, and so on. Robert Ekvall, who lived with these herders, says that the economic conditions of the herds determine the patterns of marriage in particular tents.

This can happen because people don't equate sex with marriage, so there's a lot of sexual activity between people who aren't married to each other. The birthrate is also low, so there aren't many children, and people value them highly. People don't have to be married to be sure that any children they have will be taken care of. The important thing is the management of the herd. That does require the stability of marriage.

The management of herds requires a partnership of men and women working together. Women take care of newborn and young animals and do all of the milking. This gives them the right to veto any livestock decisions any of the men might make, which, Ekvall (1968:28) says, "she can press with emotional intensity."

The important thing here is that the particular form of marriage depends on what is going on with the herds. As situations change, so will the marriage form.

So the forms of marriage are as varied as the forms of gender practices. In February 2004, the American Anthropological Association's executive board issued this statement when there was discussion of a constitutional amendment to limit marriage in the United States to one man and one woman:

> The results of more than a century of anthropological research on households, kinship relationships, and families, across cultures and through time, provide no support whatsoever for the view that either civilization or viable social orders depend upon marriage as an exclusively heterosexual institution. Rather, anthropological research supports the conclusion that a vast array of family types, including families built upon same-sex partnerships, can contribute to stable and humane societies.

Anthropologists may disagree about why this is so, but most would not disagree about whether it is so. Comparative studies of sexual practices challenge our own ideas about what is sexual let alone what is normal.

Some New Guinea people believe that girls don't need any help developing because they naturally become women, but, because women also raise boys, this view holds back the development of the boys' masculinity. Initiation rituals separate the boys from women. In the rituals, fully developed men instill men's values in the boys and give them the strength of warriors. Boys get this strength by consuming the semen of older unmarried men in oral sex. The men believe that they control everything through their control of semen. Only the men can drink the sap of a special tree that restores their semen. Their semen creates babies and feeds them because it causes breast milk to flow. It turns boys into men; it turns girls into wives; it keeps the whole society going. Women say they create milk by themselves and don't need any help from men.

In another New Guinea group, the boys get the semen they need to grow into men from older bachelors their fathers select to have anal sex with when they are about ten or eleven. But, according to these people, virgins make the best hunters because animals won't appear to men who are having sex with women.

We've called these practices oral or anal sex, but it isn't clear that the New Guineans think of it as sex at all. Because our culture thinks of these actions as sexual doesn't mean that New Guineans do. These practices are parts of larger systems of exchanges between age-defined groups of men that also involve food, meat, and sometimes painful acts of inducing vomiting and bleeding. So it is very misleading to think of these as sexual in the same sense they might be to us. Anthropologists have analyzed such actions in terms of Freudian ideas that are centered on ideas of sex and the erotic but that are not appropriate in this cultural context of exchanges of substances. Furthermore, the whole idea of seeing these acts as sexual is connected to the Western idea of sexual desire as something deeply personal and individualistic. We will return to the idea of individualism later, but for now, know that even acts that look to us like sex may be part of a different system of meaning than we are accustomed to, part of a different cultural world. Anthropologist Deborah Elliston (1995) says that to think of these acts in the same cultural terms we use instead of their own New Guinean terms of exchanges of substances is to be ethnocentric.

One test for cultural relativism is the practice of female circumcision or genital cutting, the removal of all or part of the clitoris and sometimes a more extreme form of sewing the vagina together called *infibulation.* These practices are common in parts of Africa.

Some argue, in accordance with relativism, that such practices are aspects of those cultures and that it's not up to us to judge them. Others argue that the practices are dangerous because of the risks of infection, and misogynistic or antiwoman because they deprive women of an important part of their bodies. Kirsten Bell (2005) wondered why her American anthropology students found female genital cutting abhorrent but thought male genital cutting or circumcision was normal. Some international health organizations think of male circumcision as a "medical" procedure but oppose female circumcision altogether.

Male circumcision became popular in Victorian times as a way to control masturbation to ensure physical and moral "hygiene." Some people advocated clitoridectomies to keep girls from masturbating as well.

Freud taught that mature women had orgasms from their vaginas because when girls reached puberty, sexual excitability transferred from the clitoris to the vagina. In this view, the clitoris didn't have anything to do with sex. During Victorian times, doctors would cure a woman of hysteria by massaging her clitoris until she had "hysterical paroxysms," but the Victorians did not think of that as anything sexual.

Culture defines what is and what is not sexual, whether it's oral or anal intercourse in New Guinea or clitoral massages in Victorian England. By the late 1940s, clitorises became so unimportant to the mostly male medical establishment that anatomy textbooks didn't even include them.

In the mid-1970s, *The Hite Report* showed that most women's orgasms come from clitoral rather than vaginal stimulation, and people started wondering why clitoral stimulation wasn't a normal part of sex. Westerners returned to an earlier idea of understanding the clitoris as a female penis—understanding women's bodies in reference to men's.

In fact, while circumcision may reduce the sensitivity of the penis, it doesn't prevent masturbation, and cutting a woman's clitoris off doesn't prevent her having orgasms.

Today, lots of books and other media suggest that women get sexually warmed up by talking and cuddling, while men are mindlessly attracted to body parts. The twenty-first century view is that men are always ready and willing, testosterone-driven creatures who can't control their penises, but women are delicate and passive. In this view, even cutting off part of a guy's penis doesn't slow down his powerful sex drive. It's even a good thing to reduce the sensitivity of a guy's penis because he can perform longer and better. But whacking off any part of a delicate and passive woman's sexual anatomy would cripple her.

Bell says that these kinds of cultural assumptions are behind all of the discussions about genital cutting—thinking that it's bad for women but OK for men. She doesn't say that physiology has nothing to do with sexuality, but she is saying they aren't the same thing.

Doctors and policymakers are ready to condemn female circumcision and approve of male circumcision because of what they think are the *natural* effects. But that tells more about the culture of the doctors and policymakers than about physiology. Sexuality is cultural. And cultures change through time and across space. So even something as "natural" as sex becomes part of culture, and people understand it differently in different times and places.

Conclusion

Race and gender are two of the big categories for classifying people as similar or different. Some say our experience is determined by race and gender. We said there wasn't such a thing as race. How can it determine experience if it doesn't exist? Just because something doesn't exist doesn't mean some culture won't make a big deal of it. Most Americans don't think witches and spirits exist, but they are a big deal for the Lisu tribal people in northern Thailand whom Paul lived with.

Sometimes there really are things that our cultures don't recognize. For instance, Victorian doctors could massage a woman's clitoris until she had an orgasm, but neither one of them thought of that as any kind of sexual experience. So, in America there is a rigid class system, but it's almost as evil to talk about class as it is to talk about masturbation.

So just because we make a big deal out of race doesn't mean that it's real. It isn't real biologically. But it is real politically, and people experience it because we have a racist system that discriminates against people based on the color of their skin or their surname. If you're a black American, your experience teaches you that you're the one who is different. Every black person can tell a story about when he or she first figured out that not everyone was black and that being black made a difference. It's usually painful. If you're from a Spanish-speaking family in the United States you probably remember the first time someone told you you'd better speak English or that you speak with a strange accent. You may remember relatives from Spanish-speaking countries telling you that you had a strange accent. So no matter what language you speak, someone's going to be annoyed, unless it's another person from the same barrio or region of the United States.

If you're a white female, you may wonder why some things are harder for you than for males. You may have noticed it in sports or in math or somewhere else along the way. If you haven't noticed it, you will when you learn that you will probably be paid less than a guy for the same work.

If you're a white male, you probably won't understand this stuff. You'll be inclined to think that everything is fair and equal because it seems that way to you. You may wonder why people of color and women talk about a racist and sexist system. Even if you were a minority, you were from a powerful minority, the minority that runs the country. You are the one for whom the system operates best, so you never need to think about either being white or being male.

Race and gender do affect us, often in ways we never think about. It's the job of anthropology to make those ways more visible. But in addition to race and gender, there is one other thing that is more powerful than either, one thing that in America today is more invisible than either race or gender. That is class. If we ignore class, we ignore all of the causal forces that make race and gender work they way they do. So, yes, we categorize and label each other, and that very practice along with the ideologies of nation-states provides the basis for racism and sexism.

That practice of categorizing and labeling is part of our ability to use language.

Nasrudin was in the Land of Fools. Every day for days on end he stood in the square and preached, "People, sin and evil are everywhere. Sin and evil are hateful." One day he was about to start up with his usual sermon when he saw some of the Fools standing around with their arms folded. "What are you doing?" he asked. "We've just decided what to do about all this sin and evil you've been talking about," they answered. "You've decided to avoid it? To steer clear of it? To shun it?" "No," they answered, "we've decided to shun you."

Discussion Questions:

- Have a debate where one side argues that race and gender differences are real, defined by present-day understandings, and one side argues that there is no basis for them. Keep track of the arguments each side makes. Where do those arguments come from? How did you learn them? How can they be tested?
- How does your current understanding of race conflict with what you've read in this chapter? If everyone accepted the anthropological explanation of race, how would our country be different? How would our world operate differently?
- Apply these same questions to gender differences.
- Discuss how racism has reinforced or not reinforced nationalism in the past. How does it affect nationalism today?
- What are some of the ways we treat men and women differently in the United States? Why do you think we maintain these differences?
- Are there any scientific reasons to prohibit same-sex marriages? Are there political reasons? If so, what are they?
- Discuss how you feel about the ideas that anal and oral sex and massaging a woman's clitoris aren't really sexual. Why do you think you feel that way? What cultural assumptions are involved?

Suggested Reading

Stack, Carol. *All Our Kin: Strategies for Survival in a Black Community*. New York: Harper, 1974.

———. *Call to Home: African Americans Reclaim the Rural South*. New York: Basic Books, 1996.

Herdt, Gilbert. *The Sambia: Ritual, Sexuality, and Change in Papua New Guinea*. Belmont, CA: Thomson/Wadsworth, 2006.

Warnock Fernea, Elizabeth. *Guests of the Sheik: An Ethnography of an Iraqi Village*. New York: Doubleday, 1989.

———. *A Street in Marrakech: A Personal View of Women in Morocco*. Prospect Heights, IL: Waveland Press, 1988.

Talking about the past, the future, other locations, and about "what-ifs" is unique to human languages. *Photo by Suzan Erem. Used with permission of* Voices of Central Pennsylvania.

CHAPTER 4

LANGUAGE

Language was one of the elements interacting in our evolution along with tools, bipedalism, premature birth, and long periods of infant dependency. It is one of the things that made us human and is now one of the things that sets us apart from other animals.

Other animals have systems of signaling. Bees communicate the distance and direction to sources of pollen by their body motions in the hive. They communicate about the state of the hive and the queen with chemical smells called *pheromones* to let each other know what they need to do about feeding larvae and making honey or wax for the hive. Our primate relatives have ways of signaling about food, dominance, submission, danger, and sexual state. Whether they work by body motions, noises, hand signals, or smell, these systems all have one thing in common: they can only communicate about what is going on right here and right now.

Human languages take us into different places and times. We can understand stories about places we have never been and times we can never experience. We don't just talk about the here and the now but about the past and future and the "what if." "What if we used the flakes for tools?" "What if we shaped the flakes and threw away the core?" The term for being able to talk about different times, places, and hypothetical situations is **displacement**. It's unique to human languages.

That means we can say new things. In this sense, human languages are **open.**

Bees communicate by dancing faster or slower in certain directions. Their system is analog—more or less speed or north or south. Our languages are digital—based on **discrete** units of sound and discrete units of meaning, not on the "more or less" analog principle. Linguists learn about languages by comparing different words and paying attention to the smallest differences that they can detect between sounds and between meanings.

If we pair up some words, we can see how this process of comparison works. Pay attention to the sounds, not the meanings.

- *bit/bite*
- *lit/light/lite*
- *hit/height*

Time out for a footnote. We are going to be talking about language here, and we're both Americans of one kind or another, so we're going to use our own language to illustrate those points. Our language is American. It is not English. If you don't believe American is a different language from English, ask a British person. Or, consult H. L. Mencken's 1919 book *The American Language,* which is still in print and explains the differences between American and English.

If we ask someone who speaks American about these pairs, she will tell us that each one is different. *Bit* means one thing, and *bite* means something else. It's the difference in sound that tells us about the difference in meaning. In these examples we're seeing the difference between what we call the "short *I*" sound and the "long *I*" sound, a difference in sound that signals a difference in meaning. Linguists explore all of these contrasts until they can map out all the differences of sound that make a difference in meaning. It's not as straightforward as it first seems. Let's look at some more examples.

If you hold your hand in front of your mouth and say these words, you can feel the differences, but you probably won't hear them. If you say *tip,* you feel a puff of air on your hand as you say the "t" sound and not much of anything after the "p" sound. If you say it backward, *pit,* what happens? Now you feel the puff of breath after the first "p" sound but not much after the last "t" sound. Linguists call that puff of breath **aspiration** and write it with an "h." So we don't confuse that sound with the "th" sound of *the* and *thing* (two different sounds, one spelling), we're going to make it a superscript *h,* so t^h If we write the sounds that are really there, and not just the ones we hear, it would go like this:

$t^h ip$
$p^h it$

"T^h" and "t" are really two different sounds. So are "p" and "p^h." If they're so different, why don't we hear them as different? Well, a lot of people *do* hear them as different. The alphabets of Indian languages all have four different letters for these four different sounds. The reason that people who speak American don't hear the sounds as different is that we've learned not to pay attention to a difference that's really there. We group the "tʰ" and the "t" sounds together and we lump the "p" with the "pʰ."

The difference between "voiced" and "unvoiced" is another contrast that Americans use to distinguish different sounds. Think of the difference between these two words:

bit

pit

Now put a finger on your larynx or voice box and say *bit*. You'll feel a slight vibration. That's the vibration of your vocal chords that linguists call *voicing*. When you say *pit*, you don't feel that vibration. Now *tip* and *dip*. You'll see that you voice the *d* but not the *t*. That makes a big difference in American, and we use it all the time.

So, to speakers of American, this is a difference that makes a difference, but the aspirated-unaspirated difference is not. We use these differences in sounds to communicate differences in meanings.

To make a language, we only need two sounds. Morse code only uses dots and dashes and can say anything. The problem with this is if we only have two sounds, we have to combine a lot of them together to make sure that each meaning is distinct. If we use more different sounds, we don't need so many to signal a difference. Linguists call each distinct sound a **phoneme**. Human languages use between thirteen and forty of them.

When linguists talk about all of the sounds that people can make, they are talking about **phonetics**. In the days before digital recorders, even before tape recorders, they developed the International Phonetic Alphabet (IPA) as a set of symbols for every possible human sound. In those days, to practice using the IPA, students would transcribe stories in some language they had never heard before just to be sure they were getting all of the sounds right. Later, they would figure out which sounds the unknown language grouped together and which ones were distinct. Then another student could read back the **phonetic** transcription to a different speaker of the same unknown language to see whether that person understood it. If the native speaker did not understand, then the transcription was not correct.

When the student worked out all of which sounds the native speaker heard as "the same" (like our American *t* and *tᵇ*) and which ones as "different" (like our *d* and *t* or *b* and *p*), it was called a **phonemic** analysis. From this, anthropologists took the ideas of **emic** and **etic**. Emic means the differences that make a difference inside the culture; etic means all the differences that anyone outside the system can see. Emic and etic are matters of reference. Any system that you use all the time and that you're used to seems natural to you.

This is one of those questions of getting into someone else's reference point. Later on we're going to show you how this emic-etic distinction helps us understand the different ways people deal with things like which relatives they can marry and have sex with and which ones they better not even think about that way.

We've been talking about sounds and how they form into systems of differences to communicate differences of meaning. Language has two different levels—sound and meaning, each with its own system. We call this **duality of patterning**, and it is unique to human languages.

Just as phonemes are smallest units of sound, so the smallest units of meaning are morphemes. *Morph* means "form," as in sexual dimorphism or polymorphic. Morphology, for instance, means the study of forms. Think about prefixes and suffixes in American for an example.

write	writer	writing	writes
speak	speaker	speaking	speaks
sing	singer	singing	sings
lead	leader	leading	leads
hit	hitter	hitting	hits
kick	kicker	kicking	kicks

We see that there's a verb that we can change into different meanings by adding suffixes—*-er* means "one who"; *-ing* means "in the process of doing it"; *-s* means "it's happening now." Linguists analyze languages into their morphemes like a verb plus *er, -ing,* or *-s.* In American, each verb is a separate morpheme. So we have morphemes: *write, speak, sing, lead, hit, kick.* We can use these to make adverbs, as in "She spoke singingly." And so on.

Some languages make verbs out of nouns. Americans do that a little bit, but it's usually really annoying, as in making the verb *surveil* out of the noun *surveillance,* which comes from the verb *survey.* Turkish uses a bunch of suffixes stacked onto the ends of verbs to indicate who is doing what to whom, when, and how many of each.

The last thing about human languages that makes them different is that they are **arbitrary, learned, and traditional**. There is no necessary relationship between a thing and the word for it; there is no necessary reason to use aspiration or voicing as a way of making a difference between consonants. These systems are arbitrary. That means since they aren't coded into nature or our genes, we have to learn them. Learning our languages is part of that long maturation period when our nervous systems are linking up and making connections and pathways based, in part, on our early experiences.

When we're children, what we hear is a lot of noise, but we notice that somehow it seems meaningful to the giants around us. That doesn't come from experience so much as from our genetically wired-in ability to make theories about experience. The first thing we figure out is that the noise is significant. Then we have to make theories about just what is significant in what way. Because kids do this in regular stages about the same way at the same ages, we think that it is connected with the maturation of the brain and nervous system.

For instance, kids notice the difference between *talk* and *talked*. They see the same difference in *walk* and *walked*. And in *smile* and *smiled* and in *help* and *helped,* and many more examples. So they figure maybe the *-ed* part is a morpheme about something in the past. So they experiment with constructions like *go-goed*; *buy-buyed*; *hold-holded*; *have-haved*. These are reasonable applications of the same principle ... at least the way the kids look at it. The giants can tell the kids until they're blue in the face that "It's *went,* not *goed*," but the kids won't get it until their brains are ready to try out a new theory with something that weird in it.

Kids develop a more and more complex theory of the relationships between sounds and meanings as their brains develop and as they experiment with more and more examples. Linguists call the theory of a language that a grown-up speaker of the language has a **grammar**. A grammar specifies the relationships between sound and meaning in a language. It determines how we can combine morphemes to make words. For us to be able to use a grammar and agree on it, a grammar has to be finite in size. If it were infinitely large, we could each use a different part of it, and we couldn't understand each other at all—there would be no system. And it uses the same rules over and over, like the rules for combining morphemes.

But this finite set of rules can describe all possible sentences in the language. There may be new sentences that nobody has ever heard before, but people can understand new sentences because they fall within the rules of the grammar. And there are a potentially infinite number of new sentences in any language. So finite rules describe infinite sentences. Here's a simple example from arithmetic: Imagine a rule that says "Add 1." That's a simple rule that can describe an infinitely large number of numbers. Start anywhere you want, and add 1. And again. And so on.

We've already looked at systems of sound and seen that when there is a contrast between two sounds that people hear, it's a difference that makes a difference, a *phonemic* difference. When there is no such contrast, it's the *same* phoneme, as in our aspiration examples when we showed you that, to Americans, the *t*ʰ in *tip* is the same sound as the *t* in *pit.* There are also systematic relationships among meanings—for instance, among the one who does something, the thing she does, the thing she does it with, and the thing she does it to.

> Sally—the one who does something
> Sally threw—the thing she does
> Sally threw the ball—the thing she does it with
> Sally threw the ball to Bill—the thing she does it to.

These are, roughly, the subject of a sentence or actor; the action or verb; the thing she does it with or direct object; and the thing she does it to or indirect object. In American, most nouns are the same no matter what their function in the sentence is. We could say, "Bill threw the ball to Sally," or "Sally threw Bill to the ball" if she's practicing karate on the beach, for instance. But in Icelandic, people have to indicate the role of the noun with a specific ending or suffix. So there's one ending for actors, another for indirect objects, and a third for direct objects. In American, we know the role of the word by where it comes in the sentence. In Icelandic, you know the role of the word by the ending on it.

In American, we could put *ball* first and say, "The ball was thrown to Bill." Did you ever notice that bureaucrats do that a lot? The reason is that they don't have to say *who* did it, and these folks are aces at avoiding responsibility. So they say mealymouthed things like "The decision was made," "The policy was adopted," and "The deed was done."

The American language lets them side-step responsibility as slickly as karate Sally side-stepping Bill's charge at her after she threw him to the ball on the beach. We use exactly the same logical relationships to ask questions just by putting in a question word. In American, we do this by raising the intonation at the end of the sentence. Listen to your voice when you ask this as a question: "Sally threw the ball to Bill?" In Chinese and Turkish, they add a question word to the end of the sentence. In printed Spanish, you get the hint first because the question mark appears upside down in front of the question. It comes to the same thing.

All of these sentences have different word orders, but they are built on the same logical relationships. Linguists call the logical relationships **deep structure**. They call the particular word order **surface structure**. Both of these together, the two parts of a grammar that determine the way words fit together into sentences, linguists call **syntax**.

Now, let's go back to the beginning—we're trying to understand how human languages make the connections between sounds and meanings. Language is digital, a phonological system specifies all relationships among any sounds we can hear—phonemes. In the same way, meaning comes in discrete digital segments. A semantic system specifies all possible relationships among these units of meaning. We hear sounds and somehow connect them to meanings. Linguists say that a **semantic system** specifies all the possible relationships among meanings just as a **phonological system** specifies the relationships among sounds.

The grammar is the system of matching up sounds and meanings. So it includes all of these components in a system as shown in figure 4.1.

Linguists borrow the idea of "mapping" from mathematics. In our example of odd and even numbers, we can say that the rule "add 1" maps all the odd numbers onto all the even ones. All that means is that if you take any odd number and add one, you get the even number that goes next. It sounds a little simple-minded, but so is all mathematics. It's all a matter of stating the obvious. The question is "Obvious to who?" (Or is it "whom"?)

In this model of language, a grammar is several systems working together. A phonological system maps sounds onto surface structures. Here come some sounds, "yackety yack." The phonological system maps those onto surface structures. "Sally threw the ball." A syntactic system maps surface structures onto deep structures. "Sally is the one doing; what she's doing is throwing; what she's throwing is a ball." A semantic system maps deep structures onto meanings. "Who is Sally, and what is a ball, and who cares if she's throwing it?"

All of this knowledge is unconscious, so we can't just ask people, "Please tell us your grammar." They can't bring all of these details to consciousness without a lot of practice with the kinds of analysis we've been discussing—figuring out all of the sounds and how they contrast with each other, all of the morphemes, all of the meanings and how they form a system, the logic of sentences, and all of the arrangements of words. If they do that, then they're linguists.

Even if we find a person who is a linguist and can tell us the grammar of the language, it wouldn't be of much use to us because it wouldn't

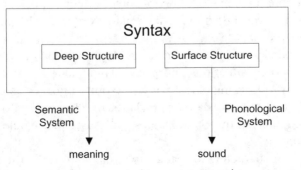

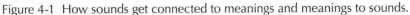

Figure 4-1 How sounds get connected to meanings and meanings to sounds.

help us learn the language. Learning a language is different from learning *about* a language. The only way to learn how to ride a bicycle is by riding one. Nobody can explain it to you. It's the same with language. To learn a language, we have to do what kids do, build an unconscious theory of the language by hearing a lot of examples and letting our brains develop a theory of how they all work together.

Linguists work out the details of different languages and describe the details of just how the grammar maps sounds onto meanings so we can, at the same time, understand what other people say and say what we are thinking—work the system from both directions.

If we compare the grammars of all languages to see what they all have in common, we can talk about the grammar of all human languages, or **universal grammar**. Linguists have concluded that all languages have similar deep structures, but they can have quite different surface structures. We are born with the capacity to construct a grammar of any particular language because the universal grammar, the capacity for language, any language, is built into us by our evolutionary history. What children learn is the details of their particular languages. This view of language is one that was proposed by Noam Chomsky in the 1960s and that he and others have developed since then.

Sociocultural anthropologists consider language to be one dimension of culture. Like language, other dimensions of our cultures are largely unconscious patterns that we learn in much the same way we learn language—by our brains working out theories of the regularities we experience while our nervous systems are developing when we are kids.

So far, we've talked about what language is, how it's different from other systems of communication, its role in the evolution of our species, and how it works. Most anthropologists are willing to let linguists answer the questions that are just about language. But that's only half the story. The other half of the story is what we do with language. We've already hinted at some of that when we said we were writing in American and not English.

Some people say that lots of people on our planet speak English these days. If you've ever talked to an Australian, you probably got lost somewhere after the first "g'day." If the sounds didn't get you, the different use of words may have. They started with some version of English and adapted it to their situations and needs. They made it up as they went along. Just as Americans did. If we wrote our languages as they sound, we'd be in trouble. There'd be several languages just in the British Islands and a bunch more in the United States, and Australian would be its own language, too.

Chinese use characters instead of an alphabet to write their language. So spelling isn't an issue. They don't pretend that the characters have much to do with sound. You have to learn a different character for each word. So it doesn't matter what it sounds like. That's the reason that no matter what dialect of Chinese you speak, you can get along with other people who can write some kind of Chinese. The writing unifies diverse dialects. Japanese imported the Chinese characters, and even Japanese speakers can get along to some extent with Chinese speakers by "drawing" the characters with a finger on the palm of the other hand.

English does pretty much the same by not insisting on a tight connection between sounds and spellings. Kids learn the languages they hear. If they hear one language at home and another at school, they'll learn both. One will be the home language; the other will be the school language. Anthropologists who have kids with them in the field are often amazed that the kids learn the language of the folks they are with faster than the grown-ups. One of the things the kids are learning in addition to all the stuff about sounds and meanings that we discussed earlier is the rules about when to use which language. This is like Paul knowing when to drop into Texan and when to try to speak American.

Sometimes language differences are stigmatized. If you're speaking Texan in the Northeast, people are likely to think that you're an ignorant hick. And if you're trying to speak New Yorkese in Texas, people may not think too well of you, either. So, along with grammar, kids learn when to use what languages.

Some people think that English should be the only language that we allow in the United States. There may be a few Americans who can manage English, but mostly they want American to be standard and to outlaw any other languages, such as Spanish, Navajo, or any dialects of Athabaskan, Polish, Italian, Yiddish, and other languages from schools, and to ensure that everyone speaks American. They are the ones who don't want multilingual education in schools. They say that kids who speak Lao or Vietnamese or Spanish or Polish should just be forced to speak English for their own good.

There's a destructive and malicious form of unlogic that says whatever you are whining about is your own fault. One label for this is **blaming the victim**. A woman wears a short dress, has a drink in a bar, and walks home alone. A man rapes the woman. It's her fault. A National Guardsman gets killed in Iraq. It's his fault? Well, he was there. He was dressed for it. He was in the wrong place at the wrong time wearing the wrong clothes and looking the wrong way. It's his fault.

It doesn't make sense in either example. Nor does it when it's applied to kids in schools. Another label for this is **deficit theory**. That's the idea that if some group of kids doesn't do well in school, there's something wrong with *the kids in that group*. There's some deficit. They may be stupid or lazy, but whatever it is, it's about them, not about the policies and the schools and the system they're in. Someone ought to teach these kids to be more energetic, to speak clearly, and educate them better so that they're not so stupid.

Black kids, for instance. Here's where it comes back to institutional racism that we discussed earlier. You don't need to think of anyone as a racist. You can think that if people just keep on doing their own jobs and are nice, there won't be any racism. You can teach people to be nice in seminars on how to tolerate people they can't stand. You don't have to change the system of funding for schools that uses meager tax revenues from poor neighborhoods to try to keep open decaying schools in those neighborhoods. You can keep the tax system in place that lets rich neighborhoods buy computers and science labs, and pay good wages to good teachers, and even buy toilet paper and soap for the kids. There's no need to change that system if the problem is with lazy and stupid kids.

A lot of this comes back to language and stigmatization of certain dialects. We mentioned earlier that the British base a kind of racism on language use. So do Americans. So do lots of people. Icelanders are no exception.

Remember how in Icelandic you can tell the role of a word by the ending? There's a different ending for subject, indirect object, direct object, and possessive for nouns. Add to that singular and plural versions. Add to that whether it's masculine, feminine, or neuter, and you have about a gazillion possibilities. Foreigners find it all a bit daunting, but kids learn it all without any problem. Unless they are from working-class families and use some word forms that the better classes haven't approved.

For instance, if you say something like, "Me and my boyfriend ... ," that's a big mistake in Icelandic. It's almost a mental disease. At least it's a linguistic disease. The better class of Icelanders think of their language as being like their environment—beautiful and unpolluted. They want to keep it that way by being sure that all Icelanders speak the language properly. Gísli Pálsson points out that this is related to the idea that all Icelanders are equal. The ideology of egalitarianism is even stronger in Iceland than in the United States. And to be fair, they are a hell of a lot more equal than Americans are. But there are still class distinctions, and you're stigmatized if you don't get the cases right. The better classes also think that you're just lazy if you voice some of those unvoiced consonants—if you use a *d* in place of a *t,* for instance. They call it being "slack jawed."

This isn't a question of language; it's a question of economic systems and political systems and classes. To understand how language works sociologically, we have to understand the dynamics of economic systems and states. We'll be explaining these in the next chapters.

Language is also connected to nationalism. Similar things happen in other European countries. Every valley in Norway has its own dialect of Norwegian. In olden days, at least some Norwegians thought that Icelandic was just another dialect of their language. When Norway became independent from Denmark, they couldn't agree on which dialect to use for the whole country. A country has to have a flag and a song and an army and a language. So they made up what they call "Book Language," or a standard form of Norwegian to use in schools, books, and media.

The same thing happened in other European countries. When Israel needed a language, they invented modern Hebrew. Indonesia invented Indonesian. In Thailand, the state supported the use of Bangkok Thai or central Thai as opposed to the more Lao-like dialects of the North and Northeast.

When linguists studied the actual dialects of Europe, they couldn't figure out where to draw the lines between different languages. The definition of the "same" language is one that all the speakers can understand. So if a Texan talks to an Australian, two different languages, right? Or a person from Canton talks to a person from Beijing? If there's one English language and one Chinese language based on this criterion, then there'd be maybe two European languages: Latin and Norse. Latin would include all the dialects of Latin that different nations have claimed: French, Italian, Spanish, and Portuguese. The Norse would include all those dialects in that family: German, Dutch, Norwegian, Danish, and Icelandic. Maybe there'd be a separate Slavic for Russian, Polish, Croatian, and Serbian.

So when people say they speak seven languages and they're all as different from each other as American, Texan, and Australian, we might wonder why they're so proud of themselves.

Linguists couldn't find the single-language communities that were supposed to go together with the nations. Someone said that the real definition of a language is a dialect (like central Thai) with an army behind it. So what most folks think of as languages have more to do with nationalism than anything else. To understand that point, we have to understand how states work, and we'll explain that in a later chapter.

Languages also have to do with gender. There's a whole industry of "Mars/Venus" stuff based on the idea that men and women live in very different worlds. Lots of that comes through in language use and what people use language for. We bet that every one of you has been in one of those conversations that went from bad to worse because the other person did all the wrong things. The woman may start out talking about the difficulty with relatives. The guy will figure out some way to fix the trouble, such as, "Why not just avoid all your relatives? I can't stand them anyway." Then the woman gets miffed because the guy doesn't like her relatives, and he doesn't understand why that should be an issue since she just said it was a problem.

The difference is that the woman just wanted to talk about it, but the guy wanted to fix it. That goes back to those gender roles we discussed earlier. Those are culturally defined, and one of the ways people act them out is in how they talk to each other, even if it sometimes doesn't work very well. Goldschmidt (2006:143) says, "Anyone who thinks that language is a useful way to communicate feelings has never had a lovers' quarrel or been to a faculty meeting."

These are some of the things that anthropological linguists work on—language and ethnicity, education, nations and nationalism, and gender. They study how people use their languages to live out their cultures. Another place for the study of language is in understanding how people think.

Discussion Questions

- Write a story about your first memory of language. When you're done, pull out the details that explain how your experience with language was arbitrary, learned, and/or traditional.
- How does our capacity to learn and use language make us different from bees, ants, or dogs?
- A number of scientists have performed experiments to prove that dolphins and chimps have the capacity for language. Look up some of that research and argue the case for or against that work.
- If you're learning a second language or have a native speaker of a language other than American in your class, write a sentence in that language and translate it directly in English underneath. Discuss the order of the words and how they translate. Why doesn't this method work very well as translation? What do you need to do to make it a better translation?

Suggested Reading

Lindquist, Julie. *A Place to Stand: Politics and Persuasion in a Working-Class Bar.* New York: Oxford University Press, 2002.
Tannen, Deborah. *Linguistics, Language and the Real World: Discourse and Beyond.* Washington, DC: Georgetown University Press, 2003.
———. *Talking from 9 to 5: How Women's and Men's Conversational Styles Affect Who Gets Heard, Who Gets Credit, and What Gets Done at Work.* New York: Oxford University Press, 1993.

————. *That's Not What I Meant! How Conversational Style Makes or Breaks Relationships.* New York: Ballantine, 1986.

————. *You Just Don't Understand: Women and Men in Conversation.* New York: Ballantine, 1991.

————. *You're Wearing That? Understanding Mothers and Daughters in Conversation.* New York: Random House, 2006.

5

Ideas about kinship are different in U.S. society today than they were in our grandparents' day. This
young girl is enjoying cocoa with her two moms.
Different societies define kinship in different ways.
*Used with permission of the photographer and the
family in the photo.*

CHAPTER 5

HOW WE THINK ABOUT KINSHIP

Sociocultural anthropologists are especially interested in systems of meaning. We've discussed the difference between the sounds we really make and the sounds we actually hear and use—phonetics versus phonemics. Sociocultural anthropologists extend the idea from language to the rest of culture with the ideas of emics and etics. Here we're going to explain how these ideas help us understand how people know which relatives they can marry or have sex with and which ones they have to avoid. This will provide us with some hints about how to understand other relationships between the realities we live in and the various ways we understand them.

Everyone has relatives, and we can make a genealogy of any person that goes as far back as memory can take us, if not all the way back to our first ancestors. We use triangles to represent males, circles to represent females, an equal sign to mean marriage, and vertical lines to indicate descent—whose son or daughter a person is. As you go up the diagram, we say you *ascend*—Latin for "go up"—and as you go down the diagram, we say you *descend*—yep, Latin for "go down." Every genealogy has a reference point, an "I" that defines all of the relationships. We call that "I" by the Latin word for "I," which is *ego*.

Here's a hint on how to read this next part. Make a copy of the diagram (figure 5.1) so you can keep it close to the book and don't have to keep turning back to see it. And don't be afraid to use your finger (*digit*, if you want to be Latin and fancy about it) to point to (*indicate*, if you want to stay in Latin) things as you work through them.

This diagram defines what most Americans think of as a family: a mom, a dad, a brother, and a sister who are kids of the mom and dad. We can link such relationships up to make larger genealogical diagrams as is shown in figure 5.2.

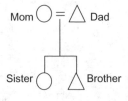

Figure 5-1 Elements of genealogy.

This diagram shows an ego, her brother, mom, dad, aunts, uncles, and cousins. (We'll get to the superscript *X*s, *Y*s, and *?*s in a minute.) At least that's how most Americans would see it. But not everyone on the planet would agree. For instance, a lot of folks would say that it's pretty weird to lump all of those people in ego's generation, A, B, C, D, E, F, G, and H, into the same category and call them the same thing because they are so obviously so different. They are as different, some might say, as that "th" in *tip* is from that "t" in *pit*—that is, different from the emic perspective. What makes them different, from a lot of points of view, is that they belong to different lineages. Remember, a **lineage** is a group of people who trace descent from a common ancestor. As we said before, they can be **patrilineal** if people trace descent in the male line or **matrilineal** if people stress only the female links. Think in terms of a matrilineal lineage like the people of the Pacific Island of Truk do. They get their lineage affiliation from their mothers, which means ego and her brother belong to the lineage of their mother. Mother's brother and sister also belong to that same lineage. We'll call that "Lineage X" because they only stress the female links; cousins C and D also belong to the same lineage. Cousins A and B belong to the lineage of *their* mom. That will be a different lineage because of the **incest prohibition** on Truk that prohibits people from marrying other people of the same lineage because an X man cannot

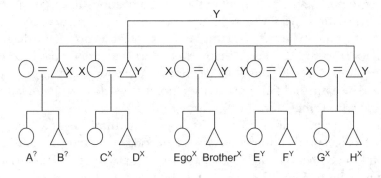

Figure 5-2

marry an X woman. Ego will call her brother, "brother." But she will also call D "brother" and C "sister," because they are in her lineage and in the same generation as she is. B is a guy she can think about for a husband.

Lineages are the important units when people think about "family." So a person's family is not just her mother, dad, and siblings; it is all of her lineage mates that are brothers and sisters as well as the women of her mother's generation that are the same as her mother. Ego's dad has to belong to a different lineage (Y) from her mom, or else it would be a brother marrying a sister—if they were in the same lineage. He gets his lineage affiliation from his mother, so he is in the same lineage with his brothers and sisters—all of them are Ys.

Because it is lineages that are families, it is lineages that have relationships with other lineages. If ego's dad married her mom, that is a relationship between those two lineages—X and Y. Suppose Dad's lineage is supposed to marry women from Mom's lineage. Then all Y men marry X woman as in this diagram (figure 5.3).

Then Dad's brother, the father of G and H, would also marry a woman from Mom's lineage. So G and H would be in Lineage X and therefore be brothers and sisters of ego, and their mom would be ego's mother's sister.

So, ego would call C, D, G, and H her siblings, and she can't marry them or even fool around with them. Let's call ego's lineage the X lineage and her Dad's lineage the Y lineage. Then we see that Y men marry X women. E and F are of lineage Y because their mom is Y. That means the father of C and D is also from lineage Y.

Get this: That means ego is likely to fall madly in love with F and F will fall madly in love with ego, and they are going to be married. Why? Because X women marry Y men and Y men marry X women, and ego has known and experienced this all of ego's life. Ego could also marry B because he is from another lineage, and he's not a brother, but that would break the pattern of exchange. It wouldn't be consistent with family values.

So what Americans call cousins, the Trukese people think of as either brothers and sisters or potential spouses, but surely very different from each other and not at all the same kind of thing. Anthropologists call the ones that Trukese think of as potential spouses **cross cousins**. (Now is a

Figure 5-3 Women of Lineage X marry men of Lineage Y. Men of lineage Y marry women of Lineage X.

good time to pull out the copy of the earlier diagram.) Here's the formula. Cross cousins are the children of ego's parent's siblings of the opposite sexes. That's Dad's sister's kids and mother's brother's kids. Anthropologists call what Trukese think of as brothers and sisters **parallel cousins**. They are all of the children of the parent's siblings of the same sex—father's brother's and mother's sister's kids.

The only reason this is a little confusing to Americans is that we don't think in terms of lineages and because we think of all cousins being the same kind of relationship, and probably nobody you'd marry.

Americans and Trukese all have relatives. All of anyone's relatives are a genealogy. We can break all genealogies down into "mother," "father," "brother," and "sister," "son," and "daughter." Anthropologists call these M, F, B, Z (for sister), S (for son), and D. So cross cousins are ego's MBD, MBS, FZD, and FZS. Parallel cousins are MZS, MZD, FBD, and FBS. What we are doing is using genealogies to represent lineage relationships.

What kind of lineages do Americans have? We don't. Our last names work somewhat like patrilineal lineages, but they don't define groups. Americans and most Europeans have what we call **kindreds**—that's the group of all relatives within a certain genealogical distance that are related by any link at all. All the cousins, for instance. Only siblings have exactly the same kindreds. Americans' share exactly the same cousins only with brothers and sisters. Kindreds were important to the medieval Icelanders for vengeance. If someone hurt one of "us," then we would get our kindred together and hurt them back. But you can only go so far up the genealogy before you run into people who are equally related to both kindreds, so feuds can't spread too far.

The genealogical diagrams define an *etic grid*—that is, an outside view or a universal system of kin relationships. The international phonetic alphabet defines the etic grid for the sounds of languages. Like the etic genealogical grid, it is outside any given language. Just as each language has its own phonemic system, the sounds and meanings that matter to only that group of people, different people have different ways of organizing genealogical relationships into emic patterns that are meaningful to them.

Remember the problems with Freud in our discussion of gender? That was the problem of assuming that everyone's culture defines sex in the same way Victorian Viennese people did, that their cultures defined the erotic and the sexual in the same way Freud did. So Freud was assuming there was an etic grid for this stuff, but in fact, he was being ethnocentric because he was thinking that *his* way of thinking about things was the natural way, the only way to do it.

We have to be careful not to be **ethnocentric** when we talk about emics and etics. Ethnocentrism is thinking that your own emic system is a universal etic system. For instance, when people get married, they have to figure out where to live. If there is some pattern to it, we call it a **residence rule**. If the newlyweds usually live with the guy's people, we say they are **patrilocal** or **virilocal**, depending on which Latin word for *dad* you like better. If they live with the wife's people, we say they are **matrilocal** or **uxurolocal**, depending on which Latin word for *mom* you like better. If they live in a different place from the family (remember, this is usually a lineage) of either mate, then we say they are **neolocal**.

What difference could any of this make? Anthropologists have tried to figure out whether the kind of residence is necessarily connected to anything else, like the kind of lineage (it's not) or the way they get their food—from gardens, from plowing farms, from foraging.

An anthropologist named Ward Goodenough (1956) was working in Truk in 1947. He did a census of all the households on the island and figured out which people followed which residence rule. When he got done, he compared his results with those of another anthropologist, J. L. Fischer, who had done another census of the same people just three years earlier. Goodenough found that the same people were in the same households, but he and Fischer had counted differently, so their results didn't agree. For instance, in one household lived an old man and his second wife, his three sons by his first wife, and the wife of his oldest son. This looks like it is a patrilocal extended family—a patrilocal family of more than one generation, since the son's wife had joined the household. Both of the wives had moved to the same household when they married men from the household.

But it wasn't that simple. Remember that family in Truk means matri-lineal lineage. Land belongs to lineages, not to individuals. The father had married a woman and moved to her lineage place to live in a house that her lineage owned. The first wife's lineage sister lived nearby with her husband and their kids. The pattern was that the women stayed put with their lineage and their husbands joined them. Now it looks like matrilocal residence. In Truk, family values means being with brothers and sisters. Nobody would want their kids to grow up separated from their siblings. So when the father's first wife died, her lineage allowed him to stay on with his children so they could be with their brothers and sisters. For the same reason, they let him stay there when he remarried.

It's important for newlyweds to think about how to make a living in Truk just as it is anywhere else. They need to be able to have access to some land. Lineages own land. So if they want their kids to grow up with their siblings, they look for some land in the woman's lineage place. If the wife's lineage doesn't have any land for them to use, then the couple can look in the husband's place. If neither of those places has any land, they can check her dad's lineage or his dad's lineage place.

Matrilineal lineages aren't mirror images of patrilineal ones because the men have authority in both. Even if the lineage is matrilineal, the men still run the lineage. In Truk, that means that men have to stay close to their own lineages so that they can take care of their responsibilities to their own brothers and sisters.

If the new husband's lineage can give the couple more or better land than the wife's lineage can give them, and the wife's lineage is far away from the husband's place, then they might live with the husband's lineage and give up on raising the kids with their siblings.

Their choice is not between living with the wife's parents or the husband's parents. Goodenough concluded that the whole etic grid for residence rules was ethnocentric. The rules that anthropologists used for residence rules weren't the same as the Trukese rules

Goodenough's conclusion was that anthropologists shouldn't use their own ideas as universal ones; we should find out how people make sense of their own worlds and not assume that they think about things the same way we do. We need to find out the emic categories that are important to the people themselves, just as we find out the sounds that are important to their languages or what relatives count as brothers and sisters.

Cultural Codes

Some anthropologists started to think in terms of **cultural codes**: not just the emic categories people use to make sense of their worlds, but how they use them, for instance, to figure out where to live after they get married. To understand this inside point of view for the people of Truk, we have to know about matrilineal lineages, who controls land, who makes decisions in lineages, family values, and the alternatives that are available to people. Cultural codes are the assumptions people use in everyday life, ideas about reality, meaning, how to divide things into categories (cousins, cross cousins), and how things are related to one another (a person marries a cross cousin).

The biological approach to curing in many industrial lands is more or less mechanical. According to this view, all of us are mechanisms that can malfunction. When our body mechanisms malfunction, we are sick. Doctors are supposed to identify the malfunction and fix it by giving us a drug to change our body chemistry or by surgery or physical therapy to rearrange some component of the mechanism or some combination of these. Even physicians like Dean Ornish, who are way out on the margins with ideas like meditation to reduce stress, operate in terms of effects on the mechanism.

In the late 1960s and early 1970s, Paul lived with Lisu people in the mountains of northern Thailand. They thought that if some malfunction causes a person to be sick, then medicines and physical therapies can fix it. They even have specialists in herbal medicines to treat these cases. They think of hospitals and doctors as doing the same kind of things their medicine women do.

But they think that no amount of medicines will help a person if a spirit is causing the sickness. Then the only effective thing to do is to find out what spirit is responsible and what the human victim did to offend the spirit, then make good the offense. In the village where Paul lived during a single year, he recorded that people sacrificed 311 chickens and 100 pigs in 411 ceremonies. They made seven visits to lowland hospitals—four for cuts, two by the same guy for a shotgun wound, and one for an intractable disease of a shaman's wife. A hundred and one people came to Paul for help, and he did the best he could with his limited skills and supplies to help people with tropical ulcers, cuts, and whatever else aspirin and tetracycline could treat. There were "injection doctors," usually former Thai Army medics who had learned a little about treating sickness in the army and decided to do it for a living for part of the year or full-time. Village people got 43 injections from these traveling medics. That came to 411 cures that involved spirits somehow and 151 that did not, a total of 562. So, about 73 percent of the curing efforts were about spirits and about 27 percent were about mechanics.

Here we want to pause and insert a note for future reference. Notice that whatever else is going on, people are killing chickens and pigs, spending time and money on medicine as well as ceremonies, and all of their actions have consequences for their households and their village. We will come back to these points later, but for the moment, think about how any time people do anything, we leave traces for future archaeologists to find. Our actions have consequences.

Industrial folks have a theory of disease that says it's mechanical. It is elaborate and has many branches to deal with cells, cell reproduction, genetics, bones, kids, moms, women, men, micro-organisms, infections, populations, hearts, lungs, and a lot of other things people can go to medical school to study. Sometimes it makes one wonder whether they got all the specialties together to make a person, what kind of creature they would come up with.

Lisu have a different theory of disease. According to their cultural code, causes may be mechanical but may involve spirits. If they are mechanical, they respond to medical treatment; and if they are not, they do not.

Somebody is sick. Lisu interpret the symptoms they see according to their theory of disease to figure out what to do about it. Since they know that spirits can cause people to be sick, they need to get some information about whether a spirit is behind this instance and what might be going on. To get this information, they ask a **shaman**, a person whom spirits can possess, to call down his spirits so that they can ask them directly. Two shamans lived in the village where Paul lived. Someone would ask one of the shamans to help, and the shaman would come to the person's house and stand in front of the altar.

On the back walls of most houses hangs a plank or two. On these are Chinese tea cups, the same small handleless cups you can find in Chinese restaurants in the United States and other countries. Each of these cups represents a spirit. Facing the altars, the cups represent, from left to right, the household head's mother, father, father's mother and father's father. If you guessed that these folks have patrilineal lineages, you were right.

Next come the spirits of the lineage. The first, right after grandfather, is the third-generation great-grandfather, the first of the ancestors who can be a lineage spirit. He is the most junior of the lineage spirits. Each lineage then has a series of spirits, each with its own name, that are ranked from least to most powerful.

So the shaman stands in front of the altar and invokes his third-generation great-grandfather spirit, the most junior of the lineage spirits, by saying, "The people have called me to help them. Someone here is sick. I am asking you to help me. Please come down." The shaman bends from the waist and holds a handful of lit joss sticks as he sways back and forth whistling until the first spirit comes to ride his horse. Then the shaman begins his "spirit singing," as Lisu call it. He speaks with the voice of the spirit who talks to the people.

"Why have you called me?"

Now several people are gathered in the house, and someone answers that this person is sick and the people need some help.

"I am just a minor spirit. I don't know much. If the spirits help you, you will have to use your pigs, use your chickens, use liquor, use joss sticks."

"We have pigs to offer; we have chickens to offer; we have liquor to offer; we have joss sticks to offer."

The people explain the problem, and this most junior spirit calls on more powerful lineage spirits, who come down one by one to see if they can help. These spirits get in touch with other spirits and ask who is causing this person to be sick in this way. They usually find an answer—it may be the spirit of the stream, the stone spirit, the hill spirit, or one of a number of others that the person has inadvertently offended, perhaps by stepping on it on the way to work. In any case, the person must make recompense.

People then use their theory of disease to interpret this information and conclude that they need to offer a chicken or pig to a certain spirit. The next morning the household may offer a chicken to the spirit. After the ceremony is done, the people eat the chicken. Or the spirit may demand a pig. Then a lot more people come to the feast that follows the offering. A male relative builds an altar like a small table of bamboo outside near the place where the offense happened and offers the animal alive. Then he kills the animal. If they sacrifice a pig, someone expert in interpreting omens looks at the pig's liver to see whether the spirit has accepted the offering, whether it was directed to the correct spirit, or whether it is the correct spirit but too small an offering. If the spirit wanted a chicken, people check the thigh bones for oracles by tapping splints of bamboo about the size of toothpicks into the holes in the bones and reading them for information. Then people cook the animal, and the officiate offers it again cooked. After that, people eat.

There are standard ways of reading oracles. They aren't random or personal opinions; they follow a definite system. People then use their theory of disease to interpret this information and decide whether more ceremonies are necessary. People use their cultural code—ideas—to understand the world (or data about it), they base their actions on these understandings, and their actions have consequences for the world.

This keeps on going until the symptoms go away or until the people have some reason to think that spirits aren't involved or until the person dies, whichever happens first. Usually the symptoms abate after a while.

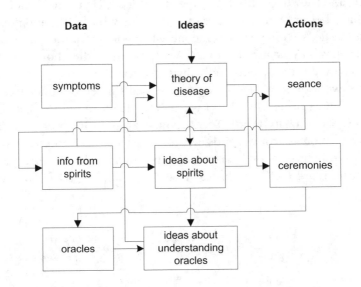

Figure 5-4 How Lisu use their cultural code to heal sick people.

When Paul discussed this with a physician, the doctor said that it was a good thing that most human ailments don't last more than about ten days, or his profession would be in trouble.

So, if we see a Lisu person get sick, ask a shaman to call down his spirits, and then offer a chicken or pig, and we want to make sense of it, we have to ask first, How does it make sense to the people doing it? What is their cultural code?

The logic of this system is that you can do things that annoy other people. When you come to know about something like that, it's up to you to do something to make it right with the other person. If you don't, they have the right to hurt you, so it's in your interest to do something quickly. Spirits are like people except that we can't see them, and they are more powerful than we are. Because we can't see them, it's easy to annoy them. Like people, they then hurt the person who offended them. That's the indication that the person needs to do something to make it right with the spirit. So the person has to find out who is offended and what it would take to make it right, and then do that.

We can generalize this approach to understanding people. There are realities that people understand in terms of cultural codes. People base their actions on their cultural understandings, and those actions have consequences for the realities.

Suppose that one of the central assumptions of your culture is that individuals are important and that their choices determine everything that happens to them. Some kids decide to drop out of high school. That's their choice, and they live with it. Some go to college. That's their choice, and they have better chances in life than the kids who finished high school but didn't go to college. Or someone who works a minimum wage job doesn't have any health insurance. Why? Because she chose not to buy it. Everything is a matter of individual choices.

Now we look at a city or region and see that some folks aren't doing as well as others. What do we do? We teach them to make better choices. We educate them. Teenage girls are getting pregnant? Teach them not to mess around. Kids are doing drugs? Teach them to just say no. Everyone has a good heart and wants to help folks do better, so they start teaching kids these things. That's the "action" part. The culture

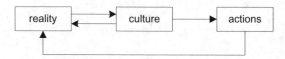

Figure 5-5 Our cultures tell us how to act and our actions change things.

tells us that we can fix any problem by educating people, so we start up programs to do that. That has consequences, too—now kids have to sit through boring, stupid discussions and classes about how to just say no and why they shouldn't be having any fun. But someone gets paid for those programs. And that means those resources aren't going somewhere else. So there's no soap or toilet paper in the bathrooms, and the school building is falling down.

We look back at the same system after our programs are working along and say, "Oh, the school is falling down. We should teach these people to keep up their schools." And so on. That's the way cultures work. We try to understand what we see in terms of the ideas we have, then we base our actions on those ideas, and our actions make a difference in the real world. And so on. Sometimes we see a problem, but instead of finding out about it, we just understand it in terms of our culture, and we try to fix it, and things get worse than they were before. That's how we can have people with good hearts working in systems of institutional racism. People don't think what they are doing is racist, but racism continues.

Maybe you're tired of hearing about racism. So, you need to get to work and to school. There's no good bus system or trains. You earn some money and buy a car. Now you can get where you need to be when you need to be there. And you have a car, and that feels good. You're in control. You can manage your schedule.

You've heard of greenhouse gases? Every time you turn the key in your car, you're adding to them. You've figured out things according to your culture; you've solved problems according to the ways that your culture makes available. And you make a bad situation worse. Is this because you just make bad decisions? No. Is it because you really want to screw up the planet? No.

For one thing, it's because the automobile companies made it impossible for you to ride a train or a bus when they bought up the public transportation systems and destroyed them in the early decades of the last century. Why? So they could have a market for their product.

So what do we do? Educate people? Teach them they're doing something bad whenever they get in their cars? Will that make any difference except to make good people like yourselves feel guilty when they drive? Does that accomplish anything?

We say no. We say we have to get outside our cultures and understand systems for what they are. To do that, though, we have to give up some ideas that we think are natural, just the way things are. One of those ideas is the idea of individualism. We'll explain more about that idea later, but right now we want to tell a story from the speech of the president on the Council on Anthropology and Education, Catherine Emihovich (2005).

There's a big hill with a beautiful city on top of it. Down at the bottom is a lake that's frozen over. People live under the lake, and the people on the hill can see the faces of the people under the ice during the daylight and in the light of the moon at night. The people on the hill feel really bad about the folks that live under the ice and want to help them. Some people write whole books about the lake people and the choices they made and say they should be educated more. Other people say they're just lazy. Any time they wanted to, they could bust through the ice and come up the hill. They're just too lazy to try.

Sometimes the sunshine warms a spot in the ice, and if the lake people are quick enough, a few of them can get out and start up the hill. The people on the hill are happy about this and even come down to help these folks climb the hill. Sometimes some lake people can put together all of their resources and work together to chop and hack a hole in the ice. The hill people are still happy about this, but in the backs of their minds they're wondering what would happen if all of the lake people ever got together and came up the hill at the same time.

The one thought that the lake people think about all the time, but the thought that never crosses the minds of the hill people, is this: Why don't all the hill people come down and break the damned ice?

Emihovich is making the point that it's not enough to study people and understand them. We need to use our knowledge to engage in action to change the system. We'll explain more about how that system works later.

The last diagram a few pages back defines the research program for anthropology. We need to understand not just how others understand their worlds, their cultures, but how their cultures inform their actions and how those actions affect the realities in which the people live.

Think about the situation facing Nasrudin when the king announced that he would hang from a gallows in front of the city gate anyone who lied. Nasrudin was the first one at the gate. The king's officer asked him where he was going. "I'm going to be hanged," Nasrudin said. "But," said the officer, "if I hang you, you were telling the truth, and I'm only supposed to hang people who lie. But if I don't hang you, then you were lying."

Sometimes it's tough to be a bureaucrat.

Discussion Questions

- A student from a tiny Lisu village just got off the airplane. You meet the student, and you both go to the downtown of a big city. Pick three things that you would have to explain to the student, and explain how you would do it. How do the concepts of emic and etic apply to these explanations?

- Discuss where the American prohibition against marrying cousins comes from. What purpose does this belief serve? (Remember our discussion in chapter 2—avoidance of bad genetic traits from in-breeding is not the answer.)
- How have our own cultural codes determined our medical practices? Consider discussing childbirth, acupuncture, herbs, and psycho-therapy as they relate to Americans' understanding of acceptable medical procedures. Try to develop an etic understanding of some of these—what would it look like?
- Imagine a Judeo-Christian tradition that considered god in the same terms as Lisu consider spirits. What would our society look like? How would it be different than it is now? How would it be the same? How does your religious background inform cultural codes you can identify?

Suggested Reading

Ekvall, Robert. *Fields on the Hoof: Nexus of Tibetan Nomadic Pastoralism.* New York: Holt, Rinehart and Winston, 1968.

Malinowski, Bronislaw. *Argonauts of the Western Pacific.* Long Grove, IL: Wave-land, 1922 (reprinted 1984).

Weiner, Annette B. *Women of Value, Men of Renown: New Perspectives in Trobriand Exchange.* Austin: University of Texas Press, 1976.

How do pigs fit into the ecological system? *Photo from iStockphoto, © Mats Tooming. Used with permission.*

CHAPTER 6

ECOLOGICAL SYSTEMS

Cultural codes, like the grammars of our languages, are mental, things in our heads. But the logic of our cultural codes is the only way we have to think things through. So we base our actions on the conclusions we can draw from the evidence we have and the logic of our cultural codes. Our actions have consequences, many of which we never notice or necessarily want to happen. Whether we understand the consequences or not, we have to deal with them. As people, the only way we have to deal with our environments is our cultural codes that define our understandings of reality. For instance, every time you put the keys in a car and turn on the engine, you contribute to global warming. It doesn't matter what you think about it. You may be "for the environment," and you may be driving a load of stuff to the recycling center or on your way to buy organic food or to camp in the wilderness. Your actions have exactly the same consequences as if you'd set out to pollute the environment.

All industrial processes are polluting. It doesn't matter whether they are in Poland or China or the U.S. of A. or Brazil. There may be different laws about how much of the pollution the process can allow into the water and air, but all industrial processes are inherently polluting. You can't make a car without polluting the environment. You can't drive a car without polluting the environment.

Some kinds of agriculture in some places may be sustainable. But not all forms are. Industrial agriculture like people do in the United States, for instance, is not. We know that because it takes more energy to produce the food than the food has in it. That's why growing corn to make ethanol to burn in cars isn't the answer to oil dependency. It takes more energy to grow the corn than the ethanol has in it.

Another corn-growing culture was the Maya, and their civilization collapsed. The descendants of the people are still there, but their kings and wars and temples—the whole complex of their civilization—are gone. Some people say the Maya rulers didn't understand that they were in trouble and didn't do anything about it. In other words, what they were doing had some negative consequences, but the people didn't notice until it was too late. Others say that they knew they had some problems with corn production and tried to increase it. According to their cultural code, the way to increase corn production would be to make the gods happy. To make the gods happy, they built temples and made sacrifices. But when they took labor away from corn production, there was less corn, and the problem got worse. So they built more temples. And so on.

The question for us is whether we're like Maya in either of these interpretations. Do we just not notice pollution and global warming? Or do we know what's going on and not do anything about it? Or is there something in the way we respond—with our political or religious or any other cultural system—that is making it worse instead of better? It's hard to know the answers to these questions from inside the system and until the story is finished, when we can look back on it with the benefit of time. Even then, not everyone agrees, as with Maya.

Sometimes people do things that work pretty well without even knowing it. How can they solve problems without knowing what they are? If over the course of years, they have tried things that turn out to work for them and continue to work for them—a kind of natural selection—then they don't need to know how the system works, it just does. Paul has a thumb drive for his laptop computer. A friend asked him how it works because there's nothing moving in there like a disk. He said that as far as he knows, it's magic. It might as well be. Paul doesn't need to know how it works, just whether it's working. People's understandings of what they are doing, their cultural codes, may be quite different from ours, but what counts is the results of their actions.

There are ecological consequences whenever Tsembaga people of New Guinea kill pigs. They kill pigs to pay their debts to their ancestors. They are in debt to ancestors because the ancestors helped them in a war with nearby groups. So they kill their pigs and sponsor a great feast to pay back the ancestors for their help and to treat their allies. But they still owe the ancestors. So they promise to pay the ancestors when they have enough pigs and start with the pigs that remain to rebuild their stocks of pigs. Tsembaga cannot go to war again until they pay the debt because the ancestors won't help them. All of this stuff about ancestors and debts is part of their cultural code. But it informs their actions, and their actions have ecological consequences.

Pigs eat the same food people do—sweet potatoes, and women do most of the work to grow them in their gardens. At the end of a war, they have few pigs. Since they only have to feed the people and a few pigs, the women make fewer gardens, and the land that they aren't using can lie fallow and recover its fertility. First, people pen their pigs up on the old garden spots to root around and soften the ground. The pigs act as bionic plows. Then wild plants take over the garden spot. The longer the land recuperates, the more fertile it is, and the women can use the most productive gardens. The longer they use the gardens, though, the less productive they become until they aren't worth cultivating and have to lie fallow again.

We can show the relationships among these elements as a system as shown in figure 6.1.

This diagram says that the number of gardens fluctuates up or down with the number of pigs; the length of fallow changes opposite to the number of gardens, so the more gardens, the shorter the fallow periods; the fertility varies in the same direction as the length of fallow; and the fertility goes in the opposite direction from the number of gardens. More pigs, more gardens, shorter fallow, less fertility, more gardens. Fewer pigs, fewer gardens, longer fallow, more fertility, fewer gardens.

As there are more and more pigs, the women make more gardens, the fallow decreases, and they need more food for more pigs but have to work harder for each sweet potato as the fertility declines. Pigs aren't very docile. They get into neighbors' gardens and root around and destroy other people's crops. When this happens, the other people complain and take legal action against the pig owner. So more pigs also means more disputes and more complaints of overwork from the women.

The elders have to hear all of the law cases and decide how to resolve them. The same guys (yes, all guys) have to deal with the women increasingly complaining about too much work. When these negative aspects of having so many pigs become intolerable to the elders, they conclude that there are enough pigs to pay off the debt to the ancestors and sponsor another big feast and kill off most of the pigs. Then they are free to go to war again because the ancestors will help them.

There's one other variable in this system—how healthy the people are. That's not so much because their health determines how hard they can

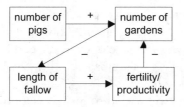

Figure 6-1 How pigs affect fertility of gardens.

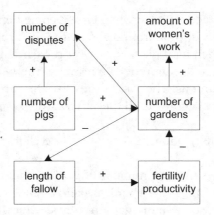

Figure 6-2 How pigs affect social relations.

work but because when someone is sick, like Lisu, they sacrifice a pig as part of the curing ritual. So if everyone is in good health, the population of pigs grows faster than if they have to kill off some of the pigs for curing ceremonies.

Roy Rapport (1967), who studied Tsembaga and wrote the book *Pigs for the Ancestors,* concluded that Tsembaga ritual was a regulating mechanism in this system. A **regulating mechanism** is a part of the system that keeps the values of variables within certain limits. The classic example is a thermostat. When the temperature in a room gets hot enough, the heat trips a heat-sensitive switch that turns off the furnace. As the room cools down, the switch turns on the furnace, and it begins to heat up the air again until the switch turns it off. The heat-sensitive switch is the regulating mechanism that keeps the air temperature within certain limits. So, the Tsembaga cultural code keeps the number of pigs within certain limits because it provides a way to turn on or off the sacrifice that regulates the number of pigs. So there are always some pigs, but they don't get out of hand and eat the people out of house and home. The critical part of the system is what is "enough pigs"? Enough pigs is the number that makes the complaints and disputes too annoying for the elders, so they are willing to flip the switch and repay the ancestors the pigs they owe them from the last war. After they do that, they can go to war again until they have enough pigs to pay the debt they got into from starting the war. And so on, as the next diagram shows in figure 6.3.

In terms of the model we developed at the end of the last chapter, we can understand this part of Tsembaga cultural ecology according to the following table 6.1.

This ritual cycle assures local groups of a supply of good protein, especially when they need it most—when they are sick. It distributes local

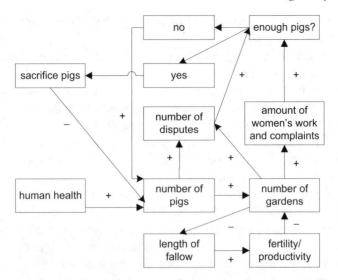

Figure 6-3 When are there enough pigs?

surpluses of pork throughout the region by the feasts so that those who have extra pigs feed those with less than enough. It facilitates trade because the allies who people invite to their feasts bring gifts. It keeps the number of people adjusted to the area of land. It limits the fighting to frequencies that don't endanger any of the groups. Finally, but most important, it maintains the environment in good condition for gardening by guaranteeing that the fallow periods don't get too short or the fertility too low.

Tsembaga warfare is not like ours. First, they can't fight another war until they are out of debt for the last one. Then, they don't use napalm and machine guns and fragmentation grenades and humvees and tanks and airplanes. They use spears and bows and arrows, not guns and

Table 6-1

Reality	Cultural Code	Action
Number of pigs	Ideas of debt	Kill pigs
Productivity of gardens	Ideas about ancestors	Raise pigs
Length of fallow periods	Debts to ancestors payable in pigs	Make gardens
Number of disputes		
Amount of work for women		
Number of complaints from women		

explosives. Their warfare is more like our football. People get hurt, and some die, but not all that many.

And, while our agriculture isn't like theirs, there are some similarities. The more livestock we feed, the more of our land and agricultural effort goes to growing feed for the animals. If you drive across the vast expanses from Illinois through Iowa early in the fall, you see the beauty of an endless sea of corn waving gently in the breeze as thunderheads gather on the horizon. This corn goes to pigs and cattle as well as to Archer Daniels Midland (ADM)—"Supermarket to the World," as they used to say on the commercials on National Public Radio.

That it is. And fixers of prices for the world, as recent convictions have shown. ADM's giant factories in the Midwest convert corn into ethanol as an additive for gasoline, and it seems to have the fix in with politicians from the area to support tax breaks for ethanol and promote this fuel additive as environmentally safe. Just outside Cedar Rapids, Iowa, is a plant that fills the sky with plumes of fragrant white vapors. At the plant they convert corn into endless tank-car-loads of corn sweetener destined for soda and bakery goods. The biggest single "food" in the United States diet is soda. It accounts for one out of every five calories that Americans consume. Some researchers think that such sweet drinks are a major cause of obesity in the United States.

Check the contents of almost any industrially produced food or drink product, and you'll see "corn sweeteners." Most likely from ADM. That's why it supports an army of lobbyists in Washington, DC, to retain a high tariff on imported sugar and work with the right-wing sugar magnates of Florida that fled Cuba and drained the wetlands of that state to reestablish their sugar plantations in the United States. Together ADM and the Cubans form a strong right-wing political block to keep Cuban sugar from lowering the prices of their products.

Just as with Tsembaga, the political decisions (How many disputes are there in the group? Can we go to war with other groups?) are connected to the economic ones (How many gardens, how fertile, and how many women work in gardens?) and the economic actions (killing pigs) have consequences for the environment (longer fallow periods, more fertile gardens).

Much of the rest of the corn from the Midwest that doesn't go for sweeteners or ethanol is destined to feed livestock in industrial animal production facilities close by or to feed livestock in Russia and other lands. One thing that's different from Tsembaga or Lisu is that it's hard to find any regulating mechanism that puts limits on anything in this system.

We'll get to the similarities between the system in the United States and others in more detail later, but here we'll just mention that the signals that go through the system determine how it will act. For instance, Tsembaga women complain of overwork. That's a signal. There are too many disputes. That's another signal. When the signals all align, the elders trip the regulating mechanism, and the feasting begins. Just like Tsembaga, our system responds to signals—some of them about pigs and their feed.

Julian Steward (1955) is the anthropologist who did a lot to develop **cultural ecology** in the mid-1950s with his book *Theory of Culture Change*. Roy Rappaport's work, and his book about Tsembaga published twelve years after Steward's, is an example of cultural ecology. This is an approach in anthropology that emphasizes that while all of the elements of a culture are interrelated, the parts that have most to do with the way people make their livings are the most important and determine the rest.

Steward called the social, political, and religious patterns most closely connected to the way people get their livings the **culture core** or central aspects of the culture. So the evolution of our biology entailed cultural variables interacting with biological ones; and while our capacities for language and culture are biological, their content is not. Different emic systems define different cultures. Steward wanted to understand the reasons these differences came to be. He ruled out the environment itself because people with different cultures live in the same environments. It could just be the history of the people, but that doesn't answer the "why?" question—it just leads to another question: why do different cultures have different histories?

Steward borrowed the idea of **ecology**—the total web of relationships among life forms in an area—from biology. Just as ecology understands a population in terms of its relations with the web of life in an area, **cultural ecology** describes the interactions of physical, biological, and cultural factors in an area to explain why different cultures take different forms. Steward suggested that anthropologists analyze the interrelationships of the productive technology with the environment—for instance, how Tsembaga men make gardens with digging sticks and how the women tend the gardens and keep them up after that; how women keep pigs, what they feed them, and where they get the food. We already see a division of labor between men and women, and we go on to see how people organize themselves for production and what the consequences are.

People solve problems, and the solutions create other problems. For instance, Tsembaga feed their pigs sweet potatoes, but the more gardens they make and the more pigs they have, the more the pigs invade other people's gardens and cause disputes. Steward suggested that after we describe the interactions of the technology and the environment, we check how the patterns of behavior involved in making a living affect other areas of behavior. For instance, Tsembaga ritual regulates the frequency of warfare, the number of pigs, the amount of land people cultivate, and the fertility of the land.

The kinds of factors that are important to cultural ecology are interrelations of land use, land tenure, kinship, residence rules—all of the emic or cultural code stuff that has consequences for how people produce things. But Steward also wanted to understand consequences of actions. For instance, he would want to understand the consequences of the Tsembaga ritual system or of the United States' love affairs with cars and soda. So cultural ecology also studies the results of people's actions, such as obesity, global warming, and environmental pollution, whether or not the people have the same understanding of these things as we do. Our understandings may be different because we develop etic understandings based on different assumptions and procedures than the ones in the cultural codes of the people in the systems. This gets tricky when we're talking about our own culture. And we're going to show you later that it's no mistake that it's so tricky because there is a very good reason for some people to try to confuse everyone else.

Each kind of technology poses different problems with different solutions. People have to do some things a certain way or not at all; other things they can do any number of ways. Steward's idea was that people solve similar problems in similar ways everywhere and at every time. That's what explains cultural similarities. And the different problems of using their various technologies in dissimilar environments cause the cultural differences.

These ideas started a lot research that's still going on.

From the point of view of cultural ecology, the environment is much broader than people's physical surroundings. It involves other social groups as well. For instance, to understand Tsembaga, we need to understand how they trade and make war with their neighbors.

Solving problems—adaptive responses—can have disadvantageous side effects. Marshall Sahlins (1968) writes, "To adapt ... is to do as well as possible under the circumstances—which may not turn out very well at all" (369). It is not to achieve a perfect fit but to find reasonable solutions to the problems that face people. We saw that different selective forces in our biological evolution worked at cross-purposes. The advantages of using and making tools selected for the restructuring of our skeleton for bipedalism. That meant our pelvises widened and our birth canals narrowed. The same advantages selected for larger brains. Narrow birth canals and large brains cannot go together. That's why we're born immature, and that has all of the consequences we wrote about earlier.

It's the same with **cultural adaptation**. Sahlins writes, "Lots of things people do are truly stupid, if understandable." Archaeologists recover their remains and try to figure out what went wrong as with Maya. Remember that there is no necessity in evolution. Just because a system needs something doesn't mean it's going to happen. Was it stupid for Mayans to continue to build temples when they were running short of corn? Maybe—from our perspective. But what would you do if you knew that the gods gave you corn and to get the gods to cooperate you had to build temples? What would you do if you knew about global warming? What would you do if you knew about the connection between politics and corn sweeteners?

Sahlins wrote about how in Fiji, people fish for food and make dried coconut, called *copra,* to sell for money. Many cosmetic products and some food products use coconut oil from this copra. Fijians use boats for fishing, but it costs money to buy and maintain a boat. Since they use boats for fishing, and fishing is a subsistence activity, all kinsmen can use the boat because there is an ethic of mutuality and share and share alike for anything that has to do with subsistence. On the other hand, people can put their money into houses with tin roofs to gain prestige. Then their kinsmen can't use the product of their work. So the question Fijians face is how to allocate their money—to houses or to boats? They put it into houses so that they can reserve the benefits to themselves in line with the individualistic market ethic of coconut production. If they use it for boats, they help themselves, but they help their kinsmen just as much, and the kinsmen do nothing for it.

Everyone continues to have relatives, but they put their resources into houses and have fewer and fewer boats. As there are fewer boats, they fish less, and their diet has less protein. Thus, the quality of their diet decreases, and they live in hot and unhealthy houses. But it is their way of adapting to the factors they must deal with in their daily lives. Is it smart? Maybe not. Is it adaptive? Yes. Is it sustainable? No.

Since cultural ecology directs our attention to those aspects of the culture most related to making a living, anthropologists need to understand economic systems. We need a framework that allows us to compare all economic systems such as Tsembaga and our own in the same terms.

Although it is important to understand systems from the inside, to understand their emic meanings, if we want to compare cultures, we have to step outside them and develop frameworks that do not depend on the ideas of any single culture. If we try to understand all languages according to the rules of Latin, we ask irrelevant questions about Chinese and Thai, languages that follow different rules. To understand languages, we have to develop a system of reference that does not depend on any single language, an outside system of reference. We have to do the same for economics. In the next chapter, we'll explain how we can understand all economic systems in the same terms. We'll develop an etic system for studying economics whether in the United States or New Guinea.

There's a story about a very accomplished dervish who was walking beside a lake thinking about absolute truth when he heard someone on an island chanting. He noticed that the chant wasn't quite right. It wasn't the way the dervish had learned it. The scholar got a boat and rowed to the island where he found another dervish chanting.

The scholar taught the other dervish the correct chant and got back in his boat to return to shore, satisfied that he had helped someone toward truth because his books said that this chant was so powerful that, if people did it correctly, they could walk on water. The scholar had never seen anyone walking on water, but he knew the difference between correct and incorrect chants.

As he rowed, the scholar heard the island dervish starting to chant again. But the scholar heard the wrong sounds again. As the annoyingly inaccurate syllables became louder and louder, the scholar looked over his shoulder to see the island dervish walking on the water toward his boat. "How does that chant go again?" he asked. "I've already forgotten the correct way to do it."

Remember this story when we tell you about how economists always know the right chants and go around our planet screwing up people's economies.

Discussion Questions

- Check the label on a container of soda or a bakery product. What does the label tell you about the cultural ecology of your country?
- What are some of the elements that make up your cultural ecology? Think about cars, fast food, grocery stores, corn sweeteners, and what's going on in Washington and your state capital.
- Among Tsembaga, the women complaining is an important ecological signal. What happens to complaints in your university? What is the ecological impact of not paying attention to signals like this? Are people who raise grievances called whiners to silence them? How do the signals flow through your university's system?
- Can some people send more powerful signals than others? For instance, compare the impact of a complaint you make versus one of a rich alum who donates lots of money to your university.
- What things do these signals regulate in the system? How does that happen?

- What are some of the similarities and differences between biological and cultural evolution? Does natural selection work the same way in both? What's being changed in each?
- Explain how some of the aspects of our cultural ecology work against one another, as in the example of Fiji.
- What's the point of the story about the dervish? Has anyone ever corrected you? Were you wrong to think or do what you were thinking or doing? Does the point of view make a difference?
- How do you think people feel when their own understanding doesn't match an etic description? For instance, how do you think American students feel when they learn that the health care system in the United States is the worst and most expensive of any developed country? That their life expectancy is lower and their infant mortality is higher than in most developed countries? That they have more people living in poverty than most developed countries? That the gap between the rich and most of them is greater in the United States than in most other developed countries? That there really is no middle class?

Suggested Reading

Evans-Pritchard, E. E. *The Nuer: A Description of the Modes of Livelihood and Political Institutions of a Nilotic People.* London: Clarendon Press, 1967.

Hanks, Lucien. *Rice and Man: Agricultural Ecology in Southeast Asia.* Honolulu: University of Hawaii Press, 1992.

Mintz, Sidney W. *Sweetness and Power: The Place of Sugar in Modern History.* New York: Penguin, 1995.

Rappaport, Roy. *Pigs for the Ancestors: Ritual in the Ecology of a New Guinea People.* New Haven, CT: Yale University Press, 1967 (reprint: Prospect Heights, IL: Waveland, 2000).

7

For the Lisu people, rice is part of the important
elements of the economic system: consumption,
production, and exchange.

CHAPTER 7

AN ANTHROPOLOGICAL APPROACH TO ECONOMICS

The economic framework that anthropologists have developed does not share much with what you learn from economists in a department of economics or business administration. There's a story about an economist, an anthropologist, and a historian who are walking together and fall into a deep, dark hole.

"We'll never get out of here," said the historian. "This is precisely what happened to Ethelred the Unready in the thirteenth century, and he died in the hole." The economist smiled.

"I think you're right," answered the anthropologist, "because on the island of Bongo Bongo where I've done extensive fieldwork, whenever people fall into a trap like this, they die." The economist smiled again.

The economist said that he wasn't a bit worried. "Don't worry," he said. "We'll get out of here."

"How?" asked his two colleagues.

"Well," he said in a cheerfully optimistic voice, "first of all, assume a ladder."

The wisdom of ethnography is "Assume nothing." Any assumptions we bring with us are likely to be based on our own cultural codes and experience and thus could mislead us in understanding the people we want to understand. We'd be understanding them in our own emic terms instead of either their emic terms or etic terms. Here we are going to develop an etic economics.

First, we do know that all societies provide themselves with the things people use. Second, we also know that all useful things are products of someone's labor. Third, we see that people exchange some things for others. These three observations define three things we need to look at to understand economic life: consumption, production, and exchange.

Everyone consumes things. We do this by direct consumption such as eating and using things to produce other things. The classic example is seed. People can eat it or plant it to grow more food and seed. Either way, they consume it.

For production, we'll just repeat the statement, because it's important, that all useful things are the product of someone's labor.

Exchange means that people trade things for other things. Anthropologists have distinguished three forms of exchange. **Reciprocity** means giving as much as you get—at least in the long run. There's usually a time delay between the giving and the getting. If I have a car and you need a ride, I give you a ride. Sometime when I need a ride, I know that someone will give me a ride. Or we may make an explicit deal: I'll take care of your kids tonight, and you take care of mine tomorrow night. Or it might just be sharing as people do when they have joint bank accounts and both put in whatever they have and take out whatever they need.

Christmas presents, birthday presents, wedding and graduation presents in the United States are examples of reciprocity with different time delays. Someone gives you a birthday present, and you give that person a present when his birthday comes along. People often compare Christmas presents to be sure they're not giving too big or small a present, considering what the other person gave them the year before.

Redistribution is based on the idea of reciprocity—give something and get something equal—but it works differently. Instead of giving something directly back to the person or group that gave it to us, we give things to some central person who then redistributes them to the people who need them. Systems of taxation are examples. We all pay taxes to various governments. In Pennsylvania, we have to pay taxes to the borough, to the township, and to the state as well as to the U.S. government. These government agencies then use the revenues for things that everyone needs, like water, sewer systems, and roads. The U.S. government uses a lot of our taxes to support a war machine. Some people who disagree with this redistribution become "war tax resisters" and don't pay their taxes in protest at the risk of being fired or jailed.

The third form of exchange is the one that's most familiar to us: the market. In **market exchange**, people exchange things for money. One of the things that people exchange for money is their labor. A **commodity** is something that people can buy and sell on a market. Most of us don't think that everything is a commodity—for instance, justice is not supposed to be a commodity that people can buy or sell. But there's that saying that in the United States you are entitled to as much justice as you can afford. A vote in a state or federal legislature is not supposed to be something someone can buy or sell, and when it comes out that legislators are taking bribes, they may go to jail. But there's no doubt that labor is something we can buy and sell. You can hire someone to fix a broken electric switch. Or someone can hire Paul to teach anthropology courses or Suzan to write a newsletter or a speech.

What determines the price of things in markets? Things are valuable because of their uses, the needs they fill. This is **use value**, and it's **qualitative**, not something we can count or quantify. If we want to rake leaves, a rake is useful for that. It may be useful for batting a ball or swatting a groundhog, but other things are more useful for those tasks than a rake. And rakes aren't very useful for driving nails or digging holes. A broom is useful for sweeping. A rake might help, but it's not very good. A coat is useful to keep us warm. We can't really compare the use values of rakes, brooms, and coats except to say that they are different. We can't say one is more useful than the other except in terms of what we use it for. For keeping warm, a rake is no good. For digging a hole, a coat won't help.

People exchange things with one use value for things of different use values. So, people might trade a rake for a coat. If people can do this, the ratio of exchange—how many rakes per coat or coats per rake—is the **exchange value** of the two things. This is **quantitative**, something we can count. People may have to trade five rakes for one coat. Or people can use money to keep track of these relationships. If the value of a rake is $1, then the value of a coat is $5. So our question is, where does the exchange value of things come from?

The one thing that all useful things have in common is that they are the product of someone's labor. The amount of labor that it takes to make things is their exchange value and sets the ratio of their exchange in markets. So, if it takes the same amount of labor to produce one pig, twelve bushels of rice, two hoes, five rakes, and one coat, people would exchange them at those ratios, either directly or by using money.

To repeat, the exchange value of things comes from the amount of labor it takes to produce them. We have to talk in terms of long-term averages. Furry boots may come into fashion when a movie star wears them. So lots of people want to buy furry boots, and they are expensive. Soon every company is making the boots, and the price comes down. And finally the boots are out of fashion, and you only see them at thrift stores. The **price** of things can be different from its value because of these kinds of processes. But the exchange value of things is determined by the amount of labor they contain.

What is useful—that is, what has use values that determine consumption—depends on what people need and want beyond food. This sets the needs people have for production. So consumption, production, and exchange are related in such a way that if one changes the others also change, they form an **economic system**. How the things are produced is the cultural core, the most important dimension of the system, since it conditions how people can exchange and consume. The task of anthropology is to figure out the systematic relationships.

We can look once more at Lisu whom Paul lived with. The feasts that go with curing ceremonies provide a way for people to enter into reciprocal exchanges. If I invite you to a feast today, then I expect that you will invite me to your feast when you sponsor one.

People grow rice, opium poppies, and corn on slash-and-burn or **swidden** fields. They cut the trees, let them dry, burn them, and then plant rice, corn, or opium poppies in the field. The people of the household provide the labor, but sometimes they need to have a lot of labor in a short time. When they need to concentrate labor at one time such as harvests, they ask neighbors to come help and promise to help them with their harvests. These are reciprocal exchanges too. But people also hire some help, especially from opium addicts who live in nearby villages of other groups. Everyone produces more than just enough to eat. To be able to sponsor feasts for curing ceremonies, people have to keep pigs. And, just as with Tsembaga, someone has to grow the food to feed the pigs—or at least enough of it to keep the pigs coming home for supper every evening.

The pigs stay in pens near the houses, but people let them forage freely in the forest during the day so that people don't have to feed them so much. To get them to return to the pens, people feed them corn, and, like U.S. farmers, they have to grow the corn to feed their pigs. If they are going to sponsor feasts, they also need to have enough money to buy home-distilled liquor from whoever may have recently run off a batch at the village still.

Figure 7-1 shows how people allocate their labor to grow different crops and what happens to the product of their labor.

This means that 62 percent of the labor went into opium production, 9 percent into corn production, and 28 percent into rice production. The rice went for subsistence and was 41 percent of the total value produced. Corn went to pigs that people used for subsistence—eating—and reciprocity through feasts. Five percent of the total value that people produced was pigs for subsistence. People used cash to buy liquor and bamboo shoots for feasts, and together the liquor, food, and pigs for feasts accounted for 18 percent of the value produced. Twenty-eight percent of the value produced went for consumption goods such as cloth for clothes, needles, thread, kerosene, lamps, soap, and other things people bought in the lowlands. Finally, 8 percent of the total value they produced went to purchase the labor of neighboring opium smokers to help, especially with the tedious harvest of the opium from the poppies.

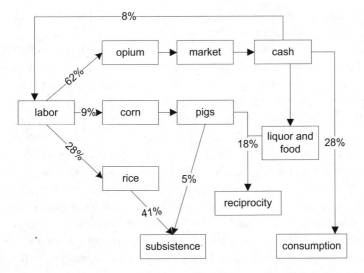

Figure 7-1 What Lisu labor produces and what they use it for.

Like Tsembaga, Lisu have a cultural code that makes it reasonable to sacrifice pigs to make sick people well. But sacrificing a pig sends another message, too. It lets people know that the household is keeping up with its responsibilities to other households, that it is keeping its place in the reciprocal relationships. When someone in a household falls ill, the householders have to think about when they last sponsored a feast and who has sponsored feasts lately. If the household is falling behind, they will sacrifice a pig. If they are already even or a little ahead, they will sacrifice a chicken. So the curing ceremonies also have a political dimension. They are the way everyone keeps up with everyone else in this egalitarian society. This provides the motive to produce pigs, rice, and opium. "You can't be a poor Lisu," one person told Paul. "You have to have pigs to sacrifice." And you have to have good clothes to wear to festivals, guns, and silver ornaments. To stay equal, everyone produces rice and pigs and opium so that they can sponsor feasts.

In this system, we see market transactions and reciprocity but no redistribution. Notice that because the land is freely available to anyone who wants to clear and use it and because people rely mostly on household members for labor, there are no categories of capital, rent, and wages. This can sometimes be a little bit confusing to people raised with the idea of markets and economics, as people in the United States are. Thinking of kinship in terms of kindreds, all of our cousins on both sides, makes it difficult for us to understand lineages based on the father's or the mother's side. But anthropology helps us move beyond this kind of ethnocentrism so that we can understand other cultures.

There are two ways to study economic systems. One is as a business tool. To anthropologists this seems like Ptolemaic astronomy that puts the Earth at the center of the solar system. It works quite well for navigation on our planet, so there's no need to challenge it if that's its use, but it won't work for going to the moon or keeping a calendar so that religious celebrations like Christmas and Easter always fall in the winter and in the spring. And it may not be the best scientific knowledge. Just because some system of knowledge is not scientific doesn't mean it's not useful. But just because it's useful doesn't mean that it's scientific. We'll explain later why economics is more like a religion than a science and how it got to be that way.

So economics may be sufficient as a tool for business calculations, but that doesn't make it adequate to describe real economic systems or useful as a framework for comparing economic systems. Anthropologists have developed other ways of seeing economies as cultural systems, as parts of cultures so we can compare them with others. It's this etic system we're explaining here.

In some systems, market exchange is the main way of organizing production. This doesn't mean everything is done by market principles, but it does mean that the market organizes most production. For instance, someone in every household has to wash dishes, cook food, and do the laundry. A married couple may share these tasks. That's not a market exchange. Or the husband or the wife may do most of it. That's not a market exchange, either. Or they may hire someone to come in and clean and cook for them. That is a market exchange.

Someone has to take care of the kids. The mom or the dad may stay home and do that. That's not a market exchange. If the parents put the kids in day care or preschools, that is a market exchange. So some of these tasks may be more or less organized by the market. But in this example, if we look at the whole economy—all of the houses and cars and food production and everything else—it's fair to say that the market is the major way of organizing production. There is money, and people buy and sell commodities, including most raw materials, tools, machines, labor, and almost everything else.

If there is market exchange and people buy everything for production, then labor is a commodity just like coal, sand, and steel. People use labor, tools, and raw materials to produce commodities with different use values and sell them. In this kind of system, they use money to buy commodities (labor, machines, raw materials) to make commodities (products) to sell for money. But the reason people do this is not just to get the same amount of money but some extra that we call **profit**.

Where does profit come from?

Remember that the exchange value of commodities comes from the amount of labor they contain. If you buy all of the inputs, even the labor, where does the value of labor come from? This is a little bit like a riddle. The value of labor comes from the same place as the value of any other commodity—the labor it contains. How can labor contain labor? People must consume to work. The amount of things others produced that we consume so we can work is the value of our subsistence. That is what determines the value of labor for a period of time—the amount of labor it takes to produce all of the things someone needs to work for that period of time.

Think back to the household where the worker lives. The house, the food, the water, the fuel, the car—almost everything in the household is a commodity. The domestic partner is probably not a commodity but a commodity worker—a maid—who may do the domestic jobs. Most of us aren't that rich, but even if we're talking about ordinary people who do their own work, the point is that they could have been working for money, so that household work has value, too.

If we buy labor at its value, we pay for all of the necessary subsistence goods for the time we use the labor. Necessary subsistence goods may include the value of a house, a car, television, food, cooking, cleaning, child care, and education for kids. That amount is what we call **wages**. Put the other way around, wages is the value that a worker needs to keep on working. So that's where the value the employer pays to the worker comes from—the value of labor is the labor it contains, just like any other commodity. But where do profits come from? We're getting there.

When we hire workers, we ask them to produce the amount of value of their wages and some more. Remember, if we're just producing the same amount that we put into the process, there's no point to it. So we ask people to put in enough work to equal the amount of their wages and some more on top. That "more on top" is the profit.

It works like this: We call the amount of value to pay for wages **necessary value** and the amount of work to produce it **necessary labor**. It's necessary in the sense that without it, there couldn't be any labor at all. The extra value the labor produces beyond that is the source of profit. We call that work **surplus labor** and the value it produces **surplus value**. We call it "surplus" because it is above and beyond the amount of value that is necessary to pay for the value of the labor.

Some people figure out how long they have to work to pay their income taxes. Suppose you pay 25 percent of your income as taxes. Then the first three months of any year you're working for your government. Only after you pay off the government can you start working for yourself. You can think of dividing the working day in the same way. Think of necessary value as the amount of value the workers you hire have to produce just to pay their own wages, to produce the amount of value they need for the day of work. After they are done with that, the rest is yours. That's the surplus value; that labor is surplus labor, and that's where the profit comes from. Figure 7-2 shows how this works.

Most of us aren't bosses who hire other people to work for us. So let's turn it around and think of it from the worker's point of view. If it takes me half a day to produce the value of my wages, then I'm working for myself that half of the day. The rest of the day's work, the boss gets to keep in return for letting me come to work and get any wages at all. In the old days, this was pretty clear. You could see how much coal you dug, you knew how much it cost to buy, because you had to heat your own house and cook, so you could know when you started working for profit for the boss instead of for yourself. But what about the mine's clerk? Or the railroad engineer who drove the train to take the coal to where someone needed it? That gets more complex. It's the same set of relationships, but it's more difficult to see because it involves lots of steps. Here we're just working on the basic ideas.

If two firms are both producing the same thing using the same machines and raw materials, they will offer their products on the market at the same price. If one of them invests in a process that produces the same things with less labor, it can sell the products for less. Then the first firm can either imitate the second or improve the process of production even more or go out of business. The same amount of labor produces more of the product—the productivity has increased, just as when Tsembaga have longer fallow periods in their gardens. Now the amount of labor in each thing is less and the value is less, so the firm can sell it for less.

Through this process of competition, the production processes come to use less and less labor. Anything that consumes less labor has less

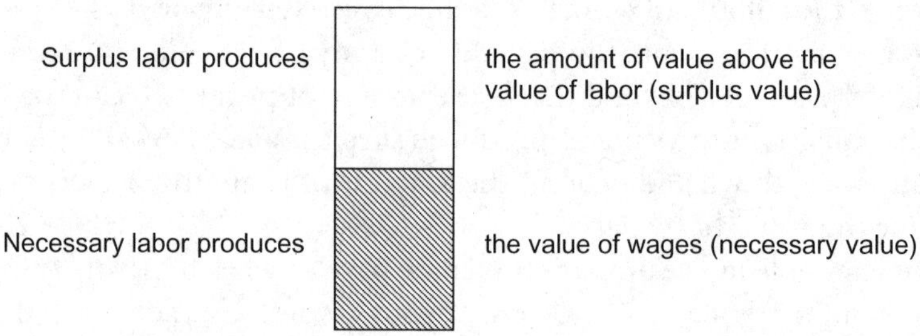

Surplus labor produces   the amount of value above the
                                value of labor (surplus value)

Necessary labor produces   the value of wages (necessary value)

Figure 7-2 Necessary and surplus labor.

exchange value and is less expensive. As this happens throughout the whole society, the value of the things necessary to support workers decreases and the value of labor decreases. As the value of labor decreases, the surplus value increases.

Think about the first automobiles that people built by hand piece by piece. Then came Mr. Ford with his assembly line that radically improved productivity and lowered the value of cars until Americans could imagine everyone owning a car. Then came the Japanese with their robot factories that could build cars with just a couple of folks to watch the computers. But people had to build Mr. Ford's factory and the Japanese robots. More of that later.

Think about farms mechanizing at the same time that automobile production was mechanizing. First people were using horses to plow and pull implements. In those days there were lots of farmers for everyone who wasn't. In 1900, 39.2 percent of the U.S. population lived on farms, and 38.8 percent of the labor was employed on farms. Then they got tractors and could do the jobs faster, with less labor because they didn't need to grow oats for horses or take care of them. Productivity increased. By 1990, 1.8 percent of the population was living on farms, and 1.8 percent of labor was employed on farms. As the machines got bigger and more powerful, the productivity increased to such an extent that there are just a few farmers now. Some people talk about replacing people with technology. In what's called the *industrialization of agriculture,* productivity increased as people invested more and more in technology.

It's important to keep basic relationships in mind. One is that labor creates all value. As we've explained, profit comes from people's labor. We'll explain later why some people are confused about this and think that profit comes from money. But money can't produce things. Only labor does that. That's why it's important to keep the basics in mind. So where do the machines, factories, and robots come from? People can use profits to invest in research and development to increase productivity. But it's the labor of the working people that created the profits that bought the machines.

We call the money that goes into production **capital**, and we call any system organized in this way a **capitalist** system. Among the many advantages of such a system are greater specialization, productivity of labor, and efficiency. Before this dynamic can take hold in the system, a capitalist system has to be in place.

The preconditions for capitalism include

- market exchange,
- labor that is available to hire,

- the possibility to expand labor time beyond necessary labor to create surplus value, and
- no interference with the process.

Firms that produce exchange values produce most things in capitalist systems, but there is also a previous kind of production that we call **household production**. Households don't produce exchange values, only use values; if they produce things to sell—like Lisu producing opium—it's so they can buy commodities they need. The usefulness of the things households produce is relative to the needs of the people. What's the value of washing the dishes after supper? Of cooking supper? Of shopping? Of taking care of the kids or picking them up from day care? Their value is the use to the people in the household. People don't sell these things. They aren't exchange values.

How can we compare the usefulness of a bushel of rice when there is no rice in the household versus the same bushel of rice when the granaries are full of rice? The usefulness of goods declines as you have more of the goods. The more of something you have, the less you need the next one. This is what economists call **marginal utility**, or the usefulness of the next thing compared with the one before. Accountants used to keep track of such differences by putting the difference in the margin of the account book, hence the idea of marginal utility, the usefulness of the next thing.

If a person has a beer on a Friday night, it might go down pretty well and feel pretty good. The second beer is less urgent and the third even less. Depending on the person's tolerance for alcohol poisoning, each beer is less useful than the one before until some point where the next beer is worse than useless; it has the person hugging the toilet and puking. That's what economists in their optimistic way call **negative utility** but what ordinary folks might call damaging.

Figure 7-3 is a graph of that process. The horizontal axis is the amount of value people have produced. At the left they haven't produced anything, and they have great needs. The more they produce, as we go along the horizontal axis toward the right, the less they need to produce any more.

The amount of work people want to do runs in the opposite direction. The more people work, the less they want to work any more. Figure 7-4 shows this exponential curve of increasing **drudgery** of work. At the left, when people haven't produced anything, they haven't done any work. The more they produce, the more work it takes, and the less they want to work any more.

Figure 7-5 puts the two curves together to show the point at which it is no longer worth a person's while to produce any more—when the marginal utility

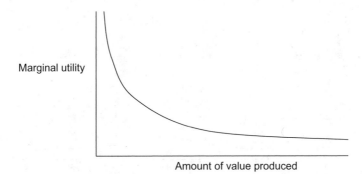

Marginal utility

Amount of value produced

Figure 7-3 How much do you need the next one?

of the next unit of value produced is just equal to the drudgery of the work it takes to produce it. That's when people in households stop working.

In figure 7-6, you see that drudgery of labor is inversely related to productivity. If the same amount of effort produces twice as much value, then the drudgery of labor is cut in half.

Here, each value of drudgery in the dotted line is half the value of the solid line for each unit of value because the people have some way to double productivity. Perhaps they have access to an irrigation system or a harvesting machine—something that doubles the amount they produce in the same time. Notice that while people increase production with the new technology from point A to point B, they do not double it. So the increase in production is not doubled even if productivity is—the relationship between productivity and amount produced is indirect.

Marginal utility is relative to needs: the greater the need, the higher the curve of marginal utility.

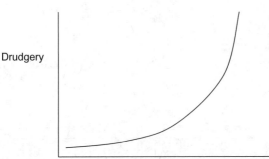

Drudgery

Amount of value produced

Figure 7-4 How much you don't want to do the work to get the next one.

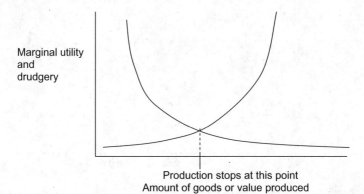

Production stops at this point
Amount of goods or value produced

Figure 7-5 When you quit.

In figure 7-7 the dotted line shows an increase in the marginal utility of the value produced; that is, these people need the product more than the people with the solid line. This could be because they have more mouths to feed, or it could be because they have to pay taxes for the irrigation system or a note on a harvesting machine. It doesn't matter the source of the need. Any increase in need acts the same way as adding mouths to the number of consumers in the household. Again, the production increases from A to B.

When we put the two curves together in figure 7-8, we see that the overall level of drudgery with the new technology—the drudgery (on the vertical axis) to produce up to the level of C—is higher than without it—the old system where they only produce up to the level of A. So in this

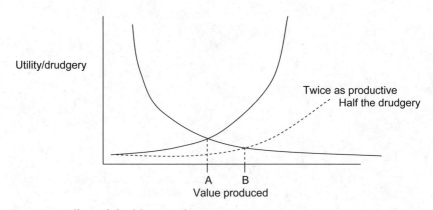

Figure 7-6 Effect of doubling productivity.

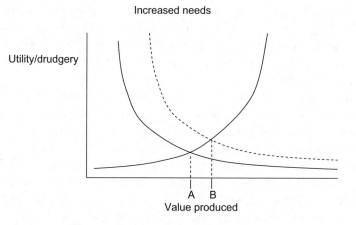

Figure 7-7 Effects of increased need.

example, given a choice, people wouldn't accept that alternative; they'd keep doing things the old way. B would be what they would produce if they could get an increase in productivity without having to pay for it.

A. V. Chayanov (1986) is the person who put these observations together on the basis of his empirical studies of Russian peasants in the early decades of the twentieth century. He was an agricultural economist. After the revolution of 1918, there was a great food shortage in the new Soviet Union. The country was being invaded by England and the United States. The supporters of the czar started a civil war, and the peasants stopped producing much of anything beyond what they needed for their families. That contributed to the shortage of food for everyone who wasn't a peasant. Stalin wanted to start large industrial farms that would

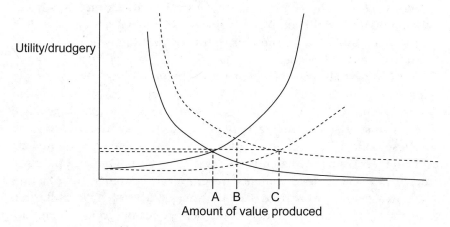

Figure 7-8 Costs and benefits of new technology.

operate like factories and be done with the reactionary peasants once and for all. Chayanov thought that peasants would respond to the needs of city people better if they could organize into cooperatives and sell their food, but Stalin disagreed. Stalin solved the Chayanov problem in his typical way, by having him shot in 1931.

Paul and other anthropologists have done lots of ethnographic work around the world to check out these ideas to be sure this is the way household production units actually work. So this isn't just theory.

Let's go back to the preconditions for capitalism. There has to be market exchange, and there have to be people willing and able to sell their labor. This wouldn't work in prerevolutionary Russia because the serfs were not free to sell their labor. In fact, capitalism would rarely work if people were given the choice. To understand this, we have to think about it from the point of view of people working in terms of the logic of household economies.

Someone sets up a factory with the most advanced technology there is, something like the water-powered textile mills of Lowell, Massachusetts. The owner offers to pay a worker maybe the amount of necessary labor, but it takes twelve hours of labor to produce that. If the owner is only paying the value of necessary labor, there is no profit in the system, so it's not worth the owner's while. If the owner can get people to work one extra hour, however, there's some surplus in the system. But why would anyone trade what they had in their household economy for the monotonous and dreary work of a factory?

They wouldn't. The best the factory owners could do is to hire the daughters of farmers. From the point of view of the farmers, the daughters could earn a little extra income without hurting the household economy too much. From the point of view of the girls, they could set aside something toward getting married and maybe get out of the house. From the point of view of the factory owner, he could start extracting surplus value. And they could control the value of necessary value by providing dorm rooms and food for the girls, so the owners knew just how much their necessary value was.

But it wasn't always so nice an arrangement. In most places, people simply refused to work in factories until the government drove them off their land with policies that kept them from being able to produce their own subsistence and gave them no alternative. We will see some of these policies at work in chapter 16. When people were denied access to their land, they had no other way to make a living except to sell their labor. These developments were no less draconian than Stalin's measures, but they were necessary for the capitalist system to get started, and once it did get started, there could be very fast progress through the technological developments that came with the process of competition that we explained before.

The point here is that labor is not naturally a commodity that people can buy and sell on markets. There has to be some government policy that makes that happen, that changes the structures of choice so that most people can no longer satisfy their subsistence needs through their household economies.

So when people say, "Isn't it better for an Indonesian peasant girl to work for a couple of bucks a day than to have no job at all?" we know that's the wrong question. The question we need to ask, and to answer, is, Why can't the Indonesian peasant girl work on her own family's farm? Maybe her dad is a tyrant, and it's no better on the farm than in the factory. We have to actually do the ethnography and find the facts of these cases. That's what anthropology is about—finding facts, not making assumptions.

One of the consequences of these political and economic developments was ideologies and institutions to make the new system of production possible and to make it seem reasonable. One of these ideas was the idea of freedom. Free people are people who are not bound to lords or land-owning farmers or lineages or tyrannical dads or anyone else. They are free to sell their labor. Thus one reason to oppose slavery was that it stood in the way of free labor that producers could hire, a critical commodity for capitalism to develop.

In capitalist systems of production, there are people who sell labor and people who buy it. Where is the middle class? The middle class is in our imaginations. It's one of those ideological myths that was made up to make the system seem reasonable. We'll come to that in a bit.

Discussion Questions

- Draw your own diagram that describes your definition of drudgery. Explain how much you would work, for how much and when you would quit. Do you think that is the same for either of your parents? Your grandparents? Why or why not?
- Iceland's constitution does not include the right to freedom of expression, or religion, or even the freedom to own a gun. But it does include the rights of health, education, a job, a place to live, and security in old age. Discuss the difference between these rights and the freedoms that the U.S. Constitution provides. What are the benefits of each? What are the costs? What does the economy have to do with any of this?

- If the reasons for the difference are economic, why can a small country like Iceland grant such rights while a large rich one like the United States does not?
- Check the local or international business news this week and find a story about wages, stock prices, productivity, and/or profits. Apply what you learned about economics in this chapter to any part of that news story or stories and discuss.
- Can you think of an example of household production from your family? How is that different from earning a wage? Describe the lifestyle, the level of work, the quality of work and lifestyle, and any other comparisons you can make.

Suggested Reading

Browne, Katherine E. *Creole Economics: Caribbean Cunning under the French Flag.* Austin: University of Texas Press, 2004.

Newman, Katherine S. *Declining Fortunes: The Withering of the American Dream.* New York: Basic Books, 1993.

Wells, Miriam J. *Strawberry Fields: Politics, Class and Work in California Agriculture.* Ithaca, NY: Cornell University Press, 1996.

White, Jenny B. *Money Makes Us Relatives: Women's Labor in Urban Turkey.* Austin: University of Texas Press, 1994.

Yates, Michael D. *Naming the System: Inequality and Work in the Global Economy.* New York: Monthly Review Press, 2003.

The 2004 "Rally for Women's Lives," held in Washington, D.C., is an example of how people in the United States voice their political views. *Photo by Suzan Erem.*

CHAPTER 8

POLITICAL SYSTEMS

One key to capitalism is the availability of people who are willing to work for a wage—or who have no choice except to work for a wage. Such people are called **free labor** because they are not tied to the land or to lineages and are not slaves. They are free to be hired.

As we saw in the last chapter, surplus labor is the source of the profits that drives the whole system and creates the dynamic of expansion. Households stop production when they reach a definite level of well-being, so they produce no surplus value unless a government or someone else forces them to. Then the amount they are forced to produce is, as Chinese peasants say of their government, "another mouth at the table." Household systems are static unless something changes their needs. Having children is one way this happens. Taxes and the demands of government are another.

In spite of its dynamism and potential for progress, capitalism can never compete with households for labor. Households never benefit from sending people to work for wages as a major means of subsistence unless they have no access to resources to use for their own production. Think about it in terms of the logic of household production from the last chapter. A person's wages is what the person produces. It's always more advantageous in terms of the curves of productivity and drudgery to work for yourself than to work for someone else.

The places where capitalism can get people to work are those where the conditions of work are so bad that working for wages looks good. That's what happened in nineteenth-century Iceland when if you didn't have land, the law said you had to work for someone who did. All you got was enough to get you barely through the year. The landowners did everything they could to keep commercial fishing from getting started because they knew people would go work in the fishing industry for wages because anything was better than working on a farm. That would deprive the landowners of their inexpensive supply of labor. Landowners were in the Parliament and made the laws. But people finally just disobeyed the laws and went to the fishing villages to work. Life was hard, but it was better than life on the farms if you didn't own any land.

Government and Capitalism

In the mid-1970s, Paul lived in a village of people called Shan in northwest Thailand. He first visited the area for a summer in 1967 before he began his work with Lisu. Back then, people leveled rice fields in the floors of the valleys, dug irrigation ditches, and built small dams across streams and rivers to irrigate their rice. In the sixties, they were able to get two crops of rice from these fields, but later, when a bridge across a major river and roads made the provincial capital of Maehongson accessible, people began to grow garlic and soy beans to sell at the market in town. When pickup trucks could drive to the villages from the capital to buy crops, the villagers could do better selling these crops than growing a second crop of rice during the off-season, so the agricultural system changed.

There weren't enough irrigated fields for everyone to make a living, so people who didn't own land made swiddens, like Lisu, in the hills nearby. In Thailand, all forests belong to the government. The government can grant the right to use trees for timber and, if it has the power to enforce it, can dictate everything that happens in the forested hills. Not long after the new roads connected villages to the capital, a new airport with long cement runways replaced the grass field where, in the sixties and seventies, World War II–vintage twin-engine DC-3s had landed.

We have to interrupt the story here for some background. Since 1961, there has been a revolutionary war—or, depending on how you look at it, several of them—in Burma. Burma's name is not really Myanmar, like you see on some maps these days. Myanmar is the name the military dictatorship made up for propaganda to make it seem like things were better than they are. The people call it Pama Myo. *Myo* means "country"; *Pama* means "Burma." To the English who colonized it as part of their Indian Empire, that sounded like "Burma," and it's not too far off. Some of the revolutionary armies in Burma are made up of Shan from the Shan States in the northeastern part of Burma. They and others financed their revolutions with opium.

The revolutionary groups and several opium-trading warlords, as well as remnants of Chiang Kai-shek's U.S.-supported Nationalist Koumintang who fled China after Mao Ze-dong's victory in 1949 to trade opium and guns in northern Thailand and Burma, occupied the border areas along with the peaceful rice-growing peasants who sold them rice. One motive for the bridge, roads, and airport in Maehongson was so the Thai could exercise greater control of the area and ensure that the Shan people living there didn't get any ideas about joining with the Shan in Burma to make their own separate country.

The Thai government improved health services and provided schools so that the Shan people would learn to speak, read, and understand the related Thai language with its different alphabet but familiar sounds (remember what we said about schools earlier?). The Thai Army radio station broadcasted its version of news and other programs in the area, while Burmese radio broadcasted propaganda in Shan.

In the sixties and through the seventies, Shan could make swidden fields to supplement their irrigated rice crops or, if they owned no irrigated fields, as their only source of rice. Slowly, the Thai state asserted its authority over this remote and formerly independent Shan state.

When Paul was there in the sixties, villagers sold rice to the rebel army in Burma by the elephant load, and members of the Shan States Army came to visit relatives or settled down in border villages. In the seventies, the occasional thumping beat of helicopters announced that the Thai Army was in the area, watching.

In the capital's open morning market, representatives of a dozen or more rebel groups and warlords shopped, and after a coup d'état in Bangkok, a Thai Border Patrol Police guy showed up to drink and gamble with the young men in the village where Paul lived. The government tried with little success to organize a border guard from the village men. The headman was appropriately enthusiastic, but there was not a military bone in the body of any of the village farmers, although one kid was drafted and went on to make a career in the army.

Now we come to the punch line. In the seventies, a few people owned much more land than they needed, and some people owned none. But the people with extra land could not hire people to work it. People could do better working for themselves on swiddens. Remember, a hired worker gets necessary value as a wage but, in return for that, has to produce surplus value. A worker in a household system only has to produce necessary value without the demand for surplus value. So while there was a market and other preconditions of capitalism, it wouldn't work because people had the alternative of making swiddens instead of working for wages. In the eighties, with more control, the government was able to assert its power over the forests and prohibit swiddening. Then those people who did not have enough irrigated rice land to feed their families had no choice but to work for the people with more land than they needed. When some people are directly or indirectly forced to sell their labor rather than use it for their own households, we see the beginnings of a system of classes in which some people buy labor and some sell it.

The Transition from Feudalism to Capitalism

In this small corner of the world in the late 1900s we see the same drama that unfolded across Europe in the 1700s. After the collapse of the Roman Empire, the rise of Islam reoriented commerce toward the Islamic world. Local lords, not that different from the warlords of northwest Thailand, dominated Europe with their system of feudalism and incessant warfare until some could make good their claim to being God's chosen kings.

These aristocrats required exotic goods beyond those that ordinary peasants produced and used. Merchants began to supply them with these goods from the East, and new **markets** developed. Money began to circulate, and banks developed to help merchants handle it. Then began a process we now call **import substitution**, making the things for yourself instead of importing them. Not that aristocrats worked, but they had their peasants do it for them. Crafts developed and then workshops; this was the beginning of the factory system.

Royalty controlled the economic and political system. The sources of wealth were taxes, skimming from traders, and warfare, not production of surplus value. Aristocrats did not control production, but they wanted to control wealth. So, as people experimented with new ways of producing things and found better ways, the political system was increasingly at loggerheads with the cultural core.

It wasn't the kings and aristocrats who grouped craftsmen together into workshops where they experimented with new and more productive technologies. The rulers just wanted the products—they didn't care how they were produced. But the people who were producing things were developing new technologies and new ways of organizing production and beginning a factory system. They were on the verge of capitalism but had to play by the old rules of the aristocracy.

Throughout the eighteenth century in Germany, France, and the English colonies in America, there were revolutions to break the power of the aristocracy and change the rules of the game to allow the people who were organizing the production of wealth to control it.

But these would-be capitalists faced the same problem the Shan land-owners in northwest Thailand faced. As long as people were either tied to the land as serfs or peasants or had access to land for their own household production, they wouldn't work for wages. If people had access to land, they would not sell their labor, and there would be no commodity labor. The solution was to deprive people of access to land. That's what the enclosure acts throughout the nineteenth century in England were about. They enclosed the land people had been using for their own subsistence and gave them to large landowners for their sheep herds. The people who had been farming were left with no alternative but to go to the towns to look for work. There were similar policies throughout Europe.

By one means or another, governments across Europe made policies that made cheap labor available. They changed the structure of choice. If people could work for themselves in household production, they would never work for wages. The new governments systematically prevented that option. They drove people from farms to cities.

Some argue that what makes America different from any other place is that we had vast amounts of land available on our western frontiers. That's why a lot of people went to America in the first place. There was so much land that this policy wouldn't work at first. For labor, industry had to rely on new immigrants coming to the cities. But by a hundred years ago, most of those lands were no longer available. The land grabs of railroads, coal mining companies, and other corporate interests caused the almost immediate imposition of a system of taxes, permits, and deeds, all designed to limit access to land, on pioneers heading west.

Hollywood's Wild West was short-lived compared with the capitalism that quickly followed. There had been the great Civil War to decide whether slavery would continue or whether people would be available to sell their labor as a commodity—the only two choices for the majority of people living in the South—and it's not quite right to call either one a choice. Even if America was the exception, as these "exceptionalists" claimed, it hasn't been for quite a while.

So there's a thumbnail sketch of European and American history from the fall of Rome until now. A historian would have a stroke over this abridged version, but the point here is that because of the attractions of household production, capitalism can only be established by government policies. That's why there were revolutions in the eighteenth century to establish new governments friendly to capitalism. Those governments made household production impossible for most people and provided the labor the new capitalists needed for their factories.

After capitalism develops, it has to be maintained by government policies such as antitrust laws, labor laws, banking and contract laws, laws against lying, and other rules of the game. Americans grow up knowing these rules from being exposed to mass media that tell what happens when people break them.

It seems as natural to Americans to separate politics, religion, and economics as it seemed to Aztecs to sacrifice human beings to their gods. But the lesson of comparative anthropology is that economic, political, and religious systems are closely linked. Cultures are systems.

So, to understand how economic systems work, we have to understand how political systems work. To anthropologists, that means putting them in comparative perspective so we can talk about the whole species.

Egalitarian Systems

We're not sure it ever bothered Americans, but one of the things that really puzzled British anthropologists was how people could get along without kings and aristocrats and governments. They called such folks **acephalous**, which is a Latin word that means "headless."

The answer is that as long as everyone depends on everyone else, as long as everyone needs everyone else, they will find ways of getting along with each other and don't need judges, cops, courts, and armies to make them behave. It's called reciprocity. Do unto others as you would have them do unto you. And the converse—others do unto you as you do unto them. If everyone follows that rule, people don't need all of the apparatus of governments. It's beautiful. It's simple. It works. It's true.

Shan have a word for it: *joi kan.* The *kan* part means "each other," and they explain the *joi* part as being something like "help," but the two words together mean, "You help me when I need it, and I help you when you need it." Someone is repairing the roof on a house and needs some help. Fellow villagers show up and help out because when they need to repair their roofs (and sooner or later, everyone does), other people will come help them out. And if you don't, then nobody will help you when you need it.

We've already talked about reciprocity as a kind of exchange. This is the same thing, and where reciprocity is the main mode of exchange, there is a political form that we call **egalitarian**. The word means that everyone is equal, but that's not quite what anthropologists mean.

We understand that in every society there are differences among people. There are men and women; kids, grown-ups and old people; married people, newlyweds, and people who aren't yet married. So we modify it a bit and say that there's equality within each age and sex category. What do we mean by equality? One of the cultural ecologists, Morton Fried, gave it this definition: as many positions of prestige as there are people capable of filling them. That means that talent and effort pay off in prestige. Nobody can fake anything when everyone knows all about you from the time you were born. There's no way you can fake your résumé if you don't usually bring home the game or the vegetables or if you have no pigs.

Why doesn't the strongest person just take over and rule with an iron hand? The answer is that people wouldn't put up with it. They can leave.

They have relatives and in-laws all over the place who would be glad to see them and have them in their own groups. People depend on each other, as we saw when we discussed our evolution, so if people leave one person alone, that person won't be able to make it. When the people who leave join other groups, they won't have anything good to say about the guy they left, and none of the other groups will help him out.

Lisu say, "Whenever you keep two cups together, they will rattle." That's something elders say to people in one of their several marriage ceremonies. It means that couples don't always get along. So how can egalitarian people deal with conflict? If everyone depends on everyone else, nobody wants to split up the group. Relatives will back you up, but they will also pressure you into getting along so that you don't split up the group. They don't want your problem to become theirs, so they pressure you to solve your problems with other people. They also help you solve them in any way they can so they don't spread. (If you grew up in a very small town or a close-knit neighborhood, some of this may sound familiar.)

There may be someone who acts as a headman, but this person has no power over anyone. He summarizes public opinion, but he listens more than talks. Finally, many people have some idea like witchcraft or the evil eye. It's the notion that some people make bad things happen to others. Many people think the only way to deal with these people is to either ostracize or kill them. The people most likely to be labeled and treated as witches are what we would call malcontents who can't get along with others. So, for a lot of reasons, everybody has an interest in getting along with everybody else. Another Lisu saying is "You can't eat with one chopstick."

The most important thing about egalitarian societies is that everyone has equal access to all resources. Like Lisu, land is theirs to use while they use it, and when they stop using it, they have no claim on it. If there are fish to catch, anyone can catch them. If there is water, everyone can use it.

Reciprocity relies on a sense of obligation. If someone gives you something, you owe them something of equal value. You owe a day's labor for every day other people give you. Here we run into another contradiction because in systems of household production, not all households are equally able to produce. Imagine a household with a young couple, a five-year-old daughter and a one-year-old son, and an aging grandfather. The couple has to feed themselves as well as the kids and the grandfather. Now suppose one of the adults gets injured or sick. Then there is only one person to do all of the work. So, if there are many consumers and few workers, then each worker must work harder.

Another household may be lucky enough to avoid sickness and injury, and their children may be old enough to help. Suppose we have a similar household with teenaged kids. Then there are four workers supporting five people rather than one worker supporting five people. Health is a matter of luck.

Lisu control this factor. They set their production at just the amount the least able can produce to keep up with the obligations for feasts. That means that the households with more workers per consumer can slack off, and they do. They don't try to overproduce because that would be ostentatious. It's good to be equal; it's not good to get too far ahead or behind.

Luck comes in other ways. Take a look at a poppy seed bagel. Each one of the seeds on it is the same size as the seed for an opium poppy. (Don't get your urine tested for drugs after you eat a poppy seed bagel, by the way.) Lisu broadcast the seeds into their swidden fields just before the monsoon rains begin. How can you tell when the monsoon will begin? Everyone has a pretty good idea of the general time when the weather begins to change, but if someone plants too early, there isn't enough rain, and the sun scorches the plants as they come up. It's just as unlucky to plant right before a gully-washing rainstorm carries all of the seeds down the hillside so that all the poppies come up in a bunch at the bottom of the field and crowd each other out. It's just luck.

Hierarchy

Unless there are strong inhibitions on ostentation like those the Lisu have, a lucky household can get a little bit ahead. If they give more than they receive, the less lucky households become obliged to them. Everyone owes them, and the goods begin to concentrate with them. But they are obliged to give away what they receive. Thus, they can move into the center of a **redistributive system** of exchange. In highland Southeast Asia, everyone knows about this dynamic. Lisu don't let it happen, but some folks do.

Redistribution comes with its own political form. The central person in a redistributive system of exchange has more prestige than others. He may have titles and fancy headdresses, and people may show him deference. In these **rank** systems, there are fewer positions of prestige than people capable of filling them. There may be more than one person equally able to be at the center. Except for these differences, rank-organized societies are similar to egalitarian ones. Everyone has equal access to resources, and the center person doesn't have any power over others except persuasion.

One of the cultural ecological anthropologists, Marshall Sahlins (1989), studied the political systems of the Pacific islands. He found that where there are diverse ecological situations, there are advantages to redistribution. People can specialize to increase the productivity or efficiency of their work. If some people grow sweet potatoes inland and others fish on the shore, everyone can enjoy both seafood and sweet potatoes. The diet can be more diverse. Food may become available at different times of the year in different areas. Distributions of food may come just when people need them, so they don't have to worry about lean periods of the year. In short, everyone benefits, and they can achieve a higher degree of well-being with less labor.

In rank systems, the center person, often with a title like chieftain, has no more power than others. But in redistributive systems of exchange, there may be another development. The center person may not distribute everything that comes in—he may keep some for his own family or kinsmen and start producing less than others.

When you get exactly as much as you give, as in a barter relationship, we call it **balanced reciprocity**. When there is no exact equivalence, or people don't keep track of it as Shan joi kan or family sharing, we call it **general reciprocity**. Some things are in between, like Christmas presents. Some people keep track of them and try to make it a balanced relationship; but others do not, and it's a relationship of general reciprocity. Some relationships aren't balanced at all. In these, you give and you receive, but you don't receive as much as you give. That defines a relationship that's not symmetrical, and we call it **asymmetrical redistribution**. Egalitarian relationships are symmetrical. Reciprocity is symmetrical. But redistribution is not necessarily symmetrical. The central person may keep back some of the goods for his family.

An example of asymmetrical redistribution is the people of the Trobriand Islands where Bronislaw Malinowski (1922) lived during World War I. They had matrilineal lineages, like the people of Truk, and a patrilocal system of postmarital residence, so the women joined their husbands on the men's lineage land, unlike Truk. But the land and the product of the land belonged to lineages. The men stayed on the lineage's land where their wives, members of different lineages, joined them and worked to produce yams. Then, following their sense of family values, the men gave most of the yams to their sisters because the yams were the product of their sisters' land, the place the sisters had left when they got married. So the yams that the men ate did not come from their own gardens but from the gardens of their wives' lineages as presents from the men's brothers-in-law (the wives' brothers) who owed the yams to their sisters. So I grow yams and give them to my sister, and I eat the yams my wife's brothers give to her. That makes a great insurance policy.

If I'm a man who belongs to the Smith lineage, and my sister marries a Jones and goes to live with him on Jones lineage land, I owe her the yams from my garden. My wife is a Brown, and her brothers owe her yams. So I give my yams to my sister and eat the ones my wife gets from her brothers. This is a way to even out some of those differences in luck.

There's another wrinkle. The Trobriand lineages are ranked so that some are higher than others according to how close they are to the original ancestor. One of the men of the highest-ranking lineage is the chieftain, and he is at the center of a redistributive system that also distributes yams. But because of the prestige of his lineage and his titles, he had up to sixty wives from other lineages that wanted to make alliances with him. So he got yams from many brothers-in-law and had so many that he could let them rot in a display of wealth.

More important, he could support some of his kinsmen and didn't have to work as much as others. Some of the people he supported knew the magic that could help or harm others. So there was a sense that if you didn't go along with the system, the chieftain could hurt you. But he didn't have an army or a police force.

Stratification

When central figures take that step and start supporting kinsmen to make an aristocracy and start providing some people with weapons so they can have more force than others do—when that happens, they can deprive other people of access to resources. **Stratification** means that people don't all have equal access to resources. An example is the Shan village where Paul lived where some people owned irrigated land and others did not.

Throughout history, most stratified systems have been like an extra consumer in households or that extra person at the table. People have to produce a little extra to pay taxes or tribute. People are still involved in household production, but they produce more to support the rulers.

Stratified systems are based on **classes**. Some people have more access to resources than others. That defines two classes of people: takers and givers or haves and have-nots. The only way to keep stratified systems going is by force.

Stratification is inherently unfair because some people have the ability to deprive others of their livelihood, something that never happens in egalitarian or rank systems because there aren't the structures that make it possible and because everyone relies on everybody else. Because they are unfair, stratified systems are very fragile unless there is some means for controlling access to resources—for being sure the haves have what they want and the have-nots give the product of their labor to the haves.

In highland Southeast Asia, chieftains may try to make the shift from rank systems to stratified ones. Trobriand brothers give their sisters yams because of their family values. When Southeast Asian chieftains say that they want to change the system from one based on family values to one based on land ownership, one of two things can happen, according to Edmund Leach (1954), the British anthropologist who lived in the Kachin Hills of Burma during World War II while he was organizing Kachin guerillas to fight against the Japanese who had invaded Burma. (These same Kachin revolted against the Burmese government in 1961, like the Shan we discussed earlier.)

In those days, Kachin people could either go along with the chieftain, who tried to get them to level and irrigate land and become Shan under his leadership, or refuse and be egalitarian like Lisu. There could be advantages to either response. The Shan Paul lived with cultivated both irrigated and swidden rice. The same amount of work on an irrigated field gave people three times more rice than on a swidden field. In other words, labor on irrigated fields was three times more productive than swidden labor. In terms of the logic of household production, that's a good deal. You can afford to give away half of your harvest and still come out ahead if you have irrigated fields. But if it wasn't that way, there was no advantage to going along with a chieftain who just wanted to aggrandize himself and his family, and, because he didn't have any force, people could just refuse and not accept the idea that some lineages have more prestige than others—they could repudiate the principle of rank. Without any force, there was nothing the chieftain could do about it if people decided to go that way.

The seeds of stratification are in the system of asymmetrical redistribution. The chieftain can hold back some of the goods he collects instead of giving them away immediately. He can make the collection period last longer to get more goods. He can do things that increase production and outputs by increasing productivity or without increasing productivity just get people to work longer hours to produce more, for instance, for the glory of the kinship group. Then the chieftain can keep back some of this increased production to support himself and his family.

If the chieftain can convert his control of the redistributive system into control over resources, he has created a stratified system. Sometimes people go along with this because it benefits them. For instance, it would be a good deal to go along if you can triple your productivity by getting access to irrigated fields, even if you have to pay half your crop in rent or taxes.

If the chieftain doesn't have any force, no cops or army to call, then people don't have to go along with such a shift. Kachin, for example, often don't. If people don't agree to it, there's nothing a chieftain can do, unless he can control or get some force to use against his own people. That's what defines stratification—the ability to control access to resources by force.

When people go along with such a shift, the chieftain can quickly gain the resources he needs to control access to resources by force. Then people have very little choice. They can leave and go somewhere else if they can find a way to make a living. Or they can stay and work on the chieftain's terms.

In a stratified system, the chieftain is the ultimate giver because he gives wealth to his subordinates. He is the ultimate receiver because everyone owes him a share of what they produce. A hierarchy of chieftains may develop so people give the product of their work to one chieftain who passes it up the line to a king. The kings and chieftains use some of the wealth to support armies, palace guards, and warfare and to build forts and palaces. That's where the force comes in. They may use wealth to build churches, temples, pyramids, and cathedrals. That's also based on force, but the reason they do these things is to create or support a cultural code that makes the system seem reasonable and natural. These systems are like the feudal system of Europe and developed at different times in Africa, China, Japan, and Southeast Asia.

The Inca Empire in Peru divided village lands into three parts—one each for the church, the government, and subsistence. They drafted forced labor from villagers to build roads, great monuments, and buildings. In the center of the whole system was a god-king. The Inca had force if they needed it, but they also had religion working for them telling the people that without this god-king running the show, the whole cosmos would fall apart.

Any stratified system has a **ruling class** that has access to resources and **subordinate classes** that do not. The ruling class takes away some of the product of the labor of the subordinate classes. This isn't always a bad deal for subordinate classes, especially if there's some increase in productivity for them, but once these systems get established, they can't be undone. So far, this has proven to be an irreversible one-way process.

The unfairness of stratified systems makes them fragile unless the ruling classes develop some means to ensure their privileged access to resources. They can use two means for this. Force is one. The other is what the American anthropologist Marvin Harris (1971) calls **mind control**, or directing how people think by controlling the culture, such as Inca having a religion that persuaded everyone that things had to be that way or nature would fall apart. Mind control is a lot cheaper than force, so rulers like it better than force. The ruling classes of all stratified systems develop institutional ways of keeping control of resources.

As we've said, **hegemony** is from a Greek word meaning "authority" or "rule." It usually means the predominant power of one country over others such as American hegemony or, in past centuries, British, French,

Spanish, Roman, Ottoman, Mongol, or Chinese hegemony. Anthropologists have borrowed this word to mean the predominant power of one class—especially the power to control the content of the cultural code.

Some argue that nobody can really fool people, even through controlling their culture. People can see what's going on around them. Hegemony only works because it has force behind it, and people know if they resist too much, they'll be on the receiving end of that force. If the ruling class cannot or do not develop control by force or cultural hegemony, they cease being the ruling class, and the system of stratification collapses when ordinary people repudiate it because it is unfair.

In the next chapters, we will discuss how ruling classes control stratified societies because that's central to understanding our own modern systems of most contemporary societies. Anthropologists call the institutional means for controlling stratified societies **states**. We will give a more thorough description of what states are and how they operate later. Here it's enough to remember that states are the ways that ruling classes manage force and hegemony to control their people and their cultures and make it all seem reasonable. Stratified systems without states don't last long because they are inherently unfair, and people will refuse to cooperate with them unless compelled by force, hegemony, or both.

Edmund Leach (1953) saw rank systems become egalitarian, but in our ethnographic work, anthropologists haven't seen a stratified system collapsing. We do have historical examples, however. One of the most vivid is medieval Iceland, where there was a highly stratified system, but the chieftains couldn't get together to create institutions that worked for them as a class. That system lasted about four hundred years, from the first settlement in 870 until Iceland became part of the Norwegian Kingdom in 1262. In the next chapter we tell that story.

Discussion Questions

- Think of some present-day rules and regulations in American society that limit access to resources, including land, food, and fuel. What purpose do those rules serve? Who benefits most? Who is most deprived? Why?
- Why do people steal? Is it possible to create a political or economic system in which stealing would not be necessary? Who defines what is "theft"? What if you had a different definition? Can you think of examples of institutional or corporate theft?
- The French philosopher Pierre-Joseph Proudhon said that property is theft. What do you think he meant?

- Develop examples of redistributive systems you have seen or read about. What do they have in common? Where do you see them, and where do you never see them?
- What are some examples of reciprocity? How do they work? What would an American economic system built on reciprocity instead of money look like?
- We assert that stratified systems are fragile. Do you agree? Why or why not? If so, what are some of the mechanisms stratified systems use to maintain themselves? How do those manifest themselves in today's society? If not, why not?
- You are probably going to college so you can get a better job. Why do you have to get a job at all?
- What class are you a member of? OK, you're in the anthropology class, but in the system of stratification, where do you fit? Ruling class or working class? How did that happen?

Suggested Reading

D'Altroy, Terrance. *The Incas.* Boston: Blackwell, 2003.

Fried, Morton. *The Evolution of Political Society: An Essay in Political Anthropology.* New York: McGraw-Hill, 1967.

Weiner, Annette. *The Trobrianders of Papua New Guinea.* Belmont, CA: Thomson/Wadsworth, 1988.

9

Archeologists and anthropologists are excavating a Viking-era settlement in Iceland. *Photo by Suzan Erem.*

CHAPTER 9

STRATIFICATION WITHOUT A STATE: MEDIEVAL ICELAND

In the last chapter, we saw that stratification means differential access to resources. If a society is going to be stratified, it needs some institutional way to enforce that differential access so that some have more than others. Anthropologists call such arrangements of institutions *states*. Here we are going to see what happens to a stratified society that does not have a state. That kind of organization is very rare because it so fragile. Usually either such societies develop states very quickly, or the people don't put up with the stratification and become egalitarian. Understanding an example like this helps us understand exactly what it is that states do, how stratification works, and how societies change over time.

In medieval Iceland, we see a stratified stateless society collapse because the ruling class refuses to have a state. It is the best example of how the ruling class needs a state to maintain the stratification from which it benefits.

The story of the naming of Iceland comes from a Norwegian who went there before the first permanent settlers in 870. According to the story, he was so taken by the hunting and fishing that he didn't bother to make hay, so when the winter, came his livestock all died. When he looked out over the land, all he could see was snow and ice and no way to make it to spring, so he said something like, "This place is an ice land." The name stuck.

In the ninth century, Norway had a lot of small chieftains with asymmetrical redistribution, somewhat like the Trobriand system, except that they didn't have matrilineal lineages—they had kindreds, as Europeans do to this day. Remember a kindred is all of the cousins out to a certain distance. And they didn't grow yams but relied on wheat, cattle, and sheep. On the west coast of Norway, there was a lot of fishing as well.

One of these chieftains was named Harald Finehair. He invited other chieftains to join him to form an aristocracy with him as king. Some did,

117

but others did not see that they would gain anything for their household economies by paying taxes to a king who could do nothing to improve their productivity. He wasn't doing anything that would increase their productivity and was imposing taxes that would impose extra costs. Check chapter 7 on household production to see how this would affect them. It was not a favorable equation.

With the power he gained from his coalition, Harald fought the chieftains who would not join him and in a battle in 885 beat them and became the king. The remaining chieftains had three choices: they could join Harald, fight him, or leave.

Some fought and died; some fought and then left; some just left. Those who left loaded their livestock, families, slaves, and followers onto their Viking ships and went to the British Isles or Iceland. Some of the chieftains who went to the British Isles later came to Iceland to settle. The first thing they did when they reached the uninhabited Iceland was to claim land and define the borders of their areas. Then they parceled the land out to their followers.

They brought with them from Norway a very firm concept of land ownership as well as an institution of slavery. Both of these things show that there was a system of differential access to resources, stratification. But there was no one king over all of the chieftains. Some of the slaves rose up and killed their masters and took off for the Westman Islands off the east coast of Iceland. The kinsmen of the dead masters hunted down the slaves and killed them all. These chieftains were not going to let their slaves change anything in the new land.

People hunted and fished for subsistence, but they relied mostly on their livestock—sheep and cows. To bring their stock through the winter, they had to cut and store hay before it got too cold. Iceland was too cold and the growing season too short for grain, so they traded wool for grain from Norway.

The more hay a person could get in and store, the more livestock he could bring through the winter. People had to figure out the balance among horses, cows, and sheep. Horses could fend for themselves pretty well during the winter, but they did better with hay. People needed to keep cows and sheep inside during the winter and feed them. The more sheep a farmer kept, the less cattle he could feed with the winter's supply of hay.

The cattle and sheep as well as horses provided provisions for people. Icelanders ate horses then as they do now. Landowners used their provisions to support their slaves and followers. The slaves provided labor for haying, for managing the livestock, and for hunting and fishing.

In the early 900s, there were about thirty-six chieftains. The sagas tell us that some of the chieftains were more cunning than others, some more ruthless, some better at law, some braver, but they were about equal in their power. A chieftain had to be generous to his followers and protect their interests, or the followers would have no reason to stay with him. Chieftains also made alliances with other chieftains, especially through marriages.

If we diagram their economic system as we did the Lisu one, it would look like what is shown in figure 9.1. We can read the diagram as saying the more slaves, the more labor; the more labor, the more livestock; the more livestock, the more provisions; the more provisions, the more slaves and followers; the more livestock, the less hunting and fishing; the more hunting and fishing, the more provisions.

In this system, where the chieftains were about equally powerful, the limiting factor was access to labor. More slaves meant more labor and so on. With needs limited by the logic of household economies and plenty of land, labor was the limiting factor.

Within sixty years, by the year 930, people had claimed all the land, and the chieftains agreed to establish a general assembly where everyone would meet once a year to settle disputes and to make what they called law. Their idea of law was not like the modern one. It was a blend of tradition, custom, religion, ethics, and law. In those days, before they had writing, they sent one man to Norway to memorize the system of law from an assembly many of the chieftains were familiar with, and then bring it back with him. That man was the first law speaker, responsible

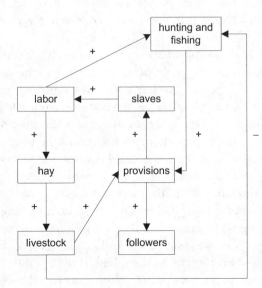

Figure 9-1 The Medieval Icelandic economy.

for knowing the law and reciting one-third of it from memory each year at the assembly. Others listened and learned the law, and then they could be law speakers for three years.

Still, there was no authority above the chieftains. There was the general assembly, but it had no authority. People could take disputes to the assembly, but winning a dispute gave the winner the right to enforce the verdict himself—if he could. If someone killed your brother, you could make a case against him and win. If you won, you could claim half his property and get him banished, but you had to go collect the property yourself, and you had to enforce the banishment yourself. If you weren't stronger than your opponent, there was nothing you could do. Almost every saga has stories of people trying to get enough force together to enforce such decisions.

So the system rested on force. The people who could maintain large followings and strong alliances could focus the most force and were therefore the most powerful. In addition to the three dozen chieftains, there were a number of independent farmers who were their followers.

Some people had settled in the highlands, and some had stayed close to the inlets and rivers where they landed. As more livestock grazed in the highlands, the grass cover diminished, and the soils literally blew away in the high winds. The loss for the highlands was a gain for the lowlands, where those soils settled out to make more productive fields. But highland people had no way to make a living.

The people from these households began to offer to work for other farmers in return for the part of their subsistence that they couldn't provide for themselves. For the first time, wage labor was available. This changed the whole system.

Slave owners had to support their slaves through the whole year to be able to benefit from their labor at peak times, such as the sheep roundup in the fall, sheering, and hay making. The slaves could produce enough to support themselves, necessary value, but not much more. It was better for landowners to hire people for part of the year when they needed lots of labor and not have to support them for the rest of the year. That way, the landowners could benefit from the surplus value the workers produced because landowners did not have to feed them through the rest of the year just to get the labor when they needed it.

When hired labor was available, there was no advantage to keeping slaves, so landowners began to free them. These freed slaves began looking for land, but there was none they could claim except the small plots that landowners offered them on the edges of their holdings. There, the former slaves could make part of their living and fill in the rest by working for the landowner, their former owner, for wages. Sometimes instead of hiring labor, landowners rented out their land. It came to the same thing: extracting surplus value from the people who produced it.

Large landowners and chieftains began to buy or take over smaller farms. If a farm was too small to support a household, it wasn't of much use, so a person might sell it and then rent land from the landowner. More and more people had less and less land. The few people who owned land owned more and more of it. There were fewer landowners, each with larger farms.

Now, access to labor was no longer the limiting factor. With plentiful labor, land was the limiting factor. But all the land was already claimed. However, there was no overarching authority; there was no state to prevent a powerful person from taking land from a less powerful one. We can diagram the system like what is shown in figure 9.2.

This system has several self-intensifying loops. More followers, more land; more land, more hay; more hay, more livestock; more livestock, more provisions; more provisions, more followers. This system depends on the availability of people for wage labor and a chieftain's ability to gain enough followers to secure and enlarge his claim to land.

The supply of labor came from the same process. The smaller the land claim, the less hay, the less the livestock, provisions, and security of the land claim until one didn't have enough land to support a household and had to sell the labor of the household.

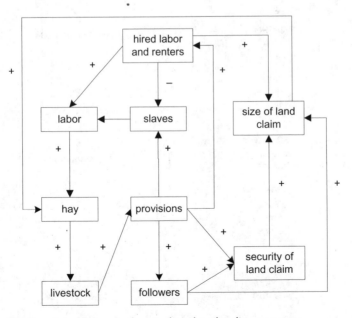

Figure 9-2 Land and labor in the Medieval Icelandic economy.

Figure 9-3 shows another way to envision the process. Because it was possible to extract surplus value from wage workers, there was no limit on the amount of land a person could use. More land meant more surplus value and more power. So chieftains started taking land from others, and everyone who claimed land had to defend it because they couldn't call a cop if someone tried to take away their land. The process became exaggerated at each turn until there were large groups fighting frequently.

As more and more farmers were drawn into fights to support their chieftains and their own land claims, they had less and less of a stake in this unstable system. A typical farmer thought, "Why should I risk my life for some ostentatious chieftain except that he will whack me if I don't?" It would have served the farmers better to have a state to protect their land rights rather than to have to fight to defend their land or to support their chieftain in his quest for more lands.

Notice, a state wouldn't have done anything for the workers, just the farmers. In fact, that's the way it turned out and the way it was for about the next six hundred years. We'll tell that story later.

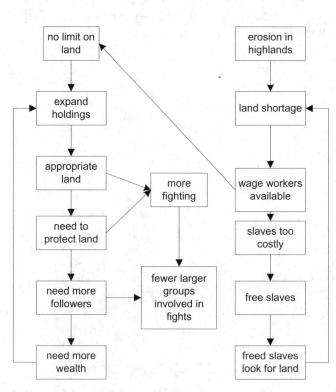

Figure 9-3 Effects of free labor in Medieval Iceland.

The chieftains had two sources of income: rents and the products of wage labor. Everything in this system rested on the control of land. A person who didn't control land had no source of income except wages or some income from working on property he rented or both. The control of land depended on the force a person could muster, and that depended on the size of his following. The way to secure a following was to be generous and "chieftainly"—to support followers in their cases and be as generous to them as one was ruthless to enemies. The importance of the followings and the trappings of chieftaincy led to an exaggerated sense of chieftaincy and more grandiose displays of wealth and of power.

The whole system rested on land ownership, but there was no institutional structure to support laws about ownership. It was every person for himself—and yes, all chieftains were "he's," although there were some remarkable women. Each person had to defend land claims on his own. Chieftains or powerful landowners took land from others by force whenever they could get away with it. At the assemblies, the most powerful usually won. Everyone was competing for land and power because the biggest and most powerful had the best chance of winning. Everyone wanted to expand, but there was no place to expand to except other people's land.

By 1220, 350 years after the first settlement, there were five big chieftains' families in the whole land fighting among themselves. Just to put the time framework into perspective, not until 2126 will it have been 350 years since the American revolution in 1776.

By 1262, one guy, Gissur, won and turned the whole bunch over to the king of Norway and became his earl. He might have become king of Iceland, but Icelanders might have resented it, and Icelanders agreed that Norway was the place where there was a real civilization. Icelanders had a long history of ambivalent relationships with Norwegian kings. They hated them, but they also loved the pomp and poetry of the court and all of its finery.

When Gissur became the king's earl, Iceland became part of a state, but it was not an Icelandic state. It was ruled by a foreign king as a colony, and Norway could enforce its power by controlling or even with holding trade with Iceland. Then, in 1380, Norway became part of Denmark, and Iceland went along and became a Danish colony until 1944, when it gained independence after more than six hundred years of colonial rule. That six hundred years of colonial rule wasn't such a bad deal for farmers; at least they didn't have to worry about the chieftains anymore. They became the power on the island and once again began to defy the king, this time of Denmark. In the eighteenth and nineteenth centuries, the king told the Icelandic ruling class that they shouldn't treat their own people so badly, but the farmers did not wish to change a system that benefited them so much. After all, they were getting virtually free labor. That was the law. The landowners controlled Parliament and made the laws.

The medieval chieftains wanted to keep the system of stratification because they were at the top. Each chieftain thought he could win in the competition for total control. Finally, they all lost because they could not agree to form a state. They wore themselves out in internecine fighting, and when the Norwegian king took over, there was the first peace in a long time, and a lot of people were relieved.

These are the lessons we learn from this story:

- Stratification without a state is messy and unstable, but it can last for a long time—four hundred years in Iceland.
- Stratified systems either develop states or stop being stratified. We don't see stratification without states today.
- States hold stratified societies together. Cooperation and reciprocity hold egalitarian societies together.

In this system, we see there is wage labor but no market, so capitalism did not develop. It remained a system of asymmetrical redistribution, but it came to be oriented around the king of Norway rather than the chieftains.

Acting on the logic of household production and their cultural code, these Icelanders created a system that did not serve anyone's long-term interests, a system that not only was not sustainable but was self-destructive. The only people who could have changed it were the ones who got the most out of it, the chieftains. Later it was farmers.

In medieval times, just because a state system would have served the landowning farmers well did not mean it would have served the chieftains well. And we have to ask how well any system served slaves and renters and wage workers who had to scrape by from one year to the next in this marginal ecosystem in a political system run by arrogant and self-serving goons. Another fact about stratified systems: adaptations of the system do not serve all interests equally. Once there are class systems, we have to ask whose interests are served by what structures and developments. There is no longer any sense in which everyone's interests are served.

In 1000, two other things happened in Iceland. One was the introduction of Christianity at the general assembly. Some of the chieftains were pagans, and some were Christians. The king of Norway was pushing for the Icelanders to convert, and he could use his clout as their major trading partner for grain and timber. At the meeting of the assembly in Iceland, people were restive and agreed that they could not live with two

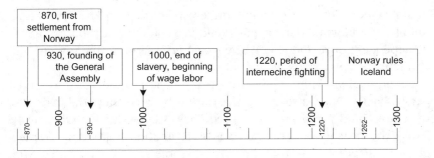

Figure 9-4. Time line for medieval Iceland.

laws—two sets of customs—one for the pagans and one for the Christians. They agreed to let one person arbitrate. The arbitrator was a pagan himself, but after a long period of thought, he decided that everyone should be Christian. At that point, all of the pagans went to a hot spring to be baptized.

Another event of that time was the outlawing of Erik the Red. When a person was outlawed, it meant that someone had won a case against him at the assembly. The person then had the choice of defending himself against the winner, leaving the island, or hiding out. If a person could remain in Iceland without being killed for twenty years, the sentence was lifted. Two people almost made it. One hid out for twenty years before he was whacked. The other made it for eighteen years.

Erik left and went to Greenland to start a new settlement there. His son was Leif Eriksson, who continued the westward exploration to Newfoundland, now part of Canada. Archaeologists have located and excavated the site of this settlement at what is now called L'Anse aux Meadows. Icelanders spent several winters there, and one woman had a child in America, but they finally returned to Greenland and Iceland rather than settle the new continent. In the summer of 2005, we worked with a group of archaeologists to locate and map her house in Iceland and to piece together this story by locating the early settlement farms and then the later ones where renters lived.

Why did Icelanders turn down the opportunity of settling in America? The Icelandic system depended on captive labor—either as slaves or as desperately poor people who offered their labor for sale. In the new world, slaves could escape. Iceland is large, but there are not that many places to make a living. The interior is all volcanic rock. There are some places to hide out, but not for long and not for many. The coastal areas are the only ones suitable for fishing and growing grass. There was no place for runaway slaves to go, as the ones who got to the Westman Islands found.

But in America, there was an indefinitely large frontier. The land was so full of fish and game that anyone could make a living without having to be dependent on a landowner. The Icelandic system of land owning and extracting surplus value would not work in the New World.

So, how do we know these stories? If the early settlers had to send a person back to Norway to memorize the law because they couldn't write, then how could they write their sagas? They didn't write them right away. Part of the measure of a chieftain was his reputation. A chieftain's reputation was made or broken in the stories people told. These stories were as important a part of the political economy as the sheep and hay. They were like a credit rating.

With Christianity, some people began to learn how to write. One of the first things they wrote was a grammar book about the Icelandic language. Another was the book of settlements that recorded the stories about the first settlers and their land claims. The sagas are stories from the ninth through twelfth centuries that weren't written down until the thirteenth century, in the middle of all of the strife as the system collapsed onto itself.

The saga writers wrote down the old stories, but they also wrote about current events. That's why we have almost ethnographic accounts of the collapse of the system. One of these writers was Snorri Sturlason, the next-to-last chieftain standing.

The end of the world for Snorri, the scholar-chieftain who wrote the story with which we opened this book, came in the basement of a priest's house in 1241. Snorri left Norway without the king's permission. That offended the king, who wrote to another powerful Icelandic chieftain, Gissur, to tell him to either get Snorri back to Norway or kill him. Gissur knew Snorri didn't want to go back to Norway, so with seventy followers and more in reserve, Gissur rode to Snorri's establishment and broke into his house, where he was sleeping.

Snorri ran to the priest's house to hide. Gissur followed him. The priest said that Snorri wasn't there until Gissur told the priest he had come to make peace with Snorri. Then the priest admitted that Snorri was in the basement, and Gissur sent five men downstairs to murder him.

Because they could not develop institutions to keep order in their stratified society, the Icelandic chieftains became absorbed into another state that could maintain order. Reciprocity and mutuality maintain order in egalitarian societies; states maintain order in stratified societies. In the next chapter, we explore how they do this, but, first, a story from another time and place.

Every Friday, Nasrudin sold a donkey in the market for next to nothing. In the same marketplace, there was a rich merchant who couldn't compete with Nasrudin's prices.

"My goons force farmers to give me the food for my donkeys," the merchant explained, "and I pay no wages to my slaves to take care of the donkeys, and I still can't sell them for as low a price as you." Finally, the merchant asked how Nasrudin could sell his donkeys for such a low price.

Nasrudin said, "You steal the food and labor. I steal the donkeys."

Discussion Questions

- In the United States throughout most of the twentieth century, people like Emma Goldman, who called herself an anarchist who supported the notion of a stateless society based on reciprocity and cooperation, were branded, brought up on charges, imprisoned, and in other ways punished. Can you think of reasons why there was such a strong response to these ideas?
- It took Iceland four hundred years to go from being stratified without a state to a state. Imagine the United States four hundred years from now. What might our society look like? If we don't manage to make our planet completely uninhabitable by then, will our government still be in place? Will it look as it does now?
- The sagas were written centuries after the events they tell of actually happened. They reflect the times in which they were written, as well as the times they tell about. Can you think of other stories that were written down long after the events? Does that color your understanding of texts like the Bible, the Torah, or the Koran?
- Why is it that stratified societies have cops and courts and egalitarian ones do not?

Suggested Reading

Durrenberger, E. Paul. *The Dynamics of Medieval Iceland: Political Economy and Literature.* Iowa City: University of Iowa Press, 1992.
Smiley, Jane. *The Sagas of Icelanders.* New York: Penguin, 2001.

10

Turkish flags fly in front of a building with a large portrait of Mustafa Kemal "Ataturk," considered the father of modern Turkey. Despite the fact that Ataturk died in 1938, his portrait is still widely displayed in Turkey. Like most contemporary societies, Turkey is an example of a stratified society. *This photo was taken a few years ago by the authors.*

CHAPTER 10

HOW STATES WORK

The American anthropologist Charles Hockett (1973) sums up states this way:

> The Mafia, General Motors, the Roman Catholic Church, and the governments of the United States and of the Soviet Union, however greatly they differ, are all cultural cousins, all specialized descendants of the arrangements worked out by the earliest successful as-yet-undifferentiated racketeer-capitalist-bishop-laborboss-governors. (549)

Stratified societies are formed of classes with differential access to resources. This creates tensions because the majority of the people would benefit from the equal access of rank or egalitarian societies, but the minority benefits most in a stratified society. The fundamental predicament of stratified societies is this inequality of distribution. The solution is a set of institutions we call states. The institutions of states solve the problem by two means, as we mentioned earlier: thought control and force.

We saw this tension among Kachin in Southeast Asia when the people repudiated the idea of ranking. The other choice they have is to create institutions of the state to maintain order and stratification, as finally happened in medieval Iceland.

Thought Control

Any university has at least one office dedicated to the task of public relations that enjoys as many resources as just about any department of anthropology. When Paul taught at the University of Iowa, he served on the faculty committee that was supposed to advise the Office of Public Information. (It's usually called something like that rather than "spinmeister central," "department of propaganda," or something more accurate.)

129

Whenever anything came up, he always suggested telling the truth as far as people could figure it out. The director, a professional information manager, could never understand that. The job of these offices is to manipulate people's ideas about the university or, as they might say, "to promote the university's interests." Penn State and other universities have several such offices—one dedicated to the sciences; one for alumni; one for athletics; one that deals with research—and others as well.

We Americans are so accustomed to spin doctors and advertising assaulting our every sense that we are like antibiotic-resistant microorganisms; a lot of it rolls right off us. But at least some of it sinks in and works. At the Superbowl of 2004, a famous singer flashed her boob at everyone watching the halftime festivities. That boob got more attention than illiteracy, racism, sexism, women's rights, and the rate of poverty for the next month and more. Maybe you've seen a magician who directs your attention to the left hand while performing the trick with the right. That's what this kind of media manipulation is all about.

George Orwell had seen a lot of the world before he wrote his novel *1984.* He had worked with the British suppressing Burmese villagers and had been with the anarchists when Franco's fascists invaded Spain in 1936. Orwell knew about the machinations of states. He set his novel in the future. That future is now decades in the past, but we've seen a lot of what he wrote about—for instance, what he called "double-speak," or reversing the meanings of words to disguise things. "Office of Public Information" means the people who don't give you straight talk. Another is "Department of Defense" for "Department of War." During the Persian Gulf War, the Reagan administration named a certain kind of missile "peacekeepers." And just think about the whole notion of "friendly fire." How friendly is it to get killed by your own side? The examples are so numerous that they have entered our language, and we no longer think about them. That's why they're so insidious, like computer viruses in our brains, misdirecting our thinking.

Think about the rhetoric of any political campaign.

Think about the messages of television commercials. "You are the ugliest, foulest smelling, hairiest, most unfashionable, undesirable worm on the planet. But our product can fix that." The media reach into every corner of our lives with their messages of insignificance and powerlessness. The rulers of preindustrial states weren't that lucky.

They used what Marvin Harris (1971) calls "magico-religious" specialists, such as the Inca priests who treated the ruler as the "son of the sun." Imagine how important it would have been to the people who farmed for a living to produce enough extra food to support the son of the sun as well as his priests. The Inca priests spread the doctrine that the order of nature depends on commoners subordinating themselves to aristocrats. If you can get people to think that way, you don't have to use force to keep them in line; they do it themselves.

These rulers didn't have television, radio, print, and Internet ads for their creeds, but they used collective wealth to spread the word through monumental structures such as the pyramids of Egypt and Mexico, cathedrals, and other great edifices designed to make ordinary people feel powerless and insignificant.

Part of the purpose of the doublespeak of today is to convince people that "we are all in the same boat," our enemies are somewhere else, some other state, some other people. They used to be Soviets; now they're Islamic terrorists. This reinforces a sense of nationalism—in other words, the state and the status quo.

Maybe you've heard about the Romans offering their citizens "bread and circuses" to distract them. What they could have done with television! With modern media, people can get the feeling of participating in something larger than themselves without ever leaving their living rooms. We can participate in the Superbowl, in the drama of football, baseball, basketball, hockey. In video games, we can enjoy our own private war, auto racing, make-believe community, or space travel. Then we can go online and chat about it. What we don't do is get in the streets.

All of us know the world through our cultural codes. They're like the grammars of our languages; we don't think about them. We don't see alternatives because we've never known any alternatives. If someone asks why we shake hands when we meet someone, we would probably say something like, "How else would you greet someone? It's obvious." We only come to see our cultural codes when we contrast them with others that are different. People think spirits cause them to be sick? The king is not a god that controls the sun and the rain?

One of Paul's most difficult moments as an anthropologist came in 1976 when he was living with Shan. A presidential election was on in the United States, and villagers had been hearing a lot about it on Thai radio. One evening after supper, he was drinking tea on the verandah of the house where he lived when the headman of the village and a group of villagers came into the compound. The headman asked whether it was true that American people really believed that "all people are created equal."

"How could that be?" he and others asked. "You can see that some are clever and others are slow; some are strong and others are weak; some are rich and others are poor." This doctrine flew directly in the face of a fundamental assumption of the villagers' Buddhist worldview—that peoples' lives are determined by the balance of their good and bad deeds in all of their past lives, their karma. That explains why the king is the king and a farmer is a farmer and beggar is a beggar. What could be more clear?

But these folks had heard from an authoritative source that some other people actually thought that the law of karma did not operate, that all people were created equal. They had come to Paul to see whether this could possibly be correct. How could anyone think such a thing?

Paul struggled to find the Shan words. He didn't know how to say "distributive justice," "equality under the law," or "equal rights for all." He didn't know how to explain how it is that black people go to jail more frequently than white ones, how to elucidate the imbalance of gender and inequality of pay for men and women, how to explain the concept that you can get as much justice as you can afford.

Finally, he said something like, "It has to do with law. We say we use the same law for everyone. We say that, but we don't do that."

Where do these assumptions come from?

When Thai people greet each other, they put their hands together in front of their chins in something like an attitude of prayer. They aren't praying, but they are making statements about their relative prestige. If their hands are in front of their noses, they are saying they are subordinate. If they are at chest height, they are saying they are superordinate. And they have to figure out which pronoun to use. They don't just say "I" and "you" but have special pronouns for higher-ups and lower-downs. Then they say, "Good day, _____." In the blank they have to put a term of address that at least shows the speaker's gender. This already indicates something about prestige and status because males are higher than females. The term of address also has to indicate something about the relative status of the two people. The tone of voice, the hands, the pronouns, and the terms of address all say where the two are relative to each other in a cosmic hierarchy of beings. No Thai person has to even think about this. It's just natural. "How else would you do it?"

But it wasn't so natural to the poor and rural Shan village where Paul lived. There, people greeted each other by saying, "Where are you going?" "Where are you coming from?" or "What did you eat?" and didn't do anything special with their hands.

When Shan kids go to school, the teachers coach them on how to greet people in the properly polite Thai fashion. The postures of respect come along with the language. It's part of being respectful. It's part of being Thai. Shan kids learn it in school because they have their own Shan customs at home, but the Thai run the country and the schools. Thai kids learn it by the time they can walk because their parents show them how to do it by moving their hands into the proper position and holding their bodies in postures of deference. So by the time they can talk, they've got the whole system of hierarchy down pat and would never think that people could be created equal.

In American schools, we have similar examples. We have a teenage daughter. The other day she came home with the assignment to imagine a colony on Mars fifteen years from now. She had to answer questions like "What form of government will this colony have?" and "Which religion will the people follow?" We suggested she ask different questions, like "What if there were no government?" and "What if there were no religion?"

We do that to her all the time. She's used to it. But, of course, by the time most of her fellow students are done with school, they will never think there could be a society without a state or without religion, yet there have been.

When you think about it, the really interesting question is why anyone ever thought that Americans think that people *are* created equal. The fact that we say that at all is testament to our ability to learn to replace our own experience with what we know we're supposed to say.

It never occurs to Lisu to think about whether people are equal. It never comes up because everyone has access to the same resources. They know they're as good as anybody else. They learn that by growing up in an egalitarian society.

Let's look at one American example. How many times do kids say, "It's not fair!" Every grown-up knows the answer to that one: "Nobody said it's a fair world, " meaning "Don't expect fairness." People who grow up not expecting a fair world are willing to accept an unfair world. It is a powerful form of mind control to tell kids not to expect a fair world. What kind of world would it be if we all tried our best to *make* it fair? What if whenever we had anything to say about it, we did the fair thing? What if our parents or our teachers and every adult we knew growing up told us, "An injustice unspoken is another injustice."

So we learn a lot of these assumptions just by growing up. Schools and religions polish and shape these assumptions. It never seems like propaganda because nobody questions it—unless the people or the assumptions come from a different system of thought and practice.

It's as necessary for Thai kids to learn how to greet people politely as it is for American kids to learn how to shake hands and to know who they can call by first name and who they have to call Mr. and Ms. and how to answer a telephone. These assumptions guide people through the complexities of social life.

In industrial societies, people also need to learn skills such as reading, writing, and math. But schools teach a lot of other stuff as well. In the United States, schools teach how to say the Pledge of Allegiance to the flag, how to sing patriotic songs, and how to do other rituals of patriotism.

We don't mean to single out American schools from Peruvian, Mexican, Chinese, Turkish, or Thai schools. Schools are part of state systems. People without states don't have schools, and they don't need them.

In 1963, the American anthropologist Jules Henry wrote a book about life in St. Louis, Missouri. He discussed advertising and schools. This is a long quote, but he sums up much experience here, so bear with it. About schools, he says:

> The function of education has never been to free the mind and spirit of man, but to bind them.... Contemporary American educators think they want creative children, yet it is an open question as to what they expect these children to create. And certainly the classrooms—from kindergarten to graduate school—in which they expect it to happen are not crucibles of creative activity and thought. It stands to reason that were young people truly creative the culture would fall apart, for originality, by definition, is different from what is given, and what is given is the culture itself. From ... kindergarten to the most abstruse problems in sociology and anthropology, the function of education is to prevent the truly creative intellect from getting out of hand.
>
> ... Learning social studies is ... learning to be stupid. Most of us accomplish this task before we enter high school. But the child with a socially creative imagination will not be encouraged to play among new social systems, values, and relationships; nor is there much likelihood of it, if for no other reason than that the social studies teachers will perceive such a child as a poor student.... [S]uch a child will simply be unable to fathom the absurdities that seem transparent *truth* to the teacher. What idiot believes in the "law of supply and demand," for example? But the children who do tend to *become* idiots, and learning to be an idiot is part of growing up! ... Thus the child who finds it impossible to learn to think the absurd the truth, who finds it difficult to accept absurdity as a way of life, the intellectually creative child whose mind makes him flounder like a poor fish in the net of absurdities flung around him in school, usually comes to think himself stupid.... If all through school the young were provoked to question the Ten Commandments, the sanctity of revealed religion, the foundations of patriotism, the profit motive, the two-party system, monogamy, ... and so on, we would have more creativity than we could handle. (286–288)

The quotation brings home the distance between our cultures as tried and true solutions to problems and creativity with all of its risks. To ensure continuity, people have to teach their kids certain things. But the cost of continuity is creativity. It's sort of like being creative with haiku. There are certain rules from the past, and the only scope for creativity is what you apply them to. But sometimes it's good to experiment with different poetic forms. It's even more important when we're talking about cultural cores and ecological consequences. These days experiments with monogamy are nothing new. We think we could risk some creativity with alternatives to the two-party system (which in the United States is really a one-party system), the profit motive, and most religious dogmas.

In her ethnographic work in central New York, American anthropologist Dimitra Doukas (2003) found that the working people she was trying to understand did not agree with the supposedly American cultural values of individualism, optimism, competitive consumerism, and upward mobility. They shun conspicuous consumption, are suspicious of upward mobility, respect hard work, are reasonably pessimistic about the larger world, and value community integrity. She argues that the culture of the people is rooted in an old economic system based on locally controlled, craft-based rural industries integrated with farming that was dominant in the United States until the turn of the twentieth century. Then there was a great cultural revolution that corporations orchestrated to make corporations seem natural and expected rather than rapacious and pathological as the older values judged them to be. Doukas locates the cultural tensions of America in the differences and contradictions between these two conflicting cultural codes.

Doukas says. "The two sides do not know each other. If they could meet, it is possible to imagine that the perpetrators of corporate abuses would face an irresistible democratic challenge in the land of their headquarters" (8). She also says that the consolidation of corporate capitalism in the United States "produced a decades-long cultural war of titanic proportions, played out on local battlefields across the United States" (7). That is the battle that we witness when, during our ethnographic work with unions, we sit at the bargaining table and see a management that embodies corporate capitalism not understanding their own American workers speaking to them in the American language because they share so few assumptions about what is natural, right, fair, and just. We will return to this later.

Doukas documents the workings of the older system and its culture based on the gospel of work, the idea that anthropologists base our comparative economic analysis on, that labor is the source of all value. The gospel of wealth, that capital is "the wellspring of national prosperity[,] was at the center of the cultural revolution that the trusts [corporations] were trying to orchestrate" (100). This gospel is embodied in the discipline of economics parading its religion as science. What makes it religion? It requires belief in the gospel of wealth. Why is it not science? It does not test its hypotheses against observable realities. This is what the Nobel Prize–winning economist Joseph Stiglitz (2003) argues in his book *Globalization and Its Discontents*. Why do so many believe in economics? Because it benefits them to do so, and it provides a bulwark to an ideology that makes these ideas seem as natural and inevitable as the god-kings of the Inca were.

Doukas documents how the trusts, emergent corporations, orchestrated a campaign to reshape American culture—what she calls a cultural revolution. They knew that for their religion to seem natural, it had to have the imprimatur of scholarship. They endowed the professorships and university chairs to make their ideology respectable.

To see how modern corporations continue to do the same thing, take a look at a film called *The Corporation* or the 2004 book that it's based on, *The Corporation: The Pathological Pursuit of Profit and Power,* by University of British Columbia law professor Joel Bakan.

Now we close the loop and remind you of your own college's or university's propaganda machine. We don't know about your school. You look for yourself. Penn State has a Schwab Hall, a Carnegie Hall, an honors college named for a beneficent donor, and a college of science named after another such donor, and it does whatever it can to court such donors. It makes strategic plans that call for transforming our Land Grant University into the research and development branch for corporations. When graduate assistants tried to organize a union at Penn State in 2002 and 2003, the administration was adamantly opposed. Who does the administration represent? Who provides the money? The universities provide the respectability for the ideologies that supports those people; universities endow those ideas with the aura of being as natural and inevitable as the rising of the sun in the morning.

Meanwhile, people learn from growing up in their own families that there really should be something like fairness, that we really do care for our neighbors, that we really do need to pull together and help each other out and can't really grasp the supply and demand stuff our schools expect us to believe. And so the older American culture lives on in spite of its retreat from the public view. But it doesn't always feel comfortable, especially when you're looking into the steely eyes of management's lawyers across the negotiating table telling you about how things have to be because that's "reality."

When the economist John Kenneth Galbraith (1992) turned to similar matters in his book *The Culture of Contentment,* he said he would "use the method of the anthropologist" to examine the "tribal rites of strange and different peoples," because "they are to be observed but not censured" (11). Cultural relativity again. He argues that because the two dominant American political parties are so similar, reasonable people do not think they have a choice, so most do not vote. The minority of adult people who do vote are those the system serves and who thus feel part of it.

This is wrapped up in our American illusion of choice. We all take great pains with our decisions. Suzan has seen Paul paralyzed in front of a case of dairy products trying to find some reasonable basis for selecting one container of milk over another. He's even worse with peanut butter. When Paul was a graduate student, he rented an apartment in a house that was managed by a guy who worked in a shortening factory. This worker explained how they used the same machines and ingredients to make every brand of shortening, they only changed the labels. That defines the range of choice. Same product, different label. Same thing with the two American political parties.

Where do we get the illusion of consequential life choices? This is one of those things that's inculcated in us from the time we are children at home, school, and church. Many of the choices we agonize over, like which can of shortening to buy or which candidate to vote for or which church to go to, are not really choices. But the idea of choice is so necessary for a consumer economy and so heavily promoted by all media that it becomes a tenet of our culture.

One thesis about American political parties is that when populists offered a real alternative toward the turn of the century when the corporate cultural revolution was under way, they showed signs of success. Grassroots organizations like the Grange and the cooperative movement were successful. They organized into the Farmer-Labor Party, the People's Party, and other populist parties. They carried some governors' offices and elected some legislators. When they became a threat to corporate America, the two dominant parties had an interest in working together to maintain their monopoly on the machinery of the American state to serve the corporations.

The premise of this argument is that both parties attempt to keep the level of well-being just high enough to prevent a majority of people from being attracted to populist alternatives. Democrats would pull it up just a bit, and Republicans would let it slip a bit. Or they can trade off and move it up and then down and then up again. And both serve the same corporations. Take a look some time at the big donors to each party and to each presidential candidate, and you'll see what we mean.

In 1930, eastern Iowa was under martial law. The National Guard manned machine guns at rural crossroads to quell a growing rebellion of farmers. When Paul began to study this populist movement, he asked students and colleagues whether they had ever heard of the main organizer, Milo Reno, president of the Farmer's Union, or whether they knew of the Farmer's Educational and Cooperative Society. None had except one colleague who was the granddaughter of a guy who worked with Reno. No one was aware that Iowa had been under martial law. That is how effectively our schools and our media eradicate the events of our history so that they don't become threatening models for the future.

We have countermoves in books such as Howard Zinn's (2003) *People's History of the United States* or in movies like *Matewan* and *Norma Rae* and, more recently, Michael Moore's documentaries and books, but they are few and far between. So we're not saying that the state or corporations control your brain from the time you're born. They try, for sure. Sometimes it takes some real effort to bust out, but that's what you're doing here.

One of the corporate countermoves to populism was to organize a "safe" alternative for farmers. The Sears-Roebuck Company and several railroad companies joined together to form the Farm Bureau. Later, they gave their ideological organization more clout by getting it grafted onto the agricultural extension service of the Land Grant Universities. These universities—such as Penn State, the University of Illinois, Texas A&M, and Washington State University, just to name the ones Paul is indebted to for his job or his education—were supposed to be the bastions of the yeoman farmers who were supposed to be the backbone of our country. Congress gave them federal lands to support them and gave them the mission of doing the research and development to support small farmers. To get the newest research speedily into the hands of farmers, they organized the extension program with the U.S. Department of Agriculture. The extension program worked through the Farm Bureau. If a farmer wanted the latest developments, he had to belong to the Farm Bureau. Even today, many think of this right-wing ideology mill as speaking for farmers.

As a historical footnote: in their championing of corporate agriculture, both the Farm Bureau and the Land Grant colleges have done more to destroy small farmers than to preserve them. We'll pick up that story later.

These are not things of long ago. The same cultural mechanics are operating today. Lewis Lapham (2004), for instance, documents the successes of the ultraconservative millionaires in orchestrating a massive propaganda program from endowing foundations and think tanks, sponsoring publications, books, briefings, and mass media campaigns to make *liberal* a bad word. He attributes the successive dumbing down of our public discourse to this extension of the cultural revolution that Doukas describes. He concludes by pointing out that both candidates in the 2004 presidential election presented themselves as embodiments of "values" rather than proponents of any ideas. Critical thought wilts under such a barrage. Intelligent political discussion dies. And of such machinations are the cultures of states made. Of these machinations are our cultures made.

Industrial and preindustrial states alike use mind control. Schools and media are one avenue, but states also sponsor religions that preach that if you tolerate poverty and misery in this life, everything will be better in the next life, that people deserve whatever hardships happen to them, and to question it or feel guilty if something good happens. When we look at the topic of religion later on, we will see that there are two major types of religions: state religions and nonstate religions. All of the state religions share one thing in common: they demand that their followers believe something.

This is one of those elements of cultural codes. You're probably thinking, "That's what religion *is* after all, belief in something." For now we'll just say this: what state religions ask people to believe isn't as important as that they ask people to believe *something.* That is because all state religions ask people to accept ideas that are contrary to what they experience in everyday life. Belief is based on faith, not experience. The only way people can accept such counterexperiential things as their state religions teach them is if there is some way to *disconnect* those teachings from experience. Belief and faith do that. Some state religions have or had institutions to enforce compliance, such as the Inquisition. Others are more subtle.

The stance toward belief is what makes science different from religion. Science teaches us to believe nothing, to be skeptical of everything, to check whether everything anyone says is true against our own experience to see if it matches what we observe.

So, media from inscribed stones to Internet, families, and churches are all forms of mind control that states have used since ancient times. Schools are a more recent secular addition to the machinery.

Seeing the world this way can make a person feel pretty hopeless sometimes. If we are all controlled by these kinds of mind control, what's the point? All of us have deep-down feelings about fairness, and we know that even if we don't experience a fair world, we want it to be fair. Cooperation is one of the things that made us the kind of species we are. We can't just deny that because our experience runs against it. Everyone who has been treated unfairly or has seen others treated unfairly knows those feelings. A lot of times there is nothing we can do. But sometimes there is.

What we can all do is to first try to understand how our own societies work and why they work that way so that we can understand better what we can do to make the world more fair. We've mentioned the idea of agency before, and we'll come back to it again, but right now we want you to remember that the more aware you become, the more you can move these feelings and thoughts from the back of your mind to the front, the more you can move them from being unquestioned assumptions of our culture to being questions you ask, the better able you are to see alternatives and to give yourself agency.

We know it's hard to see these things "from the inside." But it's not impossible, if you keep your mind open to it. That's why so many anthropologists over the years have gone to exotic places to study people—it gave them that automatic outsider's view that also made it easier to see their own culture in a new way when they came back. When you see that outside view, you can help others. We're just showing you how to make those nagging doubts into questions that you can answer and that you can act on the answers you develop. It's that knowledge that states try to suppress when they rewrite history or only ask you "which" instead of "whether." They don't want kids growing up challenging the system the way Milo Reno did.

Want to read something really radical? Get a hold of the Declaration of Independence sometime. Those guys went way out on a limb. But, if you don't like the tree, out on a limb is a good place to be.

Force

All stratified societies also make use of coercion. Force. The political scientist James Scott (1984) found that Indonesian peasants aren't fooled by state propaganda. They see through it and understand their situations quite well. And to the extent they can, they resist. But, he points out, they know that they don't have a lot of agency, don't have much space to act because the state will use force on them to keep them in line.

The state wants to draft young men for an army or work detail? Send the youths away when the government agents come. The government wants to tax your land? Lie about how much of it you have. Be too stupid to understand what the government agents are telling you. In the Icelandic sagas, there's an archetype of the stupid slave. To believe the sagas, these guys were just barely aware that they were alive, much less able to follow the instructions of their owners. This is what Scott calls resistance. But take it too far, and they kill you. Force.

We see this in its starkest forms when societies are in transition. Remember Stalin and Chayanov? Stalin had millions killed to gain compliance to government programs. The emperors of China were as nasty as any when it came to using force against anyone who disagreed with them. Their Communist successors were no better. The English used force to ensure compliance to the enclosure acts that drove people from their land into the cities to sell their labor. When they couldn't make a living selling their labor, people started stealing, which the English punished by banishment, imprisonment, and hanging. In the first third of the nineteenth century, the English hung more than twenty-five thousand people for theft.

In America, the corporate cultural revolution wasn't just a matter of talk. The corporations used guns as well. They killed innumerable working people who had tried to organize unions. Not until 1935, in the throes of the Great Depression with Roosevelt's New Deal being enacted, did the Wagner Act give American working people the right to organize. After World War II, in 1948, the Taft-Hartley Amendments to that act pulled the teeth from the Wagner Act, and there has been a concerted war on the labor movement ever since. In addition, the expansion of the United States to the west entailed the massive killings of the Indian Wars. So, in the use of force, archaic empires, revolutionary states, and parliamentary democracies are pretty much the same.

Coercive political and economic powers are means states use to control stratified social orders. In states, kinship is not an important organizing principle. Trobrianders and Kachin have ranked lineages and ranking within lineages. When the highest-ranking people of all lineages share more in common with each other than they do with their lower-ranking lineage mates, when they can think of making kinsmen into renters rather than relatives, then kin groups fall apart. Then the important groups aren't lineages but classes—aristocrats and commoners. This is the move that Harald Finehair accomplished in Norway in a system based on kindreds. When he got all of the high-ranking people together, they formed an aristocracy of a kingdom. The kindreds ceased to be important because the high-ranking kinsmen had no interests in common with low-ranking ones.

We can understand these developments in systems terms as self-intensifying loops similar to the ones we've discussed before.

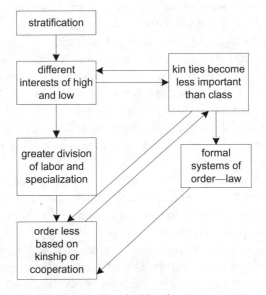

Figure 10-1 How stratification makes kinship less important.

Because stratification defines different interests between people with privileged access to resources and those without, kin ties become less important, and order is less based on kinship, mutuality, or cooperation. That makes kin ties even less important and differentiates the classes even more. The differential interests contribute to an increasing division of labor that erodes kin relations in favor of occupational ones. As kinship ties become less important for maintaining order, formal systems of law develop and these begin to replace the role of kinship and cooperation in maintaining order. This is more or less what was happening in ninth-century Norway but not in Iceland. Iceland, with no state, had no mechanism for the universal application of law.

States maintain order in stratified societies by upholding three principles by mind control and by force:

- Hierarchy is natural. Some people have more power, prestige, authority, and access to resources than others.
- Property is natural. Some people have the *right* to use certain things, and others don't.
- The power of law is for the good of everyone. There are universal rules to govern property and social relations. They are not personal, they don't depend on who you are, and they are for everyone of the same group—all commoners or all aristocrats.

There are many ways to legitimate hierarchy. One is the idea of closeness to an ancestor to define hierarchies within and among lineages. This is an integral part of redistributive systems of exchange. But with the development of states and the waning importance of kinship groups in stratified societies, religious ideas can support hierarchy with concepts such as god-kings or the idea that some gods or god gives the kings the right to rule and makes aristocrats better than ordinary people. State religions often communicate ideas such as that if common people interfere with the operation of the state—by resistance, for example—or don't do proper rituals, pay taxes, and obey their rulers, the gods will be unhappy and punish everyone.

Revolutionary ideologies can enshrine hierarchy as well. In Mexico, the Soviet Union, and China, the rulers ruled in the name of the revolution, and if you disagreed, you were counterrevolutionary and had to be shot. We see examples from Tiananmen Square to Stalin.

The American form is "democratic." Americans are supposed to all believe that our rulers represent the will of the people. They were elected in one-person, one-vote elections that give them the authority to rule by "majority rule" even when less than 50 percent of the eligible population ever votes, or when the president can lose the popular vote and still win the election thanks to something called the Electoral College, which was supposed to be something like a parliamentary system but has now ceased to have any real function.

Not everyone has a concept of property. Remember Lisu, who have free access to agricultural land if they clear it for their own use. Property is the idea that some people have the right to use something and others don't. Here we aren't considering small things like arrows or clothes but basic resources like land. If someone can use the land and someone else cannot, if there is privileged access, then there is property. Icelandic chieftains, for instance, established this principle when they first landed and claimed land.

In medieval Iceland, law was not universally applied. If a person had sufficient force of arms to impose a penalty, he could justify it by appeal to a decision of the assembly and law. *Universal application* means that the same law applies to everyone of the same class equally. When that happens, people don't settle disputes by feud, as they did in medieval Iceland, or by consensus and public opinion, as among Tsembaga, but by law and the officials who decide how to apply it on behalf of the state. Feud is against the law because it is disorder. To control people, the ruling classes concentrate force and monopolize force and maintain order through law enforcement. Everyone must follow the same rules.

This is an example of the way law does not and cannot work. Recognizing his wisdom, the sultan made Nasrudin a magistrate. The plaintiff in the first case he heard argued so eloquently and so persuasively that Nasrudin said, "I think you must be right!" The clerk of the court explained that the magistrate should hear both sides before he made any pronouncement on the case. When the defendant presented an equally well-argued case with equally persuasive evidence, Nasrudin said, "I think you must be right!" Then the clerk of the court explained, "Your honor, they cannot *both* be right." Nasrudin said, "I think you must be right!"

To maintain order is to keep a stratified society working. No longer is it sufficient just to cooperate, as in nonstratified social orders. States are the institutions that the ruling classes devise to accomplish the tasks of maintaining order by ideas and practices of hierarchy, property, and the rule of law.

States and Labor

The ruling class uses the labor of a subordinate class. The subordinate class provides labor for the ruling class. Another way of saying this is that the ruling class appropriates surplus value from the subordinate class. The state provides institutions that govern the subordinate class, and the subordinate class supports the state. For this to seem reasonable to people, they have to accept the legitimating ideology of the state whether it be religious, revolutionary, or democratic. The state promotes this ideology via its schools, churches, and media, and the ideology justifies the state and makes it seem natural and inevitable to the subordinate class. Meanwhile, the state protects the interests of the ruling class, and the ruling class controls the institutions of the state. The legitimating ideology justifies the ruling class and makes them seem natural, invisible, ordained by god, or justified by a vote or the revolution, and the ruling class promotes the legitimating ideology via media, schools, and other forms of thought control. Is this some grand conspiracy? You might think so, but it's more like an interest-assisted evolution, with the ones who have the power doing the assisting.

Here is the natural, inevitable, and if not God-given, at least author-provided, diagram that shows how these parts all form a system and how if one of them changes, the others change, too (figure 10-2). As Hockett suggests in the opening quote to this chapter, all states do not operate in the same way, but this much they all have in common.

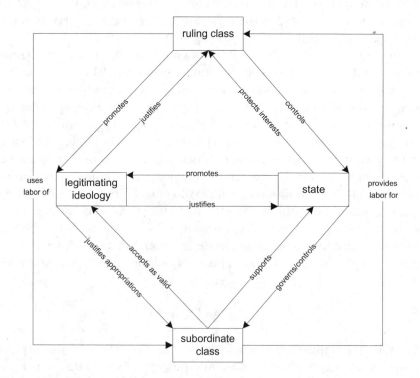

Figure 10-2 How stratification makes kinship less important.

Discussion Questions

- Remember when you were a kid, or watch parents with their kids when you can. What rules do parents enforce (aside from those that keep their children safe)? Why? What would happen if they didn't enforce those rules?
- Whether or not you believe in a religion, you are probably familiar with some of the basic tenets of the major religions in the United States. List those, and discuss what makes those tenets so valuable to a state society. How do you think people would behave without those tenets given them by formal religion?
- What are some ways that college students "resist" certain laws? (Consider speeding, underage drinking, and other common infractions.) Can you think of any ways Americans work collectively to resist the rules? Is there a difference between individual resistance and collective resistance? If so, describe it. If you can't think of any examples of collective resistance, why do you think that's so?
- Seek out one event in history that you weren't taught in school. Talk to your parents and grandparents, or look in Howard Zinn's *People's History*. It should be an event that affected a large number of people or an entire community, like the "cow war" in Iowa. Research it, and then discuss why you believe that event didn't make it into the standard history textbooks.
- If you have classmates who are from the North and from the South, have a conversation about the basic facts surrounding the Civil War, or the War between the States. Or use events from elsewhere in the world such as the division of India and Pakistan or the Palestinian intifada. Identify the differences in different peoples' understandings of that historic event. Why do those differences exist? What do they have in common?

Suggested Reading

Berdan, Frances. *Aztecs of Central Mexico: An Imperial Society.* Belmont, CA: Thomson/Wadsworth, 2004.

Bonanno, Alessandro, and Douglas Constance. *Caught in the Net: The Global Tuna Industry, Environmentalism and the State.* Lawrence: University Press of Kansas, 1996.

Chomsky, Noam. *Necessary Illusions: Thought Control in Democratic Societies.* Cambridge, MA: South End Press, 1989.

Doukas, Dimitra. *Worked Over: The Corporate Sabotage of an American Community.* Ithaca, NY: Cornell University Press, 2003.

White, Curtis. *The Middle Mind: Why Americans Don't Think for Themselves.* San Francisco: Harper, 2003.

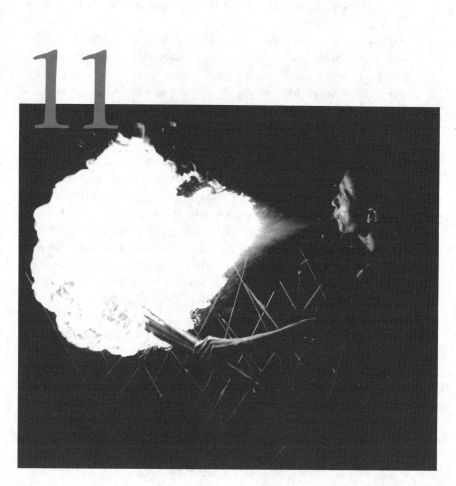

A Lisu shaman chases bad spirits.
Photo by E. Paul Durrenberger.

CHAPTER 11

THE ANTHROPOLOGY
OF RELIGION

When a sing-song wail breaks the night silence in a Lisu village, people are likely to go to the house the sound is coming from to see what is happening. A man dressed like any other man will be bent from the waist in front of the altar at the back of the house. In his hands will be a bundle of smoldering incense sticks adding their smoke to that of the fires for cooking and making tea. This is the shaman we saw in chapter 4 when we discussed systems of knowledge. Listen to the words of such a meeting of spirits and people.

> Spirit: I, Third Generation Daughter, have come down. People, why have you called me? ...
> People: Come down quickly. We do not know where we offended. . . .
> Spirit: People, people, she has been sick for many days. I will tell you about the offense.
> People: What should we do for it to be good? Please tell us. People do not know.
> Spirit: Altar spirits, keep soft hearts. If you keep soft hearts, you are honorable.
> People: What should we do to have honor?
> Spirit: If you keep long hearts, you will have honor. People do not know, cannot do. . . . If you altar spirits sent this sickness, you do not have honor. More than this, Third Generation Daughter will tell.
> [. . .]
> Here the spirit coughs and stumbles.
> People: Hold your horse, do not let it fall.
> Spirit: I will tell you. I will tell about people who do not know.
> People: Please tell us how to cut away this sickness.
> Spirit: . . . Three generations, four generations [ancestors], you look after your children. . . . If your descendants are sick, you have no honor. This is the country of other people. There is much sickness. The people will

laugh at you. The descendants of others do not get sick. The descendants of others are not sick.

People: You must have a soft heart....

Spirit: I, the daughter, will tell you.

People: If you have something to tell us, please tell us everything....

Spirit: There, where you cut wood, call my friend and make a ceremony there. Before, Third Generation Daughter told you and you did not keep it in your hearts. You have big hearts. What has happened to you now?

People: People are like pigs and dogs....

Spirit: People, I have told the altar spirits to keep soft hearts. Now they have soft hearts.

People: If you tell them, may they have soft hearts.

Spirits: Now it will be good for the people. It has become well. People, I do not know, I cannot do. I have told you much.

Another man stood behind the shaman to catch him when the spirit left. If some of this is confusing to you, know that it was just as confusing to the people who heard it. They thought the shaman's spirit had told them to make an offering to the spirit of a certain hill and that the disease stuff, the essence of disease, should be sent from the house.

But here are some of the other things we learn. Spirits can lose and gain honor by their actions just as people can. If the ancestors don't take care of their descendants, they lose power and honor. The power and honor of spirits depends on their being able to do what people expect them to do. We see that nobody has any special awe of spirits and that spirits are fallible just as people are. Paul shortened the transcript of this séance because it is very repetitive. But to get a sense of it, go back and read it again with these ideas of honor in mind, and see where the spirit or the people mention it.

The Lisu world is populated with spirits, as it is with people. The spirits are about the same as people except they are more powerful and people can't see them. Paul never saw Lisu being reverent about spirits. True, they kneel and bow and say amen when they are supposed to in a prayer to make offerings to spirits, but Paul never noticed anything that looked like reverence as distinct from the respect that people owe to those who are more powerful, like Thai officials. Nor did Paul notice anything like awe, fear, dread, or trepidation with respect to spirits.

If you do something to offend a person and you want to make it right, you take a bottle of liquor to the person and offer to sit down, have a drink, and talk about how to resolve the matter. That's the responsibility of the person who commits the offense. If the person who is offended has to wait too long for an apology and a settlement, that adds to the injury and makes it worse.

Remember that Lisu are egalitarian people. They don't have any cops, courts, judges, or juries. The last recourse you have, if someone has done you harm, is to harm that person back. Anthropologists call it **self-help**. And that can lead to **feuds** that get ugly for everyone. So everyone has an interest in seeing to it that people settle things short of self-help and try to help people come to terms with each other. But people can't do that for spirits. The only way you know you've offended a spirit is when the spirit attacks you by making you sick.

So, people can offend spirits, but we never know what might have offended them. When Paul asked the abstract question, someone told him that just about anything could offend a spirit, that to avoid offending spirits a person would have to stay in bed all day long—and *that* would probably be offensive to some spirit. To be alive and moving around in the world is to risk offending spirits.

What can anthropology say about this that could have anything at all to do with Christianity or Islam or any other religion? What do all religious traditions have in common?

We have the same problem with religions that we have with economic and political systems. To understand religion in comparative terms and from the point of view of the people we want to understand, we have to guard against imposing our own categories on other cultures. By now you know that we do not all believe in one god any more than that we all have one spouse at a time or buy all our food in markets for money.

"The supernatural" is one way to answer the question of what religion is about. This assumes that everyone thinks in terms of a distinction between nature on the one hand and something else, "supernature," on the other hand—something beyond nature. For the Lisu villagers that Paul lived with, there was no such contrast. Spirits are just a normal everyday part of life and just as natural as other people, plants, and animals. Robert Lowie wrote a book about the anthropology of religion in the 1940s. He said that to understand religion, we have to study a number of different religions to see what they all have in common. But then he had to figure out what to study in different cultures. He suggested that feelings of awe and mystery were central. But Paul didn't see any awe or mystery with Lisu.

Some have suggested that religion has to do with the ultimate. Melford Spiro (1966) points out that if baseball is your ultimate, that makes it a religion. Others say religion makes us feel safe and explains things we can't understand. But religion raises more questions than it answers—what do you do with issues like Job, the Trinity, and Immaculate Conception, or shamanistic séances nobody can understand? Some say religion makes people feel safe. In the words of the country and western song, "I don't care if it rains or freezes long as I got my plastic Jesus riding on the dashboard in front of me." The problem is that religion may make people afraid in other situations. It may offer guilt instead of security.

So defining religion in terms of what it does doesn't really give us much to go on. Religion may do a lot of things, but other institutions do at least some of the same things, and we can't point to one thing that religion does that no other institution does.

Spiro (1966:96) suggests that religion is "an institution consisting of culturally patterned interactions with culturally postulated superhuman beings." An institution is something people learn by growing up when and where they do, like their language or lineages or kindreds or schools. Spiro talks about two different kinds of interactions: one is doing what superhuman beings want or like, and the other is doing things to influence these beings. For instance, Tsembaga don't go to war until they pay off their debt to their ancestors. It would make the ancestors angry if they started a war before they paid off their debt, and the ancestors wouldn't help them. A sure way to lose. Tsembaga also sacrifice pigs to the ancestors to please them so that they will help cure sick people.

The interactions are culturally patterned. That means that what people think their superhuman beings like and don't like and what they think influences them are all matters of their cultural codes. The ideas that ancestors can help you in a war and that giving them pigs gets them to help you are both parts of the Tsembaga cultural code. Lisu think that they can offend spirits and spirits can hurt them. They think that people can give spirits liquor and animals to make them stop. This is part of their cultural code.

Superhuman beings are beings that people think have more power than they do. Because people get their ideas of superhuman beings from growing up in groups, these ideas of superhuman beings are something that is reasonable in that cultural code.

A lot of times we explain what people do in terms of what they believe. People cheer at football games because they believe it will help their team score. As anthropologists, we have to ask how do we know the people believe that. We have two ways of knowing—either they say so, or they are doing it and we can't think of any other reason they might be doing it. They *must* believe it helps. That is, we assume they believe it. But this violates our first principle of ethnography—assume nothing.

Many people have ideas and practices similar to Lisu ones about spirits. Some also participate in one of the major religions such as Islam, Buddhism, or Christianity. One of the things that puzzled Spiro when he was studying religion in Burma was how Burmese villagers could at the same time believe in the doctrines of Buddhism and believes in spirits.

This seemed to him such a contradiction that he concluded that there are two different religions, each answering to a different part of people's emotional needs. Buddhism provides explanations for long term and abstract things like life and death and why some people are rich and some are poor. Belief in spirits helps people deal with concrete problems such as sickness in the here and now. What puzzled Spiro was how people would express skepticism with regard to spirits but act as though they believed in them.

Lisu expressed the same kind of skepticism. One man told Paul that he disbelieved in spirits so much that when he died, he would not return to the ancestor altar at all. But he did the same ceremonies as other people did. How can people kill a pig and make an offering to a spirit they don't believe in?

In the same sense that many of us would take an antibiotic even though we don't especially believe in it. Nobody asks us to believe in an antibiotic. The doctor doesn't check to see whether you believe in a certain antibiotic before prescribing it. It just doesn't matter whether or not we believe in it. Another example: you don't have to believe in gravity for it to work. Even if you stop believing in gravity, you're not going to float away.

The point about antibiotics is that we have some reason to suppose that they might help us. It's not a question of belief. It might be a question of finances if you don't have health insurance that covers drugs. You might not be able to afford the expensive antibiotic that the doctor prescribes. You may not even be able to afford the doctor. But it's not a question of belief.

A belief is something that's beyond evidence. It doesn't depend on experience or arguments or facts. It only depends on your opinion about something. For instance, some people hold deep religious convictions about the creation of the Earth and all of its inhabitants. They don't rely on scientific evidence but on their religious opinions. And no amount of arguing or proof will change their minds. That's what belief is—something that's beyond any evidence.

Sometimes people say they don't believe something but act as though they really do. Folks in Burma are Buddhists, but they also make offerings to spirits—something that's not in Buddhist doctrines. They act as though they believe in spirits.

In fact, some anthropologists discuss religion as a belief system. A lot of times we can't show that anyone believes anything in particular. Do people really believe that cheering helps their team score? Burmans said they didn't believe in spirits, but they made offerings to them. Lisu don't believe in spirits, either, but they make offerings to them and talk about them.

When Paul asked Lisu about these things, they said they believe what they can see. They can't see spirits, so they don't believe in them. Lisu aren't Buddhists, so they don't have to worry about doing things that don't match up with some standards of religious practice.

One time a Thai guy came up to the Lisu village where Paul lived and said he had a very powerful talisman that would protect people from gunshot wounds. Lisu asked him to put it on and let them shoot at him to test it. If their bullets couldn't hit him, they'd know the talisman worked. The guy didn't want to risk it. So the Lisu folks said he could put it on a pig instead and they'd shoot at the pig. If the pig wasn't hurt, they'd know the talisman would work for them, too. The Thai guy was grossed out at the idea of putting a powerful religious thing on a pig. That was just too disgusting to think about. So he didn't sell any talismans.

Lisu do say that their shamans can see spirits and ghosts. One time, after a guy was accidentally shot and killed, Ngwa Pa, a shaman, came into Paul's house and said he'd seen the ghost of the dead person behind the house. Paul asked Ngwa Pa to show him the place. The other Lisu sitting around in the house laughed and said Paul wouldn't be able to see the ghost because only dogs, horses, and shamans could see ghosts. But Paul went with the shaman anyway. The shaman pointed at a place behind the house and said, "Right there, see?" Paul said, "No." Just then all of the horses started stamping and neighing, and all the dogs started barking. There may have been a ghost, but Paul couldn't see it.

In the same way, most Lisu never see spirits and have no reason to believe in them. "So why do you do these ceremonies?" Paul asked. "What else can we do?" they would ask back. "This is what we do."

If nobody believes religious ideas, how can we explain religious actions like sacrifices?

One way is by their ecological consequences. For instance, Tsembaga have ancestors in their cultural code, so they will participate in a ritual cycle that regulates their ecosystem for them and keeps them from destroying the land by farming it too much. Nobody invented it; nobody thought it up. But because they do it, and because it works, they continue to do it.

The second kind of explanation is in terms of social consequences. People believe in witches so that they can kill malcontents and others who can't get along. This lets them maintain order without courts and cops and states.

Both of these are etic ideas. They rest on some ideas that don't belong to the cultural codes of the people we are trying to understand. We can put this in terms of the system we developed earlier when we were discussing cultural ecology (table 11-1).

The ecological consequence is that Lisu keep pigs so they can offer them. They're like health insurance. The social consequence is that everyone can stay even with everyone else and nobody gets ahead of anyone

Table 11-1

Reality	Cultural Code	Action
Sickness	Spirits make people sick	Call shaman
Spirits speak	People have offended a spirit	Make a sacrifice

else in feasting and obligation, so no redistributive system can develop, and hence no rank or stratification can develop.

Anthropologists try to understand what people are doing from their own point of view, in terms of their emic systems, in terms of their cultural code and worldview. Lisu act as though there are spirits because according to their understandings of social life, it is reasonable to think that there might be spirits, whether they know it or not. It doesn't matter to anyone whether someone believes in spirits or not, whether anyone does a certain ceremony or not. Because of certain other ideas, ideas about how people get along together, it is reasonable to think that there might be spirits. And people act in terms of that idea. Nobody asks you whether you believe in gravity when you get on an airplane.

We can ask why Lisu have that kind of cultural code. Lisu spirits can cause people to suffer, and offerings can make the spirits stop bothering people. These ideas follow from ideas about how people are. It's obvious to Lisu that a person's productivity is related to wealth. The more you work, the better off you are. Americans say that, but it's obviously not true because the richest among us work the least, and the ones who work the most are not the richest. But it's different when everyone has access to all of the same resources, as Lisu do.

People use their wealth to sponsor feasts, as we discussed earlier. When you sponsor feasts, other people eat your food, and their sense of obligation gives you power. It's that power that gets hurt if someone offends you. They take away some of your power if you let them get away with it. So it's up to them to restore your power by apologizing—bringing a bottle of liquor to your house and talking about it—and then by compensating you to make it right again. If my pig roots up your opium plants, I apologize, we talk until we agree on the amount of damage, and I make it up to you by giving you a pig or two or maybe some opium or money.

Remember what happens if I don't do this. You can try to hurt me. Self-help. Just like a spirit.

The productive part of a person is the soul. If your soul goes away, you don't want to work. If you don't work, you don't have wealth; and without wealth, you have no power. If your soul stays away, you die. You can't see souls, but you can tell when they're gone because people have bad dreams, don't sleep well, and don't want to work. It's similar to what

Americans call depression. You fix it by getting the soul to come back. Maybe a spirit has captured the soul; maybe it has just left because, as Lisu say, "Sometimes you wake up in the morning, and all you can see is pig shit."

You can make a small ceremony and tell the person's soul, "Come back, come back from wherever you are. Come look at your beautiful family, your rice in the baskets. Come look at your pigs and your wealth. Come and be with your family. We all want you to be with us." That's just got to make a person feel appreciated.

Or you can do it up grand, if you need to sponsor a feast, by killing a couple of pigs and having everyone in the village make a similar prayer.

So, by this logic, anything that's productive must have a soul. Like a soul, you can offend it; and if you do, it will hurt you. Nobody has to believe anything. It's the same logic for people and for spirits. People take the logic of social relations for granted—it's just the way we are—and assume it is true, but they don't believe it or not believe it. It's no big deal. It's the same kind of thing as being patrilineal. You don't have to believe anything to be patrilineal; it's just one way of doing things. Lisu are patrilineal, but they also know about matrilineal systems and can explain them to you.

So, a couple of points. First, if we want to understand other religions, we can't be ethnocentric and let our categories guide our understanding. For instance, belief may be important for some kinds of religions, but it isn't for all of them. This is the same as Goodenough's conclusion about residence rules. Rather than assuming a set of rules works everywhere, we should find out how the people we want to understand actually think about things.

Second, remember systems? The economic, political, and social are really all one thing. They aren't separate. When Lisu sacrifice a pig, it's a medical event, a religious event, a political act, and an economic phenomenon all at the same time.

Third, to understand what people do and why they do those things, we need to understand their cultural code from their point of view.

But remember Julian Steward? His idea of the cultural core is that the way people make a living is the most important part of their cultural system. So why are we even talking about religion? Because shamans' séances, monks' sermons, offerings, and other kinds of ceremonies all offer anthropologists a rich field of symbols to understand. These symbols are good places to start understanding people's cultural codes. If we understand Lisu spirits, for instance, we understand a lot about Lisu politics and economics and the important points about being Lisu—things like wealth and productivity and honor.

The central part of this system of symbols is productivity. Remember our discussion of household economies? There, one of the central ideas was also productivity because people's judgments of drudgery depend on the productivity of their labor, and the amount they produce depends on the intersection of the curves of their need—or marginal utility—and the drudgery of the work to produce that amount of value, whether it be rice or money.

People symbolize things that are important but that they can't articulate very well, like the relationships among marginal utility, drudgery, and production that are at the center of household production. One way they symbolize these things is the way Lisu do, with the idea of some kind of power that people and spirits share. Shan do the same thing, and their ceremonies to spirits aren't very different from Lisu's. In fact, wherever people are involved in household production, they have some kind of religion based on spirits or something like them. It might be jinn in Islamic societies or saints in Christian ones.

Why make such a big deal out of belief? Because we want to understand the difference between religions like Lisu that demand no belief and those like Buddhism that do.

What kinds of religions do demand belief? The one thing all of these religions have in common is that they support state systems, as we explained in the last chapter. Is it natural for some people to have more and others less? No. But to support systems of stratification, the ruling classes of states support religions that say it is natural and necessary. Listen to the teaching of a Buddhist monk as he delivers a sermon to Shan people in a temple:

> If you live in the village, you follow the ways of the village; if you are a housewife, you keep the place of the housewife; if you are a house husband, you must keep the place of the house husband; if you are the children of parents, you must keep the place of the children; if you are the headman of the village, you must keep the place of the headman; if you are village elders, you must keep the place of the elders. If you know the appropriate place, you can stay together peacefully as the Buddha taught. If people cannot live together, it is because they do not keep the appropriate places; the young act like elders; the old people act like young ones; men act like women; women act like men; common people act like kings; kings act like common people. All are opposite. They do not know their places. We do not respect or believe each other. If we do not keep our places, we cannot live together. We would be like animals.

The lesson is pretty clear. Know your place and keep it. If you're a king, act like one; if you're a common person, keep your place. Or else you'd be like an animal.

State religions demand belief because they teach their people things that do not match their experience. If your husband beats you or is a drunk, you're still supposed to stay in your obedient wifely place. If your government is getting into wars and drafting your kids or brothers, you're supposed to keep your place as a commoner and not question it. Buddhism promises justice in the end. The laws of karma work the same for everyone. Everyone is rewarded for good deeds and charity. Everyone is rewarded for bad deeds. It's automatic. Do we see such justice around us? Neither do Shan. But Buddhism assures them that everyone gets what they deserve in the long run. And for Buddhists, that's a lot more than just one lifetime because you get reincarnated many times.

Shan even told Paul not to worry about government corruption. It wasn't his problem. It's a problem only for the officials involved. Why? Because it's their karma that's at stake, not Paul's. If they do bad things, it's bad for their karma, but it's not our business.

Remember that if there is commercial production where everything that goes in and everything that comes out is a commodity, then there must be markets. If there are markets, there is ownership. If there is ownership, there is stratification. If there is stratification, there are states. If there are states, there are ideologies to support them. One of these is religion.

Most people these days live in some kind of state society. Remember that capitalism takes surplus value from those who produce it, but household economies do not. That's the reason capitalism can't compete with households for labor. So there are usually household production units even in state societies. Shan are an example. That's the reason they have both forms—state religion and one based on the logic of household production. The Buddhist part is the state religion, and the spirit part comes from symbolizing household production.

But just because something is symbolic doesn't mean it doesn't have power. In 1956, Anthony F. C. Wallace wrote a paper about revitalization movements that has been reprinted so many times that it has become the standard reference. Revitalization movements, he observed, reorient cultural codes overnight when people's expectations no longer match their experiences. So one of the problems that state religions face is that if their teachings are too far off from people's experiences and if the people find themselves in dire straits, the people are likely to change their religion and then change realities to match the new religious ideas of a better world. This often happens when a colonial power has moved in on a people. In its beginnings, Christianity was one example of such a radical change of religion that was also a revolutionary movement to change realities.

Marvin Harris (1974) thinks that these kinds of revolutionary religious movements in medieval Europe were related to the witch hunts of the time. Feudalism was falling apart, and people had no way to make a living under the old system. But they had no way to make a living under the new market system that was coming in either. They were in dire straits. People created the religions we now know as the radical reformation. We know their descendants today as Amish, Hutterites, and others from the same roots.

Harris's idea is that the ruling classes wanted to control these revolutionary movements, so they tried to divide the poor against themselves by getting poor people to accuse other poor people of being witches. Who caused your misery? Was it the ruling class? No, it must be witches. Kill another poor person. It worked.

This chapter has several lessons. One is that we cannot understand other religions in our own terms. We must use the peoples' own emic terms. Another is that we can understand why they have such cultural codes if we connect the cultural codes to other dimensions of the people's lives such as their social and political organization. We can understand the cultural codes also from the point of view of their ecological consequences—the results of the actions people do because of the way they understand their worlds. This takes us back to the diagram (figure 11-1) of the relationships of reality, cultural codes, and actions that then have consequences for the reality, a feedback loop.

We see that spirit-based religions are symbolizations of the relationships of household production and that people who are involved in household production have similar cultural codes that center on power. We also see that those religions that demand belief are the ones that teach things that run against peoples' everyday experience, things like "If you keep your place, everything will be good," and "There's justice in the long run." These religions are the parts of state systems that make them seem reasonable, inevitable, and just even though they are not any of those things.

Finally, the lesson about anthropology is that the answers we get depend on the questions we ask. If we ask "What do people believe?" rather than "Do people believe anything at all?" we don't see the relationships among states, belief, and stratification.

Time to lighten up a little before the next chapter.

Author Pierre Deelattre tells a story about the current Dalai Lama. When he was a boy, before the Chinese came, he had to answer a riddle each year. All of the scholars and monks of Tibet would gather at the Potala, the central monastery in Lahsa, to hear the god-king's answer to the

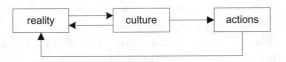

Figure 11-1

riddle and learn from it. A tutor would always clue the incarnation of past lamas into the riddle and the answer. He had the riddle and the answer, but he didn't want to do this again. He worried so much that he looked much older than his years. He told the regent that this year he wanted a better question, a question about something real that would make him more aware of the conditions of life here on Earth, not a stupid riddle that nobody could understand.

Then, he appeared in front of all of the monks and scholars and waited for a new question, for a question about something real.

Nobody dared to say a thing. It got later and later and nobody said a thing. The sun went down. It started to get cold. Finally, a young monk said, "Aren't you cold? Shouldn't we go inside?"

"Yes," said the Dalai Lama, "I'm cold. Aren't we all?"

Everyone agreed.

Then the Dalai Lama said, "Let's go inside."

When everyone was inside and drinking tea, the Dalai Lama had returned to his young self, smiling, and said, "That's the kind of question we should ask each other, and that's the kind of answer we should give."

That's an important lesson we need to remember in anthropology.

Discussion Questions

- List the ways an anthropologist's approach to religion challenges your own belief system. What basic assumptions have you made about religion and the supernatural? How would an anthropologist describe the emic cultural code of your religion?
- How would an anthropologist describe how your religion fits the rest of your culture as part of a system? What would the etic description of your religion look like?
- Religion and politics often intersect in American public discourse these days. Offer some examples of how one amplifies and supports the other. Discuss the contradiction between those examples and the fact that our Constitution requires a separation between church and state.
- In these examples, substitute Islam for Christianity, and discuss how a government that intersects or overlaps with Islam as much as ours does with Christianity would look and act. Discuss the similarities and differences between the two.
- Attend a church, synagogue, or mosque this weekend, and compare and contrast the service with one of the two quoted events in this chapter (the Lisu shaman or the Buddhist sermon).

Suggested Reading

Ekvall, Robert. *The Lama Knows*. Novato, CA: Chandler & Sharp, 1981.

Evans-Pritchard, E. E. *Nuer Religion*. New York: Oxford University Press, 1971.

————. *The Sanusi of Cyrenaica*. ACLS E-Book Project. Ann Arbor: University of Michigan Scholarly Publishing Office, 1999.

————. *Witchcraft, Oracles and Magic among the Azande*. New York: Oxford University Press, 1976.

Gottleib, Alma, and Philip Graham. *Parallel Worlds: An Anthropologist and a Writer Encounter Africa*. New York: Crown, 1993.

Sandstrom, Alan. *Corn Is Our Blood: Culture and Ethnic Identity in a Contemporary Aztec Indian Village*. Norman: University of Oklahoma Press, 1992.

Tannenbaum, Nicola. *Who Can Compete against the World?: Power-Protection and Buddhism in Shan Worldview*. Ann Arbor, MI: Association for Asian Studies, 2001.

12

Icelandic trawlers. Do skippers who dream about where to find fish actually catch more fish? *Photo by E. Paul Durrenberger.*

CHAPTER 12

POLITICAL ECONOMY

If cultural ecologists are right, and the most important part of any culture is the way people make their livings, as we suggested in the religion chapter, then what does that say about the choices people make? Is everything we do and think determined by something outside us—larger political, economic, or historical **structures** that we don't have any say about? Or do we have some choice in what we think and do? As we've mentioned before, anthropologists call this idea of choice **agency**.

This is a big deal to middle-class Americans because we have an ideology that the anthropologist Katherine Newman (1993) calls **meritocratic individualism.** That means that we like to think we are separate individuals who think for ourselves and that we get rewarded according to our individual merit. She also suggests that working-class people think more in terms of structures than choices because they've experienced layoffs and plant closings that they know had nothing to do with the effort or quality of their work. Where working-class people blame systems for bad things, middle-class people tend to blame themselves. "You get what you deserve" also means "You deserve what you get." We'll come back to this issue when we discuss class explicitly, but it is enough for now to hint that it is something about our culture that makes the question of agency even relevant.

Before, we asked questions about cultural codes and why they are the way they are. Cultural codes provide us with ways to think. We may be able to expand those cultural codes a little but, but we can't just make them up for ourselves any more than we can make up our own languages. Well, people can do that, and some do, but the very fact that they are making them up and that nobody else agrees with them makes them crazy one way or another.

We can understand the reasons cultural codes are the way they are in terms of the cultural core, the basic shape of the economic system. Here's an example.

161

Paul first went to Iceland in 1981 because he was interested in shamanism. Some anthropologists have written about what happens when spirits speak through shamans. Claude Lévi-Strauss, for instance, suggested that the shaman's séance gives people a story that they can tell to make sense of things and that makes them feel better about whatever it is that's bothering them. With the story, they can understand things they couldn't understand before.

When he was living with Lisu, Paul couldn't figure out a way to find out whether people felt better after a shaman was possessed. If you feel sick and see a doctor who tells you a story about what's wrong and what drug will help, do you feel better? Probably not, at least not right away. But then, most things that ail us get better all by themselves if we don't do anything.

So what does Iceland have to do with any of this? A sociology graduate student at the University of Iowa where Paul was teaching kept telling Paul about how Icelandic skippers get drunk and dream about where to find fish. Here was something like a shamanic séance—at least something that doesn't involve rational calculation. But in Iceland, it's not connected with something subjective like feeling better; it's connected with something that's easy to measure: tons of fish. It should be possible to find out whether the skippers who dream about fish catch more than others.

So Paul went to Iceland in the summer of 1981 to see what he could find out. The Icelandic sociology student introduced Paul to Gísli Pálsson, an anthropologist who had been doing ethnographic work in a fishing village. Paul and Gísli worked out a program for studying the "skipper effect," the difference in catch that the skipper makes.

First, they listed and measured all the mundane things that would affect a skipper's success: the size of the boat and the number of nets, crewmembers, and fishing trips. They decided whatever was left would be the amount of difference that the skipper made. So Paul put all of Gísli's numbers into a computer and did some statistical modeling.

He found out that there was virtually no skipper effect. If you took into account the size of the boat and the number of times they went fishing, the skippers didn't make any difference at all.

Paul and Gísli had just done themselves out of an interesting question, and they were pretty depressed about it for a while—until they figured out an even more interesting question: Why did Icelanders ever *think* there was a skipper effect if there really wasn't one?

Though fishing has always been important to Icelanders, there weren't always skippers. In the nineteenth century, the guys in charge of fishing boats were called foremen. They fished in the North Atlantic from row boats. Catching a lot of fish didn't make a foreman a good foreman. But his seamanship—his ability to get a crew out to sea and home again without losing anyone—did make him a good foreman.

At that time, there was no market for fish. People were fishing as part of their household economies, so there was a ceiling on production as we discussed in the chapter on economics. In 1920 came the first motor boat.

In the village Gísli studied, there had been a custom that when a boat got to a particular rock, the foreman would lift his hat and say a prayer for the protection of the crew. The very first guy who went out with a motor boat didn't do that. When he got back, people asked him why he didn't. He said if a guy had a motor, he didn't need to pray.

At about the same time, Iceland was becoming more independent from Denmark and controlling more of its own economy. Instead of a Danish trade monopoly, there were Icelandic merchants, and some of them started trading in fish. Thus developed an international market for fish. With the motor boats, fishermen could go farther out and catch more fish. With this technology and the developing markets, commercial production was possible.

But they had the same problem that faced a lot of entrepreneurs when they wanted to become a commercial producer: there was no free labor, no people to hire to produce surplus value. Everybody was busy working on farms. There was even a law that if you didn't own land, you had to have a contract with someone who did own land to work for that person either as a laborer or as a renter of some kind. That meant very cheap labor for landowners, which they didn't want to give up, but no labor for fishing.

Poor people started voting with their feet. They left the farms and went to the coast to work in the fishing industry. They worked as crew for fishing boats, for processors to cut and salt fish, and for all of the other jobs that keep the boats going back out to catch more fish. Since they didn't have their own means of production, it was better for them to work for wages than to work for landowners for virtually nothing—just enough to scrape by for the year.

The Icelandic novelist Halldor Laxness told about the lives of farming folks in his Nobel Prize–winning novel, *Independent People.* He told about life in the fishing villages in another novel, *Salka Valka.* In that novel, one of the characters says, "Life is salt fish." Laxness's novels like those that tell about the living conditions in Iceland made him very unpopular with the ruling class ... until he won a Nobel Prize. Then he was OK because the whole world thought he was a pretty good novelist.

During the times of household fishing, there was no idea of any skipper effect. People only started talking about such a thing during the expansive phase when commercial fishing took off and there was no ceiling on production. Suddenly there were international markets and whole indus-tries of processing fish and outfitting fishing ships. Skippers were racing for bank loans, for the backing of processors, and for fish.

Processors were important because if you could get your boat in and unloaded ahead of others, you could get back out fishing and fish more than they could. Some skippers owned their own boats, but many oth-ers worked as skippers for the owner or owners of the boat. If a skipper wanted to buy a modern boat, he had to get a loan from a bank—in other words, ask a bank to bet on him. So the reputation of the skipper was very important for getting access to a boat either through loans to buy one or through a position on a boat someone else owned, and for loading supplies and unloading fish. That meant lots of competition among skip-pers, and anything that would enhance their reputation would contribute to this "star" system.

The whole idea of mystical processes fit very well with other themes in the Icelandic cultural code, such as elves and other worlds, that are common if not dominant in Iceland to this day. Put the star system to-gether with the preexisting cultural code, and the idea of the skipper effect becomes reasonable and credible—it makes sense—in terms of the Icelandic cultural code.

But that doesn't mean there really is a skipper effect. The statistics showed that there wasn't one—that given the same size boat and the same days fishing, every skipper would catch the same amount of fish whether he was a dreamer or not. So here there was an idea of a skipper effect but no real skipper effect.

As a result of the expansive phase of fishing in Iceland when fishers caught all the fish they could, the fishing stocks were diminished to the point that the government started to use quotas to regulate fishing. The first quota said that after so many tons of each kind of fish were caught, everyone had to stop fishing because the stock couldn't survive if they took any more. Then they changed the system so that each boat got a quota based on the history of its catch in the past. Boat owners could sell or buy quotas under this system, which is called **individual transferable quotas**, or **ITQs** in government talk.

Under this system, the whole concept of the skipper effect diminished in Iceland, so that now people don't think that it is strange to say that there really isn't a skipper effect. "Of course," they say. "How else could it be? Your catch depends on your quota." But before that system was in place, people got offended if you'd suggest that there wasn't really a skip-per effect. It was something like telling Americans that the United States isn't really a democracy. Something that challenges a cultural construct always makes people feel uneasy.

The idea here is that if we understand the economic system and the cultural code that were already in place, we can explain why there was a cultural construct of the skipper effect in Iceland during one period of its history. As the economic and political system, the **political economy**, changed from household production to industrial fishing, the cultural code changed. As the political economy changed again, the system of quotas was put into place; the cultural code changed again as well.

The general point is that if we want to explain why cultures are the way they are, we ask what the connections between the political economy and the culture are. Then we ask how the political economy developed to be the way it is. Once we've done that, we have answered our big questions of what is the nature of the culture and how did it get that way.

Culture is all of the ideas we learn by growing up when and where we do. It includes lots of assumptions about the way the world is from what is a cousin, a sibling, or a parent as well as what's just and fair. People do what they do because of the way they think. Understand how people think and you understand why they do what they do. Culture is what gives people ways to think. So understand culture, and you understand what people do.

Now, we've just said that we can understand cultures if we understand how political economies got the way they are. So which one is right? Do we use culture to understand what people do, or do we use what people do to understand culture? The answer is both. This is one of those mutual determination loops we talked about at the beginning of the book. Each determines the other.

People think and act in the terms their cultures give them, and their actions determine what other people can do. And so on. We'll explain this interaction in some detail as we go along. Just remember that the loop goes both ways—from political economy to culture and from culture to political economy. People change the systems they live in, but not always in ways that they understand or that they intend. For instance, a lot of changes happen even if we don't understand them or mean for them to happen.

Here we need to stop for a moment and look at the idea of political economy a little more. The basic idea goes back to the concept of systems and holism, the idea that an economic system never exists just by itself apart from the rest of the institutions and culture. For instance, in medieval Iceland people had an idea of property that was very important, but there was no institution of a state that could enforce property law. That was one of the reasons the system collapsed into warfare among the people who were powerful enough to even claim to own property. The political institutions limited the economy. But the cultural code played a role because the landowners had the idea of ownership, one of the pillars of states. Even so, they were not able to come together as a class to create the institutions of a state. That's why their system finally collapsed. Realities, cultural codes, and political economies never line up perfectly. That's why our social and cultural systems keep changing.

We've seen the same thing in our discussion of capitalism. If the political institutions don't support some necessary part of capitalism, it can't develop. So, when there wasn't enough free labor for capitalists to hire, the system couldn't develop, as in the example of the Shan village where Paul lived or Europe before the revolutions of the eighteenth century. Those revolutions established new political orders that made capitalism possible.

For capitalism to work, everything has to be available as a commodity on a market—labor, raw materials, manufactured goods. There is a whole institutional structure that guarantees the operation of markets. As economists found after the collapse of the Soviet system, markets don't just come into being wherever there are people; governments have to create the institutions that make them possible. Americans have lived in such a system for all of our lives, so we're likely to take markets for granted or even suppose, like economists, that they are somehow natural.

Reciprocity as a system of exchange requires an institutional structure to make it work. Reciprocity also requires a cultural code that says if people do something for you, you do something for them. All people have some idea of reciprocity, but if their cultural codes about it don't match, they will be disappointed or angry at the behavior of others. It won't make sense to them.

Redistribution is related to a different institutional structure and to a different cultural code. Redistribution also requires the notion of reciprocity, but it adds the idea that some people are different from others, higher than others, or more central. So if a big man says he's going to organize a feast, you pitch in and help. You know the big man will help out when you need it, but you also know that there's something different about the big man and you. He's the guy with the feathers or the title or whatever. So there are never just economic systems or even economic actions but always political economies that are built on economic actions, cultural codes, and institutional structures.

We live our lives in terms of the political economies of the times and places in which we live. We usually think of the realities we experience as just the way things are. These experiences are so powerful that they shape the ways we think. It is the political economies that define our choices.

For example, you can't just decide what courses to take—you have to select among the ones that are available any given quarter or semester.

You can choose among the available ones, but you can't choose which ones will be available. The courses available depend on who is available to teach what and what the administration has decided is important to teach. So your agency, your sense of choice, is highly constrained by the structures in place, what courses are available. In the same way, political economies constrain people's choices and define the terms in which they can make them. Just as you come to think of the requirements you have to fulfill for your degree as just what you have to do, so people come to think of their choices and the terms of their choices as just natural.

In their study of the skipper effect in Iceland, Gísli and Paul were comparing the etic statistics with the emic cultural code of the skipper effect. When we discussed kinship, we showed that there is an etic grid in terms of which we can think about all of the different systems of kinship. The etic grid represents all possible kinship relationships just as the International Phonetic Alphabet represents all of the possible sounds of human languages. Different cultural codes may classify these relationships in different ways just as different languages classify sounds differently.

It wasn't that easy to find an etic grid about the Icelandic skipper effect. Gísli and Paul checked the Human Relations Area Files, a compilation of worldwide ethnographic information, and found that not every cultural code of people who fish has a concept of a skipper effect. They found examples where there was a skipper effect but no idea of one, where there was both an idea and a reality of skipper effects, and where there was a skipper effect but not any cultural concept of one. That is all possible combinations of a cultural concept with the reality.

There may be a skipper effect, or there may not be. That depends on the situation. In Iceland, you have to undergo a long period of training before you become a skipper, so anyone who is a skipper is already very skilled. Gísli and Paul figured that all of that training makes Icelandic skippers about equally skilled. There just aren't any Icelandic skippers who aren't good.

But in the Gulf of Mexico, you don't have to do anything to be a skipper on a shrimp boat. You don't have to do an apprenticeship or go to school. Paul studied shrimpers in Mississippi and found that they don't have any idea of a skipper effect, and they are right—there really isn't one. Why would there be a cultural concept of skipper effect in Iceland but not Mississippi? Fishing is a commercial enterprise in both places. In Mississippi, there was always more ability to process shrimp than there has been supply of shrimp. In Iceland's expansive phase of fishing, there was more supply of fish than ability to process them so there was competition among skippers. In Mississippi, because of the greater capacity for shrimp processing, this kind of competition never existed among shrimp skippers. So a difference in the political economy explains a difference in the cultural code.

If you talk to shrimpers on the Gulf Coast today, they'll tell you how independent they are, how they can't get together on anything. That's part of their cultural code. But it hasn't always been that way. In 1932, Mississippi shrimpers organized a union that lasted for twenty-three years—until 1955, when processors sued them under antitrust laws to bust their union. The processors argued that each shrimper owned his own gear and boat, and that meant shrimpers didn't work for processors but worked for themselves. Each shrimp boat was its own corporation, like General Motors. Therefore, for all of these corporations to get together to set the price for shrimp was against antitrust laws. The court agreed and disbanded the union.

That meant it was against the law to have a shrimpers union. So it's just not true that shrimpers are too independent to cooperate or to organize. The cultural code works along with the law to make organizing impossible.

Why would they believe it if it's not true? First, it's consistent with their experience because they experience themselves and other shrimpers as stubbornly independent rather than working together. But there are a number of reasons for that. One is that this cultural code works very well for processors who benefit from keeping shrimpers from organizing, and it benefits bureaucrats who have to regulate them. Processors want to bring in cheap imports of pond-raised shrimp from all over the world. That undercuts the price shrimpers can get for the shrimp they catch. But as long as shrimpers aren't organized, they can't do anything about it. Bureaucrats have to enforce regulations about shrimping. That would be a lot more difficult if shrimpers were organized to resist the regulations.

So it benefits processors and bureaucrats if shrimpers think of themselves as independent. The only way it benefits shrimpers is that they can think of themselves as somehow set apart, elite, or more independent than other people. They pay dearly for that feeling, but with the law, the processors, and the bureaucrats aligned against them, they're not strong enough to change the law or the institutional structures. So once again, we see that the political economy causes the cultural code to have the form it does, and the cultural code informs what people do. What people do then reinforces the institutional structures and so on.

When we wanted to learn how American union members think about their unions, we found that there is an etic grid in terms of which we could match people's ideas. Law and practice both define the etic grid. There is a management side with people who supervise the work, supervisors. Supervisors answer to managers. Usually there is also a vice president for human relations who handles all personnel issues.

On the union side, there are the members who voted to have a union in their workplace. There are also stewards, usually people whom the members elect to help them with any problems they might have at work. If a steward can't handle the problem, she can call a union representative. The union uses members' dues money to pay representatives, who are a little bit like lawyers to come in and help the stewards whenever they need it. The stewards can deal with supervisors and managers. The reps can deal with managers and vice presidents.

So there are two sides to this: union and management. In each side there is also a hierarchy. On the union side, the hierarchy is from member to steward to rep. On the management side, the hierarchy is from worker to supervisor to manager to vice president.

On the basis of this etic grid, we devised a way to find out how people think about their union. In spite of the etic grid, people can think in any number of different ways. Americans can put their mother's brother's kids right in with their mother's sister's kids and call them all the same thing, cousins. Lisu and Navaho do it differently.

To find out how people think about their unions, we developed a method for telling how people think about similarities. It's called a *triads test*. You ask people which of three things is the most different. For instance, if you asked which of these is most different—blue, purple, green—people might say "blue" because although purple and green have blue in them, blue is the only one that's a primary color. It might be harder if we asked, "Purple, green, or orange?" because green and purple both contain blue, purple and orange both contain red, and orange and green both contain yellow, so any answer is equally correct.

We took all of the terms of the etic grid except VP—steward, other worker, rep, supervisor, and manager—and put them into every possible combination of three and asked people which is the most different. As with the color examples, there is some similarity between the two things that someone does not select.

We did this with the staffs of three union locals in Chicago and one in Pennsylvania and found that they all agree with the etic grid. We checked to see how much all the people agreed with each other. If there isn't much agreement, then all you can say is that you aren't looking at anything that's cultural—different people think about it differently, and it's based on something individual, but you can't see any cultural code at work here. But if most folks agree, then you can say it's cultural.

While staff agree with the etic grid, as we might expect because of the work they do, we got different pictures from members at different worksites. Members at industrial worksites for one local saw themselves as way low on the hierarchy scale relative to both union and management folks and equally different from both. So they didn't see themselves as having anything in common with either management or the union.

Some health care workers at hospitals fit the staff-etic pattern pretty closely, and others did not. When we compared the different conceptual schemes with what we knew about the worksites, we concluded that it was the relative power of management and the union at the different worksites that made the difference. Where the union was powerful, members saw themselves as part of it. Where the union lacked power in the worksite, members didn't identify with it so much.

At one hospital, there was one interesting difference between what the members thought and the etic pattern. They put their steward above their rep in the hierarchy. That was reasonable because the rep was new, and the steward had been there for more than two decades and ruled that place like a grandmother ruling her tribe. When management informed her that the women in her kitchen should wash the pots, for example, she answered, "My girls don't do pots." That was the end of that.

But she had carpal tunnel syndrome from a lifetime of hard work. When she retired, another long-term steward joined her, and the workers were left with no leadership. The hospital management was building a new wing, and, in the meantime, they weren't full of patients. They said that because they didn't have enough work for everyone, they'd lay off some folks. The union countered that if they would let everyone continue working, each person would work fewer hours. Management agreed. When the new wing was finished and all the rooms were full, management did not return all of the workers to their full hours as they had initially agreed. Instead, they started hiring temporary workers, workers who were not eligible to be in the union.

Just at that time, the bargaining team was negotiating a new contract for the union members. When the bargaining was finished and the members were voting on the contract, we did another triads test and found that since the first one two years before, the members had shifted from seeing themselves as close to the union to seeing themselves as closer to management.

Because we had seen the same relationship between power and union consciousness in the other bargaining units, we knew that this shift in cultural code was because of the shift in power from the union toward management that happened when the two long-term stewards retired and the rep could not find any experienced and knowledgeable replacements for them.

So, as with the skipper effect, here with the unions in Chicago, we see that the cultural code depends on the political economy. If the political economy of a worksite changes, so does the cultural code.

This tells us that it isn't what people think or decide that makes a difference—it's their daily lives that determines how they think—their cultural codes. If we zoom the lens out a little and take a more wide-angle view, we see that the hospital is a nonprofit corporation. Here it's the "corporation" part that's important. All corporations have some things in common. One is their concern for their bottom line. That's part of our cultural code. So one group's cultural code sets the actual realities for another group.

Here class is very important, because the degree of agency you have depends on the amount of power you have as well as your awareness. So, if we changed laws or change cultural codes that define how corporations work, the realities for workers would change as well. If you can't do that, you can try to change the realities at work by showing workers that they always have some power if they stick together. They can use that power to make changes in the workplace that then affect others' cultural codes and so on. That's the job that union organizers and representatives have.

Now we're going to zoom out from the microscopic focus on bargaining units at particular worksites and look at the whole labor movement in the United States to develop a more wide-screen view, something like the scope of the view we developed for Iceland and the skipper effect.

When we were doing these studies in the late 1990s, there were two different views of what unions should be like. One view said they should be like insurance companies. You're a worker. You pay your dues. In return for your dues, you get a rep to help you out if you get unfairly fired or disciplined for something you didn't do. You also get someone to come in and bargain with management to get you a little bit better deal, or at least not a worse deal, with every new contract. Maybe you get a small pay raise. Maybe the union can get management to back off a little bit on their demand that you pay more of your health insurance so that you only pay 20 percent of it instead of 60 percent. Members pay dues and get services. This is called the "servicing model" of unions.

In the old days when unions were much stronger than they are now, when more than a third of all American working people belonged to unions instead of 10 percent, when the New Deal government of Roosevelt actively supported unions, back in the 1930s, when workers at a worksite had a problem with management, they could strike until management figured out how to solve the problem. A problem for workers very quickly became a problem for management. The union members didn't call a union rep. Their worksite leaders could call them out on strike over one person's grievance with management. They could do that for two reasons. The first is that they were well organized inside every worksite. We'll come back to the second in just a minute because it's even more important to our story here.

Today, this is called the "organizing model." That means that the union puts its effort into being sure that each unit is so well organized that it can take care of itself. Then the union can let its reps spend their time and effort organizing places that don't yet have unions. As workers at more and more places join unions, union strength grows.

Then unions can mobilize their members politically—to vote in elections and keep friendly politicians in power. The politicians who owe their positions to unions can then see to it that there is legislation that helps rather than hurts unions.

But in the 1990s, unions weren't that strong. They had declined in strength ever since 1948 when they were at their strongest ever. The original laws that allowed unions to organize, that made union representation a right of any workers where a majority voted for a union, were passed in 1935 as part of the effort to combat the Great Depression. The law is called the Wagner Act.

After World War II, the leaders of industry got together and pushed through some changes in this basic law. It was 1948 and Harry Truman was president. He vetoed the legislation, but Congress passed it over his veto. This was called the Taft-Hartley amendments to the Wagner Act.

This may sound like a lot of useless history, but it's important for developing that wide-screen view of unions we were talking about when we looked up from the worm's-eye view of the ethnography of each individual shop to try to see what is going on in the whole country.

The Taft-Hartley amendments said that unions couldn't strike during the term of a contract. As soon as the members at a worksite agreed to the contract, they couldn't strike about anything. This took away the major source of the power of unions in worksites. If there was some problem that the steward couldn't handle to the satisfaction of the members, then they could call a rep from the union. This law changed the union reps from organizers into dispute handlers and insurance people. Their role changed from organizing to servicing. Under the new law of 1948, if there was some dispute or issue that the reps couldn't handle with management, they could take it to arbitration. Both sides had to pay for half of the costs of an arbitrator, who would hear both sides of the case and then make a judgment. Neither side could appeal the judgment of an arbitrator. The arbitrator's word was final, as it was in medieval Iceland in 1000 when an arbitrator decided that everyone would be Christian.

If management's pockets were deep, they didn't mind taking lots of cases to arbitration because it would cost the union as much as it cost them. As a result, unions had to be very careful about what cases they took to arbitration. The law also set up boards of people to decide about charges of unfair labor practices. For instance, if management fires someone just because the person is active in the union, it's against the law. The union can file an unfair labor practice complaint. The problem is that the members of these boards are political appointees. So they can be more or less friendly to management or labor depending on who won the last election and appointed them.

Grievances were no longer a matter of right or wrong, fair or unfair—ideals that workers would strike over. It was now a matter of legal skill—how well each side could negotiate an agreement or how persuasively someone could argue the interpretation of the contract language.

After the Taft-Hartley amendments, a lot of labor leaders became pretty complacent. They were moving with the big boys, smoking the fancy cigars, driving the fancy cars, living in the fancy suburbs, and sending their kids to prep schools with the bosses' kids. You couldn't tell the difference between a labor leader and a boss by smelling the cigar or looking at the suit or the car.

And the unions changed from being centered on organizing and developing power in workplaces to big bureaucracies for dealing with the problems of their members and negotiating new contracts for them every few years. As long as they had enough power to negotiate a contract with a raise and some decent benefits each time around, members were happy. As long as it was cheaper or easier for the boss to give the raises instead of deal with labor unrest or a strike and still make a profit, management agreed to the increases.

Every year the management bosses gained strength and the union lost strength. The labor bosses weren't paying that much attention. Everything was fine with them. But then several things happened in 1981.

There was a big strike of meat cutters in the Hormel plant in Austin, Minnesota. About the same time, a whole new way of processing meat was coming on line. A company called Iowa Beef Processing, or IBP for short, was opening up a new kind of meat processing plant. It was automated. The plant didn't need the skilled work of butchers. It could hire anyone off the street and in an hour or two show them how to do a couple of simple things and have them doing one little part of taking apart a continual stream of steers or pigs and putting meat in boxes to send to stores.

The old-style plants sent sides of beef to stores where butchers cut off exactly the part a customer ordered. The new factories sent boxes of meat to stores. The stores didn't need butchers anymore, and neither did the plants. Instead, IBP could now hire unskilled workers at a much lower rate, undercutting (so to speak) everyone else in the industry. Hormel couldn't compete with IBP, and the workers went back into work after a long strike with a worse contract than before they went out. It was the beginning of the end of the success of that union.

This is the competitive process we described in chapter 7 on economics. Productivity increased, and IBP didn't need as much labor or any skilled labor.

It was worse at other plants. In Waterloo, Iowa, and other plants in the Midwest, Rath Packing went out of business completely, leaving tens of thousands of people out of work. More than a decade later, with the local industrial economies in tatters, IBP moved into those towns, started up their own plants, and hired workers at a fraction of the wages their uncles, mothers, and fathers had made fifteen years earlier. Safety conditions were so bad they caused high turnover, which in turn created a shortage of labor (but no shortage of amputations, carpal tunnel syndrome, and other disabilities) in local communities. Then IBP began importing workers from Mexico and other parts of the world.

In 1981, the air traffic controllers got fed up with the conditions of their work and decided to strike. They had complained for years that poor scheduling and understaffing were causing exhaustion that would lead to disasters in the air. Harry Truman and FDR were long dead. Ronald Reagan, the candidate these air traffic controllers had endorsed during the election, was president. He decided that these government employees weren't going to get away with a strike. He fired them all, replaced them, and the air traffic controllers' union was busted. Others in the labor movement, thinking those workers got what they deserved for endorsing a Republican, sat back and chuckled, never realizing the cannons were turning toward every other union in America. Sort of like Wyle E. Coyote in the cartoons right after he runs off the cliff and before he looks down, or when he lights the fuse that blows him to smithereens a couple of seconds later.

That year, 1981, was a turning point. From then on, unions were on the defensive against management. The new policy that Reagan started was that if the union went out on strike after a contract expired and before they negotiated a new one—the only time it was legal to strike—management could bring in other workers to replace the strikers permanently. Let's put that another way: the law says you have the right to temporarily withhold your labor—to strike—but it now said, according to Reagan, that you could permanently lose your job if you exercised that right.

That left unions with very little power.

Here's the point. Their power came from the law and the way the government enforced it—the policies in place. Unions lost their power as Republican politicians and others friendly to management changed the law, interpreted old laws in new ways, or enforced them differently according to different policies. That's why we can't just speak of an economic system. It's a political economy.

Now cut to the 1990s when we're working in Chicago. By then, some new union leaders were in place, and they were trying to get the unions to pull their head out of the sand enough to make an effective resistance while there was still something to work with. The ones we studied argued that unions should change their way of doing things—they should change from the servicing model to the organizing model. Unions should organize. This meant there were three things they had to do:

- organize more workers and more places and get stronger;
- organize to support friendly politicians to change the laws and labor boards;
- organize in worksites so that the stewards could help members take care of their problems without calling on reps all the time.

That meant that it couldn't be business as usual any more for these locals. They had to change and change fast. Every local would have to be involved. So the message went out (maybe *down* is a better preposition) to the locals.

The presidents of the locals got the message loud and clear. Some liked it and some did not. The presidents passed it on to the reps, and the reps told the stewards.

Here's where ethnography comes in handy. Suzan was working for a union local in Chicago at the time, so she had a close-up inside view of what was going on. She wrote about that in her book, *Labor Pains: Inside American's New Labor Movement* (2001). We wrote a book about that part of our work, *Class Acts: An Anthropology of Urban Service Workers and Their Union* (2005).

OK, we're done plugging our other books. Back to this story. To understand what was going on, we had to understand the social and political relationships inside locals. The presidents of locals are elected. The members get to vote for their president, unless the president does something wrong, something that violates the union's own rules or the law. If that happens, the international union can replace the president with a trustee—someone the leaders trust to be honest and get the local back on the right track. There was a lot of that going on in Chicago in the 1990s. But a trustee in the unions we studied could only serve up to eighteen months. Then an election would be held, and the members could decide whether they wanted to keep the same leader.

But in one union, it was so difficult to get on the ballot that you had to already be in charge before you could get your name on a ballot so that people could vote for you. As a result, there wasn't a lot of opposition.

It was sort of like those old elections in the Soviet Union with one guy running, and that one guy always won.

But there had to be an election because that's what we Americans mean when we say "democracy." One person, one vote elections. That means the members have to actually more or less vote. And that means someone has to get them to vote. Someone has to let them know there's an election and get them to vote for the president. Otherwise it would be against the union's own rules, and the law and the local could be trusteed.

Presidents relied on reps to deliver the votes for them. The reps depended on stewards to deliver the votes for *them*. So there was a kind of pyramid scheme. Stewards deliver votes to reps, and reps deliver votes to presidents. If people didn't play their assigned roles, the whole thing would fall apart.

How could reps be sure that stewards would deliver the votes? How could they be sure that members would vote the way they should? The best way was by having the stewards and members be obliged to the reps. Remember reciprocity? Reps did that by their servicing. If there was a problem, the rep would fix it. Then the member and the steward owed the rep. Folks in Chicago talk that way. When they say, "I owe you one," they mean it. And you can actually collect.

This is pretty much like medieval Iceland. There, if someone hurt you, you organized enough goons to go hurt that person back. In just the same way, "I owe you one" can cut both ways in Chicago, so reps had to be sure it was cutting their way and not against them.

If the reps delivered the votes, the president would like them and help them gain access to the resources they needed to keep their members and stewards happy—maybe an arbitration, maybe some fried chicken to help get members to a meeting. The rep might even get promoted or the president could ask her to run for office on his slate.

When the word came down about the organizing model, the reps weren't too anxious to do any of it. To do those things would mean that they weren't servicing their members as much, that they were losing touch and losing their own base of power. In Chicago, they call it their base. Different folks have different power bases.

You may have seen *Fahrenheit 9/11,* the Michael Moore movie about George W. Bush. In the movie, George W. is talking to a group of billionaires and gazillionaires, and he says they're his base. They are. But union members are the base for reps. And they didn't want to lose their base any more than W wanted to lose his.

But create a system where reps are irrelevant to anything going on at the worksite, because now stewards solve all the problems, and from the rep's point of view, it looks like she's doing herself out of her job. It's like

training all the passengers on airplanes to fly, so nobody needs a pilot.
Are pilots going to support that? Are they going to train us to fly?

So the reps all said, "Yeah, sure," and got on with what they'd always
been doing. The program hit a stump. Paul was in a rep's office when a
sociologist did a phone survey of reps to see whether they were with the
program. The sociologist asked some clever question like "Are you with
the program?" and the rep said, "Sure," and the sociologist was convinced.
Later the sociologist published a paper in which he proved that the reps
really liked the organizing program. It was another three years before Suzan left that local, and the program wasn't even up to a crawl by then.

In the meantime, we did some surveys of our own—with stewards. We
didn't ask whether they liked the program. We did what's called a *paired
comparison*. That's where you ask people which of two things is more of
something. For instance, we might ask people, "Which thing is bigger?"
and then give them several combinations:

- elephant/goat
- elephant/mouse
- goat/mouse

These are all possible combinations of two. The people would probably
select "elephant" in the first and second ones and "goat" in the third. We
give each thing one point every time someone selects it. So if we talked
to one hundred people and they all agreed, "elephant" would have two
hundred points (a hundred from "elephant/goat" and a hundred from
"elephant/mouse"); "goat" would have one hundred points (from "goat/
mouse"), and "mouse" would have zero. So the ranking would be

elephant	200
goat	100
mouse	0

And we'd conclude that these folks think that elephants are bigger than
goats and that goats are bigger than mice.

This lets people tell us what the scales are and whether there are any
scales at all. Maybe nobody agrees with anybody else. Remember, if that
happens, then there's no cultural code about that; it's just a matter of
individual opinion. And maybe there's no scale. People may like apples
better than oranges and oranges better than bananas, but they like bananas
better than apples. Anthropologists don't tell people they're crazy or what
they *should* think; we try to figure what they *do* think.

We did that with stewards and found out that the least important things for them were anything political, like helping to elect friendly politicians. The next least important thing for them was organizing other workplaces. The top things were negotiating contracts and dealing with grievances—servicing their members. So the program wasn't percolating down to the stewards.

But look at it from the stewards' point of view. Every day their job is to try to keep the peace in their workplaces. They have to know and enforce the contract. Management won't help. They'll violate the contract any time they can get away with it. So the daily life of stewards is centered on these things right in their own workplaces. After all, that's a steward's job for the union. The other parts of the program, organizing other workplaces and electing friendly politicians, are just something they heard in a speech or read about in a pamphlet or newsletter. They're not even real.

Same thing for reps. They know their jobs and do them. But what's important to them is keeping the structure of reciprocity and obligation in place with their members and stewards so they can help get their president reelected.

Here again we come to the conclusion that the political economy determines the culture. But we're down in the worm hole of ethnography again. That's where anthropologists feel most comfortable. So we'll try to get out and finish developing that big picture we promised a few pages ago.

The law changes in 1948 to make unions lumbering bureaucracies instead of organizing machines. The unions go along with that and work in terms of the servicing model. The political balance shifts from labor-friendly Democrats to management-friendly Republicans. The policy changes again in 1981 to make permanent replacement workers acceptable. That sets off a whole rampage of union busting across the country. The ruling class declared war on the working class. There really is a class war. We'll get to that later, but for right now the thing to know is that all of these legal things set the stage for the way things happen at the worksites.

The law determines what goes on in worksites, and that determines how people think—what seems reasonable to them—their cultural codes. So now we have all the links between political economy and cultural codes for working class Americans.

What's the answer to the question we started this chapter with? The question was about agency and structure. Americans like to think that everything is a matter of our own choices. That's part of our cultural code. Thomas Frank (2004), author of *What's the Matter with Kansas? How Conservatives Won the Heart of America,* says that conservative propagandists believe that thinking in terms of hierarchy is just plain

Marxist and therefore wrong. The Soviet Union collapsed, after all. So we're all in this together, one big middle class. According to conservative ideologists, the model is

> a high school cafeteria, segmented into self-chosen taste clusters like "nerds, jocks, punks, bikers, techies, druggies, God Squadders," and so on. "The jocks [he's quoting one of the ideologues] knew there would always be nerds and the nerds knew there would always be jocks ... that's just the way life is." We choose where we want to sit and whom we want to mimic and what class we want to belong to the same way we choose hairstyles or TV shows or extracurricular activities. We're all free agents in this noncoercive class system. (26)

Frank continues: "As a description of the way society works, this is preposterous. Even by high school, most of us know that we won't be able to choose our station in life the way we choose a soda pop or even the way we choose our friends" (26-27).

He's right. There's precious little choice. Our cultural codes are given by our political economies and those are given by the histories of political economies—how all of the parts of the system interact with the other parts and change each other. Remember the system diagram that went like figure 12.1. The actions impact the realities; the cultural codes give us ways to think about realities and help us decide what to do, our actions. And where you are in the class system makes a big difference in the effects of your actions and the cultural code you have.

So does this mean that we can never change anything? That we just cycle through this? No. First, this is from an actor's point of view, not from the system's point of view. We can see change and the possibilities for change better from the systems perspective than from the perspective of people in it. But even from the individual point of view, we can see that even though we are limited by our cultural codes, we can try different things. If a lot of people go in the same direction, they can have an impact on the reality. That's what happened in Iceland when the people who working for farmers for free just quit and went to the coast to work in the fishing industry.

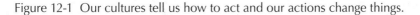
Figure 12-1 Our cultures tell us how to act and our actions change things.

That's called *collective action*. That's what the civil rights movement was. That's where greenhouse gases and unions come from—a lot of people acting in the same direction. Sometimes they don't especially mean to have that effect—greenhouse gasses are a byproduct of driving cars and industry. Sometimes they do—we get unions only when lots of people act together and mean it.

But then some people oppose both greenhouse gases and unions. How effective they are depends on how powerful they are. The more powerful, the more effective. If the ruling class of the United States were as against greenhouse gases as they are against unions, we'd sign the Kyoto agreements and reduce our air pollution. But that's not where the political base has been, so that's not where we are going.

All of this structure stuff makes us feel uncomfortable. We are used to thinking in terms of choices. But that's our culture. That's our emic system. That's our economic system based on consumption and the idea of consumer choice. Sometimes we're like Paul looking at milk or peanut butter in the grocery store—faced with lots of apparent choices but no real ones. Democrat or Republican? Half a pound or eight ounces?

The culture of choice and the illusion of choice doesn't make it real any more than the skipper effect is real because some folks think it is. But anything that goes against our cultural code makes us feel uncomfortable. That's why Icelanders didn't much like it when Gísli and Paul talked about no skipper effect.

It's OK to feel uncomfortable about things that challenge our cultural constructs. We're built that way so that we don't easily give up on things that work for us. But sometimes we find it difficult to give up on things that don't work for us, like shrimpers giving up on the idea of individuality long enough to get organized. That's especially so if there's a class dimension as there usually is. For instance, all the powerful processors and well-educated managers continually tell shrimpers they are right to think that they're too individualistic to organize.

That's where science comes in—to help us sort out the cultural illusions from the political economic realities. That's why we think it's good practice to be scientific in our anthropology. We can tell you, "This is what we found," and we can show you why we think it is valid and reliable. Then you can check it for yourself.

That doesn't mean that we don't have any choices. But it does caution us to understand what the choices are and to base them on reality as best we can know it. We showed that the realities of daily life shape the awareness of workers. But we also showed that those realities were dependent on the strength of the union in the hospital. And that's something that can change with some effort. If you ever work in a place where you find yourself saying, "We have a union, but it sucks," then consider that you can get active in the union and change that. If you work at a place without a union, and the boss can arbitrarily fire you, change your hours, or deny your vacation, you might decide to pull everyone together and form a union, but be careful, because even though the law says that you have the right to do so, bosses have a way of breaking the law.

When Nasrudin Hodja was teaching school, one of the students asked which was the best—the greatest achievement: to conquer an empire, to be able to conquer an empire but choose not to do it, or to prevent someone else from conquering an empire. Nasrudin said, "I don't know about empires and conquests and the greatness of achievements, but I know something that's even more difficult than any of those things."

"What's that?" the student asked.

"To teach you to see things as they really are."

That Nasrudin Hodja—he knew about emics and etics and the differences between them.

Discussion Questions

- Go to a newspaper or online news source and find a news story that focuses on politics. Show how that story is related to something economic. Now find a story in the business section, and show how it's related to something political.
- What are some of the things you considered in deciding which college to attend? If you had no constraints, what college would you have chosen?
- One thing that 2004 presidential candidates George W. Bush and John Kerry had in common was that they both went to Yale and both belonged to the same elite society, Skull and Bones. Was Yale one of your choices? Why not? If it was one of your choices, explain.
- If your parents went to college, where did they go? If Yale was one of your choices, explain what that had to do with your mom or dad being a Yalie.
- Can you think of something in your life that is like the skipper effect, where people get credit for a skill they don't really have? Explain it in emic terms and etic terms.
- In America, some people say that hard work leads to financial security and success. In your family, do you see the relationship between hard work and financial success? Do you think that all successful people have worked hard for their money? Why or why not?

- Make a systems diagram with boxes and arrows to show the relationships among the variables involved in the Icelandic skipper effect.

Suggested Reading

Durrenberger, E. Paul. *Gulf Coast Soundings: People and Policy in the Mississippi Shrimp Industry.* Lawrence: University Press of Kansas, 1996.

——. *It's All Politics: South Alabama's Seafood Industry.* Urbana: University of Illinois Press, 1992.

Durrenberger, E. Paul, and Suzan Erem. *Class Acts: An Anthropology of Service Workers and Their Union.* Boulder, CO: Paradigm Publishers, 2005.

Erem, Suzan. *Labor Pains: Inside America's New Union Movement.* New York: Monthly Review Press, 2001.

Pálsson, Gísli. *Coastal Economies, Cultural Accounts: Human Ecology and Icelandic Discourse.* Manchester: Manchester University Press, 1991.

13

There are two classes: the capitalist class and the working class. These members of the working class have organized into a union to protect their interests. *Photo by Suzan Erem.*

CHAPTER 13

CLASS

L.A. detective Captain Gregory is talking to hard-boiled detective Phillip Marlowe:

> "I'm a copper," he said. "Just a plain ordinary copper. Reasonably honest. As honest as you could expect a man to be in a world where it's out of style. That's mainly why I asked you to come in this morning. I'd like you to believe that. Being a copper, I like to see the law win. I'd like to see the flashy well-dressed mugs like Eddie Mars spoiling their manicures in the rock quarry at Folsom, alongside of the poor little slum-bred hard guys that got knocked over on their first caper and never had a break since. That's what I'd like. You and me both lived too long to think I'm likely to see it happen. Not in this town, not in any town half this size, in any part of this wide, green and beautiful U.S.A. We just don't run our country that way."

It's in chapter 30 of Raymond Chandler's book *The Big Sleep*. It was published in 1939, shortly after the Wagner Act but before the United States got into World War II.

That was way before Enron or Martha Stewart or Tyco or any of the other corporate or political crimes or shenanigans of the later twentieth and early twenty-first centuries. "We just don't run our country that way." Nobody runs any country that way. The kind of justice Captain Gregory was thinking about doesn't happen.

Before we go any further, we want you to know that we understand the anger that wells up in people when someone else tells them their myths are myths or that what they've believed all their lives isn't true. And if we were studying Lisu in 1970 or medieval Iceland, the people we studied might never learn that we walked away with that information. Most Lisu in 1970 didn't speak the language that anthropological journals are written in, and the saga Icelanders are dead. But more and more, thanks to technology, the people anthropologists study learn about the results, and invariably the emic and the etic run into each other somewhere.

185

When American anthropologists study the present-day United States, that collision happens faster, and it tends to happen with more force. In this chapter, you will probably experience it. Talking about class does two things: it ratifies the feelings of working people who have struggled at some level for years with the contradictions America offers ("Anyone willing to work hard can get ahead"), and it infuriates people who either refuse to admit they are members of the working class ("We're middle class") or really are in the ruling class, because anthropology bares the truth in an undeniable way.

Conservatives believe that the government is bad. They say it fails whenever it tries to do something, like managed health care. But governments of other countries manage health care very well. They have better health care systems than the United States does and operate them at lower cost. We need to understand objectively what governments can do well and what they can't do well. We can do that by comparative studies of other countries. In the Untied States, the idea that governments do everything badly is part of a political philosophy of conservatives who believe that everything should be done by markets because that's where businesses are supreme and government should stay out. The corporations promote this ideology through their think tanks like the Heritage Foundation and the Cato Foundation. Their mission is to manufacture **ideologies** to make corporations seem natural, inevitable, and good. We've used the word *ideology* pretty loosely as almost a synonym for *cultural code.* When ideologies are political—conservatism, liberalism—the people select parts of their cultural code to support one political position. That's what ideologies are.

Why would think tanks do that? Because these ideologies promote profits for the corporations that back them. They play to the elements of the American cultural code they can identify and locate. One is that people in the United States don't like negative things. If you can't say something good, don't say anything at all. There's no room for negativity. That's whining. So any reports of corporate bad behavior are just negative whining, and the people making them should just shut up.

But to see negative consequences such as global warming and pollution and increasing poverty as negative is being controlled by this ideology. What we need to do is see the facts and assess facts. We don't have room for opinions. We don't want to trade opinions and come to the conclusion that everyone's opinion is equal. First, it's not true. Second, this is the kind of cultural relativism that stifles the search for ethnographic reality. Questions of good or bad judgments aren't relevant. Those are the wrong questions. We need to ask questions of validity and reliability. That's what science does.

It's easy to see why people don't want to think about this stuff. We're surrounded by messages that manipulate us, and part of the American cultural code is to think for yourself. The easiest way is to think for yourself and reject all messages. But if we do that, we have no evidence, no ideas, no logic to work with. We have only our opinions. We need to be open to ideas, but we need to test them rigorously. If we do that, we can build understanding. The discussions and debates we need to have are not about trading opinions; they're about assessing logical and empirical adequacy.

All around us we see corporations. They are a major institutional form. Some say they treat people badly. Our question has to be whether that view is true, not whether it's good or bad or positive or negative. Those questions only matter in opinion slugfests, not in ethnographic work. The problem is that corporations manufacture culture and try to get us to accept it, just as processors and managers do for shrimpers.

Are governments or corporations more efficient at delivering health care? We know from comparative studies with European countries that governments do a better job of delivering better health care at less cost. Americans get bad health care and expensive health care because we rely on corporations. Can governments be inefficient? Of course they can. Especially if they're staffed by corrupt political appointees and cronies. Witness the U.S. government's response to Hurricane Katrina in 2005. But that doesn't mean corporate solutions are the only alternative. But corporations want us to think that, so they try to bend our culture to that image.

Here we're going to discuss class. That doesn't depend on culture or opinions. It depends on realities. So here we go.

All stratified societies have classes. That much is true by definition. In stratified societies, there is unequal access to resources. We've seen that states are the institutional arrangements to keep stratified societies working by making sure in one way or another that the working class accepts the unequal allocation of resources. People are not in the same boat. What works well for the ruling class may not work at all well for the working class.

This was clear in medieval Iceland when the chieftains landed and claimed land for themselves and began to work it with their slaves. The chieftains were as antigovernment as any of our twenty-first-century American neo-cons, so they didn't want to set up a state to maintain their system of stratification. But they didn't want to give up the stratification, either. We've seen what happened to them. They were able to keep the subordinate class in its position, but their real problems were with each other.

We have classes here in the United States, but we don't like to talk about it. In fact, we spend a lot of energy denying that we have any classes. We like to think that we're all one big middle class. We don't like to believe that a very few of us run the show and the rest of us serve them.

With Halliburton's Dick Cheney as our vice president and the oil companies' George W. Bush as our president, there's no doubt that the ruling class is in charge. What some find curious is that they were elected, at least for their second term, though they may have gotten in for the first term by less than honest means. In *What's the Matter with Kansas? How Conservatives Won the Heart of America,* Thomas Frank (2004) suggests that for some reason the Democrats stopped thinking of economics as a political issue.

We suggest that the reason they didn't make economics a big issue is because their candidate was as much a member of the ruling class—and certainly as beholden to it—as the incumbent. Because the Democrats were standing in that glass house, there weren't too many stones they could throw. So, as more and more manufacturing jobs go to the cheap labor markets in the global system (in a process that we discuss in the next chapter), people are working more for lower wages and for fewer benefits such as health insurance and pensions, and our presidential candidates are completely disconnected from that experience.

People who once had jobs in steel mills or automobile factories or making television sets are now looking for what economists politely call "service sector jobs." Flipping burgers, working cash registers, cleaning buildings, taking care of sick people. Many of those jobs are being automated. "Pumping gas" is no longer a service sector job as it was when Paul was a kid. ATMs replace bank workers. Lots of travel agents are out of work thanks to the Internet. The folks who used to have union wages with union benefits notice the difference, and they're angry. People who work all the time know they are working class. So do people who've been thrown out of work.

And they know there are snotty liberals around flapping their sandals and sipping lattes and jabbering in Latin about everything that's wrong with America. So when the angry workers get a chance, they vote against those liberals and put straight-talking neo-cons in office. The neo-cons cut taxes. The workers notice a little difference. The rich notice a whopping difference.

Under the guise of protection, the neo-cons increase military spending to give their client corporations like Halliburton and others big contracts. With less tax revenue, (caused by the ever-popular tax cuts), that military spending for their friends means less money for programs to help people, so the government cuts budgets to agencies like Occupational

Safety and Health (OSHA), Medicaid, and Medicare, and it tries to get the government out of Social Security. They refuse to consider nationalized health care like every other advanced country has and refuse to regulate pharmaceutical companies.

With less tax money, the government has to cut programs that workers and their families need, and that makes life that much worse—for workers. The **neo-conservatives** put the power of the government behind union busting, and that makes it even worse. Neo-conservatives advocate a global market policed and controlled by American arms for American ends. This translates into unlimited spending on arms, the support of Israel, and preemptive strikes against any opposition.

So working people get madder and vote out more liberals and vote in more neo-cons. This is one of those self-intensifying systems that we discussed earlier in the book. Worse conditions-more anger-more votes for neo-cons-worse conditions.

Let's take a look at the U.S. system in our systems terms (figure 13.1).

Thomas Frank is a journalist, not an anthropologist. But journalists are doing a lot of the same kind of work that anthropologists do. He thinks the corporate-backed neo-cons have successfully manipulated America's cultural codes to turn them against working people; for instance, "Liberals think they're better than you," "Liberals are pussies," "Neo-cons are as

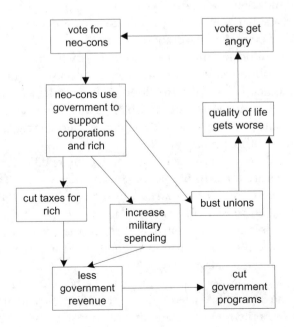

Figure 13-1 What the matter is with Kansas.

mad about it as you are," "Everybody has to look out for themselves—so if you get a cut in your taxes, it doesn't matter if someone else gets a bigger cut; you should be mad at the liberals who think it does matter." We'll come back to the American cultural code and explain where it came from later.

What we've tried to do is take some of these questions into the real world of working America to see what union people are thinking and doing. Paul picks up the story here:

A fall evening in 1997 found me sitting at a folding table at the back of a large auditorium in Teamster City, close to Chicago's Medical Center stop on the blue line train. Next to me was political scientist Adolph Reed, then at the University of Illinois, Chicago. He knew about anthropologists because he was once married to one. He's not the usual political scientist. You wouldn't find a usual political scientist at the installation of union officers that was taking place on the stage in front of us. The president of a Service Employees Union local had just won his second uncontested election after taking over a local that had been trusteed, or taken over by the international union. This was cause for celebration and for some preaching to the choir.

Well, not *exactly* the choir. All in that hall were not unanimous in their opinions about all things, even in their daily understandings of all things, as the ethnographic work I had been doing with Suzan was beginning to reveal. From the stage we heard about new directions, about organizing and other moves that would bring unions to control ever larger segments of the labor market. We heard about political action that would bring labor-friendly politicians into office, politicians who knew where their support was, politicians who would help, or at least not hurt as much as some of the neo-cons. From the floor we heard a lot of chatter about work and family, some good-natured ribbing, and, every once in a while, a question about a grievance posed to union staffers sitting at the tables, chowing down with workers they knew.

Adolph was there because he had become convinced that the only viable political future for working people in America was the Labor Party. That's why he kept in touch with labor leaders in Chicago. His writings were more familiar to readers of *The Village Voice* and *The Nation* than to those of arcane academic journals that are the literary hangouts of most political scientists. That evening Adolph and I spoke of labor, class, anthropology, and the Labor Party.

Adolph collected some of his writings into a book called *Class Notes* that warns in no uncertain terms of the political dangers of identity politics that distract from the more fundamental relationships of class and make that divide less visible or less salient. If you grow up black, you experience race and racism. If you're a woman, you know all about sexism. If you're gay, you know all about homophobia. But somehow we are all supposed to be in one big middle class, so we don't talk about class or classism. We don't experience that in the same way that we experience race or gender bias. These kinds of politics have blinded us to class politics.

I walked through the auditorium and greeted people I had met during the two years I worked with this local. There was the slim figure of the Filipina organizer displaying her femininity in her high-heeled shoes and low-cut gown. There were the more substantial African American matrons of hospital kitchens who had shown me that corner of working America. There were the organizers and reps with whom I had ridden through the further reaches of Chicago listening to story after story in my search for patterns. The pattern I found didn't have anything to do with the differences between Blacks, Latinos, or whites or men and women. The patterns Suzan and I found were based on where in the system people were looking up or down or across from; it didn't matter their race or gender.

Two years later, I sat in the butt hut behind a local hospital in the coal-mining region of Pennsylvania. Miners built this hospital for their fellow miners and their families a hundred years ago. Recently, the hospital's management had received loans from the Department of Agriculture to build a modern medical facility with the name of the old one. Now the management was in bankruptcy, and the members of the union were negotiating a new contract for a future they could not predict.

Members of these locals elected teams of fellow employees to work with their union representative to negotiate contracts. We sat in the plastic lean-to that resembled a bus stop and waited for management and the union organizer to complete a side bar, an off-the-record negotiation designed to be less unwieldy and franker than on-the-record full group discussions could be. All but me were women. All were white. They were smoking and talking. I was listening.

They had been working at this hospital for most of their working lives and told stories of various fellow workers and people in management. The conversation moved from joking with a fellow worker to the deterioration of cleaning services since it had been outsourced to what was happening in the negotiations. Would management impose their last contract offer? That was not acceptable to members. Were members obliged to work under those terms to which they had not agreed? Wouldn't that be a lockout? If they were locked out, would they get unemployment benefits? If they didn't, could they make it through the coming winter?

Some said they had freezers full of food from their gardens. Some said their fuel tanks were full for the winter. One said she had no husband

and thus no household support to fall back on. During this discussion, I learned two things:

- these women had given their working lives to this hospital; and
- from their perspective, the management of this hospital had no compunction about literally pulling the plug on their lives.

We had been sitting around the table for hours with the negotiating team. The woman in charge of the kitchen saw to it that I got fed during one of the many breaks. In the end, management announced that they would impose their last offer, but the negotiator filed requests for information that stalled the negotiations.

I left that evening with the conviction that I was witnessing class warfare. The loans that sustained the hospital had been acquired through the good offices of a local politician, a politician who was not returning or receiving phone calls from his constituents, much less the representatives of their union.

What's wrong with corporations? Anthropologists from Walter Goldschmidt in the 1940s to Dimitra Doukas in the opening years of the twenty-first century have argued that corporations destroy communities; break up the ties that bind people into local economic, social, and political systems; and in the process annihilate any hope of democratic self-determination. For example, there is no amount of Wal-Mart's feel-good advertising that changes the fact that people are so badly off that neighbors fight each other for the low-wage jobs the richest retailer in the world offers in local communities. There is no marketing slogan that lightens the heavy load Wal-Mart places on local social services because, first, most of its workers don't have health insurance and often make so little that they are eligible for food stamps, and, second, it often gets massive tax breaks to move into a town, lowering the available tax revenue that funds those services.

Or think of the IBP factories we discussed in the last chapter. Anthropologists have shown just how the importation of lots of low-wage workers damages the communities that are so anxious for "growth" that they invite IBP to come in. The schools are stretched to the limit with education in several languages, the local clinics are overwhelmed with people injured at work who have no health insurance, there is more drug use and theft due to the poverty, and the police departments are stretched beyond their limits. Life isn't very good for the workers the company brings in, either.

So, as corporations tear up the ties that bind communities, the power to make decisions is taken from people who know each other and their areas and is put in the hands of remote management elites who know neither the people nor the area. The unit of decision making is no longer the locale, the community, but the globe-spanning corporation. Labor is an abstraction, a line item in the corporate budget.

When I was riding with Teamsters, I heard British Petroleum negotiators provide Chicago truck drivers the corporate bottom line for labor for transportation. That, they argued, was the bedrock of the negotiations. All else followed from that single abstraction. Teamsters could take it as benefits or as wages, but that was a finite figure from "corporate." It came down from corporate headquarters and could not be changed without permission. To BP, the truck drivers that Teamsters knew as fellow workers were part of a complex equation for producing profit.

That formula for producing profit starts with capital and ends with profit, as we explained in chapter 7. In between is a market that organizes anonymous transactions among multiple buyers and sellers who neither know one another nor care about or for one another. To care for another would undermine the power to bargain. Labor is the only commodity that can transform others from whatever they are into what corporations can sell for money—commodities—on the same market to produce profits.

As we've said before, anthropology differs from political science and other social sciences because it is comparative as well as holistic and ethnographic. Holism means that we look for connections of everything to everything else. We don't see economic systems without also seeing the political systems that define access to resources. Ethnographic means that we like to see how things really are on the ground. We study unions ethnographically so we can see what actually happens in them rather than base our understandings on abstractions or theories that come from our imaginations. Being comparative, anthropologists put any example that we are trying to understand in a context of what we know of all other social systems ancient and modern.

So, in modern systems, the people who control capital control access to resources. The people who control nothing but their own labor and have to sell it to make a living do what the capitalist class tells them to do. That's the kind of system we have in the United States.

Is there an alternative? Yes, but it requires that people who sell their labor to organize themselves to control their own labor for their own benefit. That's what unions are supposed to do. That's also what cooperatives attempt to do.

But for any of this to have a chance, people have to understand the realities of their own social, political, and economic systems. That's what moves anthropology beyond the confines of classrooms and libraries and makes it relevant to everyday life. We understand political, social, and economic systems as they are.

That's where agency comes in. Once you understand how these things work, you can begin to change them. You can't just wish it so. Understanding why your car isn't running won't fix it. You have to do the work. In a democracy, it's the work of every citizen. To use our agency, we need to understand clearly, and we need to organize and act on our understandings.

But we have to be aware of and on guard against thought control, as we explained in chapter 10. For instance, some very abstract and complex theorizing tells us that there are four kinds of capital—**natural**, **social**, **cultural**, and **economic**. Economic capital is the kind that corporations convert into profit. The capitalist class controls that. Ordinary people don't have that.

But we have other kinds of capital. We have social relations that can be valuable. Your uncle can get you a job, or your teacher can write you a letter of recommendation. The friends of your friends can help you when you need it. So people who have more social relations have more social capital, and to be a human being, even to be a primate of any kind, or a wolf or an elephant or a wild horse, you have to have some social relations, some social capital.

Cultural capital is everything you know that might be of use to you in making a living. You know how to farm? That's a form of cultural capital. You have some friends who farm? Social capital. But you can't convert any of that into a hill of beans unless you have access to some economic capital to buy machines, seed, and get access to some land. In this scheme, the land would be natural capital. Natural capital refers to natural resources, like coal and iron ore, and isn't worth anything without the knowledge of what to do with it and the technology to do it.

What's wrong with this scheme? It suggests that everyone has access to some forms of capital. You have no friends? Maybe you know a lot. You don't know anything? Maybe you have lots of friends who can help, like George W. Bush, who was president of the United States in the opening years of the twenty-first century. And there's the third kind of capital, economic capital, that a few people have and most don't. But that's just one form of capital. So this thinking goes that people can convert knowledge, skill, and social relations into profit in much the same way as corporations convert capital into profits.

This neglects the fundamental reality that to convert capital into profit, corporations have to use the labor of people. That same relationship defines what capital really is—no metaphors here: real capital is built into the way our economic system works. It defines two classes: people with access to capital and people without access to capital. No amount of religious belief, no amount of sociological theorizing, no amount of economic hypothesizing can change that reality. And all the talk of social, cultural, and other kinds of capital distracts our attention from the realities of our class system, distorts it, makes it invisible.

That's why it's disappointing to see a whole land cooperating in their own thought control by calling themselves middle class and believing that there is no ruling class. That's why it's disappointing to see working people voting against themselves because they hate liberals.

But that's what anthropologists are here for, to bust myths.

Curtis White (2004) wrote a book called *The Middle Mind: Why Americans Don't Think for Themselves*. At the beginning of this book, we said we couldn't do anthropology without some form of relativism, but we warned against extreme relativism. That's what White is talking about. Good advice here is "Keep an open mind, but don't let your brain fall out." Descriptive and ethical relativism—not judging other people—are necessary for anthropology. But epistemological relativism—saying that everything is just the same as everything else, that we can't make judgments about what is better and what is worse—makes us into morons because that means we can no longer think. We can just swap opinions and say they're all good. They're not.

If everything is equally good, if all systems of ideas are equally good, then we can't make any political judgments. We can't decide what is good for our country and what's bad for it ... or for ourselves or the ones we love. Are we willing to say that it's OK to benefit from the misery of others? If everything is equal, then slavery is OK. Or fascism.

So while we need to be relativistic to understand others, we also need to keep our faculties of judgment strong and active so we can know the difference between bullshit and brilliance, between fascism and democracy, between a good economic program and a bad one, and, White says, between a good work of literature and a bad one. But to do that, we need to be able to "read" the works critically, to sort out and understand their messages, and we need to be willing to judge them. That's why White is against the "it's all good" approach of some of the cultural studies folks.

He has a point. When we lose track of those questions, we lose our ability to judge things on their own merits because we no longer understand what counts as meritorious. We don't follow arguments. We talk about how we feel rather than what we think. If all positions are equally good, we can allow creationism or intelligent design in our schools along with evolution. If all positions are good, we have to believe the people who say there is no global warming as much as ones who warn against it. And those who say there was no Holocaust along with those whose relatives died in it. Or those who believe slavery is OK as well as those who don't.

It's about promising individual freedom and making choice impossible. No matter what you do, it's the same thing. Go stand in front of a soap counter at a store. Read the labels. Lots of different brands. Freedom of choice. But they're all made of the same stuff, making picking one impossible. You can choose whatever courses you want, as long as they fulfill the requirements. Cars give us freedom to travel. We all get cars, and we're jammed up on big highways breathing our own exhaust fumes.

As citizens of the entertainment state, we see everything and are responsible for nothing. The media bring wars in distant lands into our houses, but we don't feel the burning of napalm; we are not responsible for those who do. That's some other place. But our movies and television programs are here. White suggests analyzing them critically, asking questions about what they are telling us—"reading" them, as he says. But this requires that we do something more than simply consume them and judge them on the basis of whether we "like" them or not. It's not just a matter of opinions.

This is all about a giant entertainment industry that keeps us occupied and amused and arguing about what we like and what we don't while we are not understanding the signals or messages we get or seeing the realities of the political and economic structures that we participate in. So we don't even think about class. We don't talk about the ruling class and the working class. It's impolite. It sounds "socialist." We don't like that. It makes us feel uneasy. Somebody might think that we're ... liberals.

Class is the most important issue for anthropology. We can't understand anything else without understanding class and how it works. No longer is there refuge for people outside a global system of information, culture, commerce, capital, labor, and feeling, all of which mutually affect the others. We'll discuss the global system in the next chapter, but class determines all of those things that make it work.

The richest 5 percent of our country owns 22 percent of the wealth. The richest 20 percent owns 50 percent of the wealth. That trickles down to the poorest 20 percent of all Americans, who own less than 4 percent of the wealth (Yates 2003). Now think about the whole world. A tiny minority of people own most of the wealth, control most of the resources. You could type their names on one piece of paper.

The rest of us? We work for them. You and us and everyone else whose name is not on the list, whether we live in the homeland in Africa or one of the places our ancestors walked, sailed, or flew to in more recent times. Your dad owns his own business? Where does he buy his supplies? Who sets that price? Your mom is a consultant? She provides a service and makes a living, but who makes the profit off her labor? Everyone who's not on that sheet of paper has interests in common. It doesn't matter whether we live in Iraq or Israel or Iceland or Alabama, what gender or color or sexual orientation we are, or how educated we are. We are in the same boat. And it's not the same boat the folks running the show are in.

Some folks were against World War I for just this reason. They said, "Why would a working person from England want to kill a working person in Germany? You folks are not enemies. You have common interests. Your enemies aren't in different countries." Their slogan was "A bayonet is a weapon with a working man at both ends." Think about it. So is a bomb, and so is a missile. The guy dropping a bomb or driving a Hummer through Iraq has more in common with the people he's trying to kill than he has with the people who sent him to Iraq to kill them.

If you've been reading all of the back and forth braying between liberals and conservatives, book after book of "I'm right and you're wrong. Nyah!" this may sound like a political statement. We don't have any interest in the liberal-conservative debate. But we do have an interest in understanding our own conditions and the human condition clearly. And sometimes that requires us to speak bluntly.

When J. P. Morgan said he could hire half of the working class to kill the other half of the working class, he was speaking of guns in the hands of Pinkertons he hired. The contemporary approach, as Barbara Ehrenreich puts it in her book on the middle class, *Fear of Falling,* is for the employing class to hire half of the working class to *manage* the other half of the working class. Anthropologists are part of that structure. We too eagerly join with sociologists to speak of "SES," socioeconomic status, or to assert that in the United States there is no class, only status.

What happened to the working class that was so clearly visible to the Industrial Workers of the World (IWW) that they could unambiguously state in the preamble to their constitution that there are but two classes—the employing class and the working class—and that they have nothing in common? Morgan furnished part of the answer. He and the employing class hired the guns and killed a lot of working people until the others got the message.

Consider the alternatives for class consciousness. One is discussion. And what your mom told you is right: "Sticks and stones may break my bones, but words can never hurt me." Or anybody else. So what you say doesn't matter. But what happens when people do what the IWW thought they should do and organize. What happens when they get angry and get together and figure our where their real enemies are? Sometimes they start shooting. But reasonable people don't do that. Reasonable people know what happens to people who do. So reasonable people sit around and talk, until talking just isn't enough.

When the rage of impotence moves people to arms, they are met with sure and swift and overwhelming violence from any one of a number of U.S. government agencies from Alcohol, Firearms and Tobacco to the Coast Guard to the National Guard or a local Special Weapons and Tactics Team likely trained, if not armed, by the Department of Defense or Homeland Security. It seems almost every agency of government has its own goon squad. For those agencies that do not maintain their own means of violence, there is the all-purpose Federal Bureau of Investigation. The examples are all too frequent in the news from Ruby Ridge to Waco to Wounded Knee to the latest worker gone postal or whacko with a gun, taking as many others as possible with him to the next life. This force and the fear of it keep our "choices" limited.

James Scott (1985), the political scientist, observed that Indonesian peasants are people not fooled by ruling-class mind control, but they also know from hard-won experience that head-on resistance only results in tragedy. It may be that every generation in every land must pay a price in blood to learn that lesson, but what the Indonesian peasants taught the Yale scholar remains universally true.

Sometimes people form new religions and revitalization movements and think they are invulnerable. The safer alternative is to remain within the law and try to organize for common purposes. Some countries such as the Scandinavian ones demand it. But even this element of corporatist states is weakening under the hammer of global economics as manufacturing moves its well-paying jobs to the cheap labor markets of the third world to achieve greater profits for shareholders, save on their tax bill, undercut the tax base, and threaten the social contract that has underwritten class cooperation on mutually agreed terms.

Other lands, such as the United States, pass laws so the employing class can systematically destroy whatever gains the working class may threaten to make through organizating. Companies and the government hire academics to make the sham complete by proclaiming learnedly that there is no ruling class, that the markets control everything. So corporations endow universities and think tanks and buy professors to tell us that there is no class, that money begets money according to natural law and that hard work pays off. We all participate in the delusion, believing that as workers and consumers we have some agency in that market.

In the last chapter, we discussed meritocratic individualism. Katherine Newman (1999) has documented the negative effects of the idea that you get what you deserve and deserve what you get. It works fine as long as you have a job, but when you lose it, it can't be anyone's fault but your own. When you've spent your whole work life preaching this and telling others that you're giving them what they deserve, it must be true for yourself as well.

We have a friend who is an anthropologist. He has a brother-in-law who worked for a big corporation. His job was to go around the country firing people as the corporation moved its manufacturing to other countries. He did this with the certainty that he was good at his work and deserved his good salary. Then, after he had fired everyone, the corporation fired him. He never saw it coming. That's how blind people can be.

The ideology of meritocratic individualism disguises the structure of classes. It says that everything is the fault of or the responsibility of individuals. If you do your part, you will enjoy the rewards. This is a good way to get people, like our friend's brother-in-law, to act against their own interests. And when they get screwed, they blame themselves. That's a pretty neat trick.

On the other hand, Newman argues that working-class people understand that some things are way beyond their control. If they get laid off or fired, they know that it's not their fault. They know that it's because of a corporate restructuring or downsizing or something structural, so they don't take it so personally.

We found Newman's ideas persuasive, so while we were working with unions in Chicago, we decided to see whether we could find any evidence that working-class people think more structurally. We did a survey and asked people what they thought the most important thing for success is. These were union stewards and activists. They were Polish, Hispanic, black, white, men, and women. They said that ability was the most important thing. This is right out of Newman's meritocratic individualism. "The most able people are rewarded."

Next they put hard work. "I worked for everything I have."

Next, they said people's own talent is important.

Everyone agreed that the structural features of race and gender were least important. Hispanics thought race was more important than gender, blacks thought the two were about equal, and whites and Poles thought gender was more important. This suggests that even working-class people buy into the ideology of meritocratic individualism.

Paul looked at a union bargaining unit in Chicago that's made up of lawyers, paralegals, and support staff. He reasoned that lawyers would be more middle class in their outlook, while working-class support staff would be more structural, and paralegals would be somewhere in between. He was dead wrong.

Most support staff and paralegals said that people who get higher salaries deserve them. Most attorneys did not agree. Support staff and paralegals thought hard work was the main reason, and talent and education were less responsible. Luck and networks, they thought to be unimportant. But attorneys thought networks were most important and put work and talent after education. So the attorneys were showing the structural way of thinking, and the paralegals and staff were showing a meritocratic individualist way of thinking.

These were some strange attorneys, though. They worked for a legal aid foundation doing poverty law—helping poor people out with evictions, cases that involved getting their kids back from child welfare, and such matters. Paul's interviews with the lawyers showed that they were very ideologically motivated—they wanted to do good and thought their law practice was a way to do that. They were paid much less than they could get in private practice.

So Paul did the same thing with some private practice attorneys in another large midwestern city. There's a joke about a lawyer and some other folks who are shipwrecked and hanging onto life preservers trying to get to a small island. Sharks are circling them, but they go to the lawyer and nudge him ashore. Some of the others ask the lawyer why the sharks helped him and nobody else. She said, "Professional courtesy." Then there's the one about the woman who was accused of being a bigamist because she said she was married to a lawyer and an honest man. Or the judge who complains that he has to deal with the dregs of society every day—and then has to meet their clients. But we've heard that those lawyer jokes are only true of 98 percent of the legal profession. Anyway, the private practice lawyers put hard work right at the top. They worked hard for everything they have. You bet! Then comes talent. And they're bright, too. Education comes in third; luck, fourth; and last, their networks.

We couldn't find any evidence that working people think more structurally than the people the ruling class hires to manage them. They've taken on the ideology of meritocratic individualism, at least some important aspects of it.

So, if everyone agrees that individual merit gets us where we are, and the lack of it keeps us back, isn't it true? Isn't that what the American dream is built on? Isn't that what our immigrant ancestors believed in and lived out? Not really. How do we know that? Because we can test it and measure it. We can look at the data and see that black folks as a group don't get as far ahead as white ones. We can measure the work women and men do at the same job and identify the one variable that causes one group to get paid an average of $0.33 per dollar less than the other. Yes, there are exceptions, and it is these exceptions—and our media's ability to magnify them—on which the American ideology of meritocratic individualism relies. It's a myth, albeit a very powerful one.

In chapter 9, we explained how Doukas (2003) argues that a great cultural revolution occurred in the United States about the turn of the last century when the trusts reorganized themselves as corporations. They did a lot of the same kinds of ruthless things that they do today, but they didn't have any way to justify their antisocial actions. So they began to peddle the idea that all wealth comes from wealth. Capital makes money, according to natural laws of economics. That's when they bought the professors and endowed the think tanks and invented a whole science of economics. The Nobel Prize economist Joseph Stiglitz (2003) calls this "market fundamentalism," equating it with a religion because facts can't change the minds of people who believe these things. Economist Michael Yates (2003) calls economics a religion rather than a science.

Before the cultural revolution, Doukas suggests, most Americans held to the gospel of work—that labor creates all value—as we discussed earlier in this book. In spite of the national-level cultural revolution, lots of people still hold to the gospel of work, and this may be the reason people identify success with hard work.

We can't sort these things out by talking about them or by making more theories about them. The only way we can sort them out is by doing more ethnography to find out just how people think and why.

If you're not a white male, you're probably wondering where race and gender come into this story. As we said in the earlier chapter on human variation, the concept of race was invented to naturalize and justify using slaves to make fortunes for their owners. But anthropologist Karen Brodkin (1988) shows us that Africans, Europeans, Mexicans, and Asians were each treated as members of inferior races when capital recruited them into the labor force. This making of racial distinctions depended on and still depends on residential and workplace segregation, so people don't mix. This facilitated the degradation of work as what unskilled people do—the mass production work of inferior people. The making of race and the making of class are two views, two sides of the same process. Brodkin says that the manufactured cultural code of the United States takes white people as the real Americans with agency. Male and female nonwhite people are savage "hands" that do the work. They are dangerous aliens inside the country. The white managerial middle class as well as the ruling class depend on the work they do. Want to drive this point home to your pals? Rent or borrow from the library the satirical movie *A Day without a Mexican* (2004).

Social movements make a difference. Some blacks enter the managerial middle class and government. Some women gain high corporate and government positions. Her main point, though, is that concepts of race and gender are based on Julian Steward's cultural core, how people organize to produce things.

No Nasrudin story in this chapter. But there is one about a follower who gave a Sufi master five hundred pieces of gold.

The Sufi said, "Do you have more money than this?"

The follower says he does.

"Do you want more?" asks the Sufi.

"Yes," says the follower.

"Then keep the five hundred pieces of gold because you need it more than I do. I have nothing and don't need anything. You have a lot and want even more."

Discussion Questions

- What is the difference between the working class that you've read about here and middle class as you understand it?
- How does the mainstream notion of the middle class benefit the highest levels of the ruling class? How does it keep working people from changing a system that is inherently unfair to them?
- Find examples of working-class role models in the media—movies, cartoon strips, television shows, and so on. What do they have in common? Was it hard to find them? If so, why?
- Find the record of major contributors in any recent election. If you can't find the exact records, look for media reports about major contributors (including for the presidential inauguration). What difference is there between who gave to the Democrats, Republicans, Greens, and Libertarians? What similarities are there? Why do you think this is so?
- What class do you belong to? Why?
- If you're not already there, do you think that hard work will make you a member of the ruling class?
- Someone once said that there are two ways to gain great wealth: steal it and inherit it. What did this person mean?

Suggested Reading

Brodkin, Karen. *Caring by the Hour: Women, Work and Organizing at Duke Medical Center.* Urbana: University of Illinois Press, 1988.

de Zengotita, Thomas. *Mediated: How the Media Shapes Your World and the Way You Live in It.* New York: Bloomsbury, 2005.

Doukas, Dimitra. *Worked Over: The Corporate Sabotage of an American Community.* Ithaca, NY: Cornell University Press, 2003.

Fink, Deborah. *Cutting into the Meatpacking Line: Workers and Change in the Rural Midwest.* Chapel Hill: University of North Carolina Press, 1998.

Ehrenreich, Barbara. *Bait and Switch: The (Futile) Pursuit of the American Dream.* New York: Metropolitan Books, 2005.

———. *Fear of Falling: The Inner Life of the Middle Class.* New York. Perennial, 1990.

———. *Nickel and Dimed: On (Not) Getting by in America.* New York: Metropolitan Books, 2001.

Newman, Katherine. *No Shame in My Game: The Working Poor in the Inner City.* New York: Knopf, 1999.

Williams, Brett. *Debt for Sale: A Social History of the Credit Trap.* Philadelphia: University of Pennsylvania Press, 2004.

Commercial agriculture is big business, and it uses big vehicles! *Photo by Suzan Erem.*

CHAPTER 14

BACK TO THE LAND

In this chapter, we use a couple of examples to bring together some of the themes we've talked about before. We discussed commercial production and how it's different from household production, how states work, political economy and culture, and how classes work. The most basic thing anyone does besides reproducing people is producing food. That's why the story in our introduction involves so much eating and drinking. Anthropologists figure out where the food in any society comes from and who controls it.

Here we're going to talk about what happens when you try to introduce commercial agriculture into places where people are producing their own food, how the idea of doing that developed in American agriculture colleges, "ag colleges," what the ag colleges are about, how they promote industrial agriculture, where the Farm Bureau came from and how it opposes farmers, and some of the ways the Soviet Union had the same response to democracy as the United States did. So, if it seems a little bit complex, that's because it really is. But it's not so complex that we can't understand it.

The goal of industrial agriculture isn't to produce food; it's to produce money, profit that all commercial enterprises seek to maximize. As we discussed in chapter 7, the goal of household production is to produce what the people of the household need. If they are on the land as farmers or peasants, that usually means that they produce most of their own food. They may produce something else to get some money. Lisu produce opium and get money. The point is that they produce the commodity to get money to buy what they need, rather than to put it back into production as capital.

We have to go back to World War II when the Japanese wanted to deprive the British of the productive capacity of India, a colony that was sending Great Britain war material from the beginning, when the United States was still neutral and not helping Britain with the war at all. The

Japanese invaded Thailand and Burma, built air strips and roads, and started a push toward India.

It was during this time that the British anthropologist Edmond R. Leach (1954) was working with tribal guerillas—freedom fighters or terrorists depending on how you look at it—in Burma. His experiences in the Kachin Hills were the basis of the book we've mentioned before, *Political Systems of Highland Burma*. The British and French both promised their colonies that if they helped with the war, they could have independence after the war.

After the war, the British and French reneged on their promises of independence. That's what got the long war in Vietnam started. Finally, the Vietnamese threw out the French only to have to face the Americans. But they finally threw the United States out as well and got their independence after about thirty years of constant warfare. In India, Gandhi started his nonviolent independence movement, and the British gave Burma independence.

Meanwhile, after World War II, Americans were wondering where global poverty was coming from. Some thought that people in poor countries were just uneducated—if Americans taught them enough of the right things, they'd create a booming economy like the United States had. These analysts hadn't figured out that it's development in some countries that drives the underdevelopment of other countries. One of the problems of taking your own myths to be true is that when you try to fix something, you get it wrong. If you think the drive shaft of your car is cooling it, you're going to put the thermostat in a really stupid place, and it's not going to do you any good.

The folks who had experience educating poor rural people were extension agents at America's ag colleges—like Penn State, Iowa State, Auburn, and the University of Illinois. So the U.S. government got these ag experts involved in creating programs to promote development in the third world.

We've seen that household production is limited—it doesn't grow. We've also seen how capitalist or commercial production does grow. The point was to promote growth so the aggies thought they'd do the same thing they'd been trying to do in the United States. They wanted to convince folks to exchange their household production for commercial production. These American ag experts helped develop markets and credit for farmers.

Suppose you were in Thailand and didn't have enough land to feed your family, but your uncle had more than he needed. It would serve both of you well if you would work some of his land and give him part of the crop in exchange for using it. You got the rice you needed; he got some extra rice. Or maybe a landowner didn't use the rice fields during the time between harvesting one crop and planting a new crop of rice. Maybe that landowner would let you use some land to grow market vegetables that you could sell in the market.

When larger landowners got capital and began to produce market crops, they had no reason to let you use their land for anything. They could produce tomatoes or tobacco to sell. The more land they had, the more crops they could grow and the more money they could make. That was the name of the game. But they needed labor, so they'd hire you and pay you the amount that you needed to get by another day—your daily rice. This was pretty much the minimum definition of necessary value that we discussed in chapter 7.

Now suppose someone gets sick or dies or one of the kids wants to go to school. You need some money, so you sell your small parcel of land to your uncle. His holdings increase and yours decrease. As this process happens, more people have access to no land. As values change from community values or family values to commercial values, wealthy people feel less and less obliged to their communities and make less land available to others.

As more people have no access to land, they are available for wage work, and the more people who are available, the lower the wages. There's less emphasis on food crops, more rural poor people, and less food. That means higher infant mortality rates, greater rates of starvation and disease, and more migration to cities. Because every contribution to the family is important, poor people have more kids, and the process intensifies.

If you've been thinking that all these things are connected into a single system, you were right. Lucien Hanks (1972) describes this process in his book *Rice and Man*. Figure 14-1 (page 208) shows what the process looks like in our systems terms.

There is more capital in play; more people are producing more commercial crops like tomatoes and tobacco. Both of these contribute to increased gross domestic production, a measure of the prosperity of a country. People are selling products to people in other countries, so the balance of trade is better—our country is exporting more than it was and getting more money. So all of the measures that economists look at are improving. Later we're going to show how this approach to development can devastate a country's economy and be damaging to the people who live there, while at the same time making them available to multinational firms as cheap labor.

As the process continues, there are more poor people, disease, and general misery. Fewer people can take care of themselves or their families, but it looks good to economists who never get out of their offices. It's the

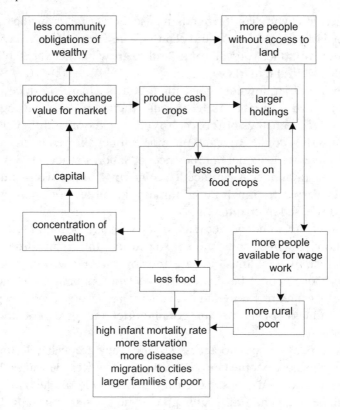

Figure 14-1 How development works.

kind of thing anthropologists see wherever we do fieldwork. From where they stand, it's hard to believe that education could solve the problem.

Why did anybody think such a system would do anyone any good? Because it's what people did in the United States. In 1861, Congress passed the Morill Act to support agricultural colleges with grants of land. The colleges were supposed to help farmers by developing agricultural sciences and teaching farmers better methods. In 1914, Congress passed the Smith-Lever Act to fund systems of agricultural experiment stations and extension agents to get the knowledge to the farmers. Notice, as we discussed in chapter 12, the relationships among law, political economy and culture.

You might know how to grow corn, hay, oats, horses, cattle, and pigs. The question for the agricultural economists was how to organize all of these into one system so that you had enough oats to feed the horses, enough horses to plow and harvest the corn, enough corn to feed the cattle and pigs, enough cattle for the milk you needed to sell for income, and enough pigs for the meat and income you needed. Farm management developed as part of agricultural economics to answer these questions. So, early in the twentieth century there was an institutional system—agricultural colleges and experiment stations—to support detailed studies of farm management.

The goal of the ag colleges was to increase production and productivity—to increase the amount of agricultural products per unit of labor and land—to raise efficiency. Between the end of the Civil War in 1865 and 1890, a farm depression occurred, and farm prices fell steadily. One reason for the fall of prices was overproduction. Farm production increased 53 percent between 1870 and 1880, mostly because people were developing new farms in the Midwest and West. During the same time, the population increased 26 percent. The increased per capita food consumption and exports were not sufficient to absorb the increase in farm production, so prices fell. This began the problem of the farm surplus.

One result was grassroots populism. Populist organizations such as the Grange attempted to regulate the railroads and to establish marketing, processing, manufacturing, and purchasing cooperatives.

Farmers realized that they could not benefit just by increasing efficiency. If they increased production, they were hurting themselves by flooding the market with cheap products and lowering the price. You might produce 100 bushels of corn and get $100. Increased efficiency might get you 150 bushels of corn, but since everyone is doing the same thing, the price falls, and you might get $90 for your whole crop. You still have to pay the same debts plus whatever debts you incurred for the costs of increasing productivity—maybe buying fertilizer or new equipment or pesticides.

Populists had the idea that if enough farmers banded together, they could impact the market by acting as one group. They could hold their corn off the market until they got the price they wanted. They could organize to make their own machines and buy, transport, and distribute other things they needed, such as clothing and farming supplies and tools.

The cooperatives were large groups of households. Each household was operating as a household production unit, but working together, they had the force of a large industrial unit. Other enterprises such as railroads, processing companies, and retailers like Sears, Roebuck and Co. were organized as commercial firms. The initial success of the cooperatives scared the firms. If the cooperatives were successful, the firms would be out of business. This was one of the reasons for the corporate cultural revolution in the United States that we discussed in chapter 10. Here we are going to see how it worked in rural areas.

About 35 percent of the wholesale prices went to farmers, but 65 percent went to railroads, elevators, and banks. The railroads, banks, and

Sears, Roebuck and Company got together and created an organization that was supposed to look like a democratic farmers' organization but would really operate against the interests of farmers. If this sounds like a big conspiracy, it's because it was. They organized the Farm Bureau as a propaganda machine against the cooperative and populist movements.

When the Smith-Lever Act passed, it connected the Farm Bureau to the extension service. The county agents from the extension service had to deal with groups of locally organized farmers to provide them with the new knowledge from the ag colleges to increase efficiency and improve farm profits. The Farm Bureau's role was to organize the local groups of farmers. And it was logical that the county agent would also be the leader of the Farm Bureau.

Farmers started losing their farms. This has been going on for so long that ag economists have names for the process. One is called the "treadmill." You increase productivity, but so does everyone else. The price per unit decreases, and your income remains the same or decreases. You are on a treadmill. More productivity, less income per unit, steady or less total income. This is a self-intensifying loop. As such, it's unsustainable, and you lose your farm.

You get caught on the treadmill, you can't make the payment on the farm, and it gets foreclosed for the debt you owe the bank for the loan that allowed you to increase productivity in the first place—the note to buy the machinery or chemicals you needed. Unless you started out a little bit ahead. Then you buy the farms that other farmers are selling. This is "cannibalism" because some farms grow at the expense of all the others.

The rates of farm ownership decreased as more and more farmers lost their farms to banks. The rates of tenancy increased, and farmers began to worry about becoming a peasant class of tenant farmers working for banks.

Farmers looked down on working people in cities who, they thought, lived the squalid lives of urban workers. There was something degrading about having so many people in one place, something decadent about cities. Farmers didn't live on wages and didn't like the idea of it. They knew that wages made a person subservient to a boss.

But farmers weren't peasants and didn't want to be. Their self-image, with the guidance of the Farm Bureau and the Extension Agency, shifted to being businessmen. The Farm Bureau tried to convince people that farmers, railroads, elevator companies, processors, and suppliers were all alike, that they were all in the same boat, that they were all businesses. Like shrimpers. And as happened to shrimpers, these interests developed cultural codes that hurt farmers.

The ag colleges wanted to figure out how to organize farms, and they also used this business model as a starting point. They assumed that all farming worked just like any other commercial enterprise—like a railroad company. A business is a business, and their job was to translate good business practices to farmers.

The populist movements of the nineteenth century failed. But early in the twentieth century, they rose again for the same reasons. One group was the Farmer's Educational and Cooperative Society of America. This group had learned the lessons of cooperatives and decided to try it again. Antitrust laws had been used against some cooperatives, as happened to the shrimpers' union, but an act of Congress in 1922 exempted cooperatives from antitrust legislation, so that couldn't happen again.

The Farm Bureau was already in place, and the ag colleges were preaching the gospels of the farmer as businessman and increased productivity.

As the population increased before World War I, farm prices recovered, and the farm situation looked pretty good for a while. As the situation improved, the populist movement declined. After the war, prices began to decline because of oversupply. Again populists proposed cooperatives. The ag colleges kept preaching higher productivity rather than organizing farmers for their own interests.

The agricultural economists who were actually keeping records and doing the ethnography of farm management made very detailed descriptions of the farms of that time, just as Chayanov had done in Russia. But they found that the farms they were studying did not fit the models they were supposed to. One of these researchers from Iowa State wrote in the late 1920s that the way they were doing the studies was fictitious because there weren't any profits. But, he said, he had to compute fictitious profits anyway. Over half of the farmers were making "negative profits."

Business can't stay in business if they are in that situation. Farmers could. Farmers could keep going by cutting back their expenses somewhere. There's always somewhere to cut. They could put off repairing the barn so that they wouldn't need to buy the building materials. But after a few years, the barn would be in worse shape and finally beyond all repair. They could cut expenses by not sending the kids to school, not buying new clothing, and growing more of their own food in household gardens.

Another study of the same period showed that if a farm kept milk cows, it did better than farms that did not. A third study showed that farmers could not sell milk for what it cost them to produce it. No business can be better off if it sells commodities for less than they cost to produce. How could that be?

For farmers, it was because the milk money gave the farm some cash income throughout the year. Farmers could use that income for things like sending the kids to school and building materials to repair the barn. What the ag economists actually doing the ethnography found was about the same as Chayanov had found in Russia. They were seeing household economies in action, not businesses.

But none of these findings, based on meticulous empirical research, could break through the assumptions of agricultural economics. Our cultural codes are that strong. They are so strong that sometimes even reality can't break them down.

When we have this kind of situation, when the data cannot affect the assumptions, we have one of two things. It could be a religion, but there aren't any superhuman agents involved here. Or it could be an ideology that is driving a policy. ***Ideology*** is the selective use of ideas from the cultural code to support one group of people. Here, it was a matter of ideology and policy to support businesses.

The ag colleges kept supporting the Farm Bureau and gave their propaganda the badge of scientific respectability. In spite of what they said, they didn't care about farmers at all. Maybe individuals did care, but this is like really nice people getting caught up in racist institutions and inadvertently supporting racism. It's not about the individuals; it's about the power of an organization controlled by a handful of interests driving the resources in the direction of those interests, often under the guise of another name.

In the 1920s and 1930s, more and more farmers were losing their land. If you had milk cows, you could sell the milk and get a little money to keep the family going, even if the banks took all of your farm income from crops and livestock. So the cows and chickens were very important elements of the organization of farms, even if they did not contribute a lot to the total income.

During that time, it turned out that a lot of cows in Iowa were infected with TB, and their milk was spreading the deadly disease. The state said it would test all the cows, kill the infected ones, and reimburse the farmers who lost cattle at the rate of two-thirds the value of the cow. The problem was that it took six to nine months to get reimbursed. If you lost your cows, you had nothing to keep your family going with in the meantime.

In 1929, a group of farmers sued the agriculture department of Iowa, talked to the governor, made a mass appeal to the legislature in Des Moines, and nothing happened. In 1931, when the veterinarians came to Cedar County in eastern Iowa to test the cattle, the farmers intimidated them. The governor called out the National Guard and declared martial law. Today, it's hard to imagine eastern Iowa, home of law-abiding farmers, being under martial law.

The authorities arrested and tried the organizers of the cooperatives of the Farmers Educational and Cooperative Society. The prosecution had to move the trial to another county because they couldn't get a "fair" trial in Cedar County, where everyone was a member of the Farmer's Union. They moved the trial to Scott County, where most people were members of the rival Farm Bureau. The jury that convicted the leaders were all members of the Farm Bureau.

The Farm Bureau was saying cooperative people were Bolsheviks, Communists, and radicals, all bad words at that time. That period was like the later McCarthy witch hunts for Communists. Businesses were trying to discredit any opposition to them and tried to get all of their opponents arrested or deported as communists.

Meanwhile, back in the USSR....

We talked about A. V. Chayanov when we discussed household production. A short review of material from chapter 7 is in order here.

Remember, there are two ways to organize production:

- household production centered on use values;
- commercial production centered on exchange values.

Remember also that there are four preconditions for commercial production:

- everything is a commodity;
- there is labor available to hire for wages, commodity labor;
- it's possible to expand labor time beyond necessary labor;
- there's no interference in the cycle of production where people use money to buy commodities to turn into other commodities to sell for the original amount of money and some more that we call profit—the dynamic of capitalism.

And remember that there can be household production units even in complex capitalist systems.

Capitalist production was developing in Russia, but very slowly. For one thing, there was a lot of interference in the process by the czarist government. In Russia, capitalists faced the same problems others in Europe had faced earlier—lack of free commodity labor, as in the Shan village Paul studied. There was no well-developed working class that would create the revolutionary conditions Marx and Lenin wrote about. There were lots of peasants and rural farmers.

The revolution happened in the name of industrial workers, but most people weren't industrial workers, and the city people who had been active in the revolution didn't know anything about rural people. The same thing happened in China, and in the next chapter we'll show you how that is working out. But back to 1918.

Europe was in the middle of World War I. The new government in the Soviet Union made a separate treaty with the Germans and quit fighting. There was no way the Germans wanted to fight in Russia, and the new government was still trying to get organized. But the British wanted the Germans to have to fight in Russia so that they'd have to throw all of their people, food, and equipment to the east and not against the British, French, and Americans. Besides, they had no use for the Communists.

The British asked the Americans to help them with an expeditionary force to go into Russia from ports on the Arctic Sea and try to get the Germans' attention in the east. They didn't get very far before the war ended on November 11. But they left all of their stuff there for the White Army to use against the Reds. The Europeans and Americans didn't trust Lenin and his Communists. They didn't much trust the czarist White Army, either. But they knew they couldn't lose if the country was torn apart by a civil war.

Americans often wonder why the former USSR would have borne them any malice or would have been paranoid about the United States having atomic weapons. From their point of view, the English and Americans had invaded Russia to help the czarists overthrow the new government. Just for comparison, imagine what would have happened if France and Germany had invaded the United States when Roosevelt instituted the New Deal. Maybe they would leave pretty soon, but not before they armed a force of Republicans who wanted nothing more than to undo the New Deal. Not a pretty picture.

There were other problems in the Soviet Union. One was that a lot of people took the ideas that they heard about during the Soviet revolution seriously. The "soviet" part of "soviet union" means something like a self-governing democratic group, something like a cooperative. So people organized free soviets of people who worked at the same place. They organized their own production and began to exchange their goods with other soviets.

This was a problem because it made fighting the civil war and recovering from World War I difficult. There was no centralized planning to connect the different parts of the economy. Railroad workers and sailors in the Red Navy organized themselves into free soviets. To deal with that, Lenin sent Trotsky to Kronstadt, the headquarters of the navy, to shoot them all. That was the end of the free soviet idea.

But food was getting tight. Peasants were not cooperating with the revolution. City people had to go to the countryside to try to buy food or get it from relatives.

We can understand this from the point of view of household production units. There's a revolution on behalf of urban workers. One of the demands is cheap food. Food prices are low. If prices are low, that's the same as decreasing productivity for farmers. If you are selling crops, money is the thing you are trying to produce. So if you could sell grain for $2 a bushel and now you can get $1, your productivity has been cut in half. With food prices so low, it wasn't worth the effort for peasants to produce any more than they needed for themselves. If you cut productivity in household production units, the production decreases, as we explained in chapter 7. That's what happened, just as Chayanov said. So there's less food available in the system.

There were two ideas about what to do about this problem. Chayanov suggested that differences in levels of production and income were largely due to different needs of different households. Households with more consumers need more income or food, so they produce more. Marxist theory told Lenin and the Marxists that capitalism was an inevitable development in the countryside. (Theory was as much a religion for them as it is for American economists.) So they believed that if one farm produced more, it was more capitalist.

Chayanov argued that the best way to increase production was to let the peasants get something out of it by empowering them to organize cooperatives. Each person would own his own farm. They would control the co-ops for their own advantage and demand and get reasonable prices for their products. Then they would increase production and there would be more food for people in the cities. Everyone would benefit.

The Marxists thought the best thing to do was nothing. Let capitalism develop and encourage it by providing easy credit and agricultural extension, just like the system that the United States exported to poor countries that we discussed at the beginning of this chapter. When capitalists had concentrated all of the means of production into a few hands, the government would take it over and turn it over to collectives to create socialist agriculture.

Lenin died and Stalin came to power, and the food situation got worse. Stalin thought, like the American ag economists, that farming was just like any other industrial process—best done on large farms or factories in the field. The government would own the farms just as it owned factories. There wouldn't be any farmers, just industrial workers producing food.

Stalin knew that if he started this program where peasants were already farming, they would revolt. The last thing he needed was another civil war. So he went to Siberia to develop the new industrial agriculture with modern equipment—tractors, trucks, railroads, harvesters. But he didn't have any farmers to work for him, so he rounded up peasants and forced them to work on the new collective farms.

But Chayanov was still arguing for cooperatives. Stalin called him a counterrevolutionary, arrested him, and had him shot in 1931. The end.

Stalin was just as successful in destroying cooperatives in the Soviet Union as the capitalists he hated were in the United States.

Stalin had one more problem. He couldn't find anybody who knew how to run one of his factories in the field. Who in the whole world had been thinking about these things—concentrating land, efficiency of farming, industrial methods, advanced technology, crop breeding, and how to organize all of these into industrial farming? American agricultural economists.

They had been writing about it for years. But industrial farming hadn't developed in the United States. Family farming was still hanging on. Some of these ag scientists were about to despair because the realities were so different from their neat theories. They didn't want to give up their ideology of serving business, so they concluded that farmers were backward and stupid. Therefore, when Stalin asked whether they'd like a shot at doing what they'd been talking about, they jumped at the chance, and Stalin got his new industrial farm managers from Iowa State University and other ag schools.

These guys wrote home, and *Wallace's Farmer,* a farm magazine, published a lot of the letters. These aggies were eager to be at the front lines of agricultural development, to put their futuristic ideas into practice. They got to Siberia and faced a surly bunch of drafted peasants, whose language they couldn't understand or speak, and an economic and political system they didn't know. Where's the lumber yard? Where does a guy get bailing wire? Where does a farmer get a tractor?

The aggies tried to help Stalin set up his collective farms because Stalin's image was just like their image of what a farm ought to be. And while the reactionary Farm Bureau was branding cooperativists Bolsheviks and putting them in jail in the United States, Stalin was calling folks with the same ideas counterrevolutionaries and killing them. Neither socialism nor capitalism could tolerate the cooperative movement.

Since those days in the 1930s, family farms have just about disappeared from the American scene. American agriculture is now pretty much what those aggies of the 1930s were thinking about—factories in the field. The policy they have been promoting for more than a hundred years has finally been borne out. Now instead of working for farmers, the ag colleges work for corporations to help them develop genetically modified organisms (GMOs) and try to get the idea of industrial control of the planet's food accepted as a scientific inevitability. The aggies work for the industrial swine industry to try to convince rural residents that "pig shit don't stink" and to develop other miracles of industrial agriculture.

Someone quipped that capitalism has achieved for agriculture in the U.S. what Communism never quite did in the Soviet Union—truly centralized industrial agriculture.

Anthropology is comparative, so let's look at a couple of other examples.

First, Guatemala, where Catholic liberation theologists organized cooperatives and unions. In the late 1960s, a big destructive earthquake took place. The government called for foreign aid to help. By the time the government organized, the cooperatives and unions already had the situation under control through their grassroots organizations. That was very worrisome to the government.

Remember chapter 10 about how states work. Now we're going to see an example. If these popular and democratic organizations could deal with the massive devastation of the earthquake, what could they do if they decided they wanted to change the government? The government began a program to discourage such organizations. The major element of this program was to kill the leaders of any organizations so that nobody would want such a job. That was the beginning of the terror and civil war that racked Guatemala for years.

There is one other place where people tried organizations like free soviets. That was in Catalonia during the Spanish Civil War.

The Spanish had set up a republic, a parliamentary democracy. The leader of the army in Morocco, who represented the ruling class, didn't like the idea, so he brought his Moorish league into Spain to overthrow the government. The "loyalists," or people who supported the elected government, fought against this army. Lots of people joined the fight—Communists, Socialists, liberals, capitalists, anarchists. All got together to protect the republic.

This was 1936, just as National Socialism, the Nazis, were getting ugly in Germany. The Nazis helped this general, Franco. The only help the loyalists could get was from the Soviet Union. Since the Russian Communists hated the German fascists, and since the Germans were helping Franco, the Russians helped the Spanish loyalists.

During this time, the anarchists of Catalonia set up free soviets. But the Communists didn't like them any more in Spain than they did in the Soviet Union. So the Communists shot all the anarchists. George Orwell was there. He wrote about it in his book *Homage to Catalonia.*

So the ruling class really does not appreciate it when people of the working class organize democratic groups for their own interests, unions or cooperatives. It doesn't matter whether it's in the capitalist United States or the Communist Soviet Union or Spain or Guatemala. The ruling class has no use for democracy.

One day four kids came up to Nasrudin with a bag of walnuts and asked him to divide the walnuts evenly. He asked them whether they wanted the walnuts divided God's way or the human way.

"God's way," the kids all said.

So Nasrudin opened the bag and gave two handfuls to one kid, one handful to another, two walnuts to the third, and nothing to the last kid.

"What kind of division is this?" the kids asked.

"It's God's way," Nasrudin answered. "God gives some people much, some people little, and some people nothing at all. If you'd asked for the human way, I'd have given you equal amounts."

Discussion Questions

- Compare the treadmill farmers get on with the kind of treadmill that credit card debt can cause. What do they have in common? What is it about agriculture that makes it different?
- Discuss how the Farm Bureau's propaganda to and about farmers is similar or different from the ideology of meritocratic individualism.
- When farmers, shrimpers, and many other kinds of "independent" workers organize collectively, they can be charged under the Sherman Anti-Trust Act. Find out more about the creation of that act and the criminals it targeted. How are they different from the family farmers or fishermen of today?
- What are the social, economic, and cultural ramifications of corporate agriculture? What are the benefits and costs of the vertical integration (where one company might own everything from the pig to the grocery store) of agriculture?
- What do you think Nasrudin meant when he said that giving the kids equal shares of walnuts was the human way of dividing them?

Suggested Reading

Bookchin, Murray. *The Spanish Anarchists: The Heroic Years 1868-1936*. New York: Harper, 1978.

Kern, Robert. *Red Years—Black Years: A Political History of Spanish Anarchism 1911-1937*. Philadelphia: Institute for the Study of Human Issues, 1978.

Mintz, Jerome R. *The Anarchists of Casas Viejas*. Bloomington: University of Indiana Press, 1994.

Orwell, George. *Homage to Catalonia*. New York: Harcourt, 1980. (Free at http://www.george-orwell.org/Homage_to_Catalonia/index.html.)

15

This ship is registered in Greece. The Greek letters tell us the home port is Piraeus, Greece's largest port and the port for Athens. The containers being offloaded are from Hanjin, a South Korean transport company, and Cosco, a huge Chinese shipping conglomerate (not the U.S. warehouse store), plus several other international companies. The port is Charleston, South Carolina. Globalization is here! *Photo by E. Paul Durrenberger.*

CHAPTER 15

GLOBAL PROCESSES, LOCAL SYSTEMS

In the last chapter, we saw how importing commercial agriculture can break up local economic systems and create the preconditions for capitalism that we discussed in chapter 7. Because there are many people with no access to livelihood, they become available as wage workers. The people without access to resources become a critical resource for corporations and an important labor pool for the global economy. In the next chapter, we're going to show how this works out for the individuals who get those jobs.

Let's get one thing out of the way right at the beginning. Some people say, "Isn't it better for poor people in the third world to have a low-paying job in a factory than to have no job at all?" Remember that the answer depends on the question. We think this is the wrong question. We think the question should be "Why do these folks need to look for a job?" Remember that to understand other people, we have to keep open minds and not judge them. But if we take cultural relativism to the extreme, as we discussed before, everything is equal, and we can't make any judgments about ethics, morals, or politics. Yet, as people, we feel that some things are better than others.

We live in state systems that administer societies built on inequality. When we see that the people who work the hardest don't reap the greatest benefits, when we see the inequalities of class and race and gender, we have to make ethical and political judgments.

How can anthropology help with this? First, it can help us to see things as they really are, to see the inequalities and the systems behind them. To do that, though, we have to see past the fog of the spin doctors and mind controllers. Second, it can give us ideas about how things could be different. Think about this: Suppose that every person deserves one share of our planet just by being here. No more, no less. That's one way to make the political and ethical judgments—to favor anything that moves in that direction and oppose anything that does not.

What kind of system has the world become with speed of light communications, computer tracking of people and things, container shipping, and computer-controlled robotics?

Because people can communicate so quickly and accurately, and because of container shipping, corporations can put their factories anywhere local governments will let them. Wal-Mart keeps its shelves full of stuff from China. As we'll show you in the next chapter, anthropologists doing fieldwork all over the world see people going to work in factories where they used to see people working in their fields. You're probably wearing something from one of those factories.

Anthropologists like ethnography. We like to get up close and understand people as individuals. That means that sometimes we get so involved with the trees that we don't see the forest. Sometimes it takes a whole group of anthropologists working in different locations to see the patterns. Richard Apostle and others (1998) got together to see what kinds of patterns they could see in the changing fishing industries they were studying in Atlantic Canada and Scandinavia (and then wrote *Community, State and Market on the North Atlantic Rim: Challenges to Modernity in the Fisheries*).

They wanted to see whether fishers and fish processing plants in all of these places were responding to the global economy in the same way. Though they focus on fisheries, their work can help us understand other aspects of the global economy. They divide the world into three dimensions.

The first is community, where people know each other and they have complex relationships and overlapping identities. So you may be someone's boss and coach the soccer team her daughter plays for. You may both belong to the parent–teacher organization at the school and see each other at band concerts that your kids are in. And you may be neighbors. We can think of a community as overlapping networks of social relationships in which the people treat each other pretty equally.

The second dimension is the state, where relationships are hierarchic, formal, and bureaucratic, as we discussed in chapter 10 on states. Relationships here are one-dimensional and professional and involve authority. Sometimes a city sends cops to a rally to direct traffic and keep an eye on things. A lot of times the cops went to high school with people in the rally or are their relatives. But as long as the cops are there as cops, they *act* like cops. Because the dog catcher is your neighbor doesn't mean she won't catch your dog.

The third dimension is the market, where there is competition, economic efficiency, and rationality. Nobody cares who you are; the only thing they need to know is how much you're willing to pay for what or how much you're willing to take for what. It doesn't matter if someone is a relative or from your town or anything else. It's impersonal. People are there for just one of two things: to buy or to sell. So it's one-dimensional. The relationships are fleeting and impersonal and lack any inherent value—you don't know or care about the other person just because you sold or bought something. Think eBay or Amazon.com.

Community, state, and market. Aztecs had all of these things. But the market was not very important compared with the state. With globalization, the market expands and the state contracts. Some people think that states will become so unimportant that they won't have much role in the future. This is reasonable when you think about economic systems. But it's not so reasonable if you remember that markets can't exist without states to enforce the laws and rules that markets depend on.

If you take out all the links that make a system work, then there's no way you can control it. It would be like driving a car where the accelerator, brake pedal, and gear shift lever didn't connect to anything. When corporations become so big that they straddle many different states, the policy of any one state doesn't make any difference to the whole economic system because the system isn't inside the state, and the connections are somewhere beyond the confines of a single state.

The connections may be inside a corporation that buys ore from one place, ships it to factories in another, and then ships aluminum to other countries where people make it into various products. This is the example that George Beckford (1972) discusses in *Persistent Poverty: Underdevelopment in Plantation Economies of the Third World*. Suppose you had a car that you thought was a regular car. It had always worked before. And then the accelerator goes out, and then the brakes, and then the transmission. If you have any sense, you jumped out of the car when the steering went out. Problem is, people can't jump out of their countries. Just as trying to drive a car like that might make a person crazy, if you thought it ought to actually work, if you didn't know it was all screwed up, so trying to make policy in a country whose economy has been disarticulated makes for crazy politics.

On the other hand, Joseph Stiglitz (2003) points out that markets aren't just there naturally like mountains, the sea, and air. There has to be a state system with policies that actively create and maintain markets. When the Soviet Union collapsed, there weren't any market mechanisms. There, markets didn't just erupt out of nothing to replace the centralized economic system. The "market fundamentalists," as Stiglitz calls economists who think the market is natural, were puzzled when markets didn't automatically come into being to solve all problems. But markets couldn't come out of nothing because there has to be all kinds of law about contracts, real estate, patents, ownership of ideas, ownership of things, and ways to enforce these laws. That requires the machinery of a state. No state, no market. No market-friendly policies, no market. The funny thing is, that in this void, something a lot like Icelandic chieftains moved in—the Russian Mafia—and to the extent it could enforce the rules, it ruled the market that had begun to develop.

If the market expands to connect more and more people, some states may become less influential, but others become more influential. There have to be some states to keep the market going. But relative to states, the market is far bigger than it was for Aztecs.

These fisheries folks also showed that it was the policies of the different states that made the differences in how things worked out in Canada and Scandinavia. There are some surprising results. Norway is a pretty centralized **welfare state** or **corporatist state**, and Canada is a **federal system**, so you might think that things in Canada would be a lot more decentralized than in Norway. But that's not what happens. Canadian fishers aren't organized—they can't get together for anything—so power in the fisheries is centralized in the Ministry of Fisheries. But in Norway, with its mandatory union structure, people have the means to speak for their interests so the power is decentralized.

What both countries share is a welfare program for corporations. Fisheries corporations have sufficient clout that they can get politicians to rescue them when they get into trouble. That's again a matter of policy, politics, and states. There is another area where the market works—finances. People don't just trade things on markets; they also trade money and stocks. These financial markets are very strange because what they trade isn't real—it's a bunch of cultural fictions that exist only because people agree that they exist.

Suppose that we all agree that what's really going on in the world is that the Norse gods are duking it out with the Greek gods. We could bet on outcomes. Thor versus Dionysus. Both of them were heavy drinkers, but we'd bet on Thor. We could have a market in god futures—what we think the gods are doing. As long as everyone agreed on the premise, it would work. That's like money. It's all a fiction. It isn't real. Money is just paper with some fiber in it so it'll survive the washing machine, but hand someone a $100 bill instead of a $1 bill for a tip, and you'll know the difference. That's only because you both agree that the paper, the fiber, and the number of zeros actually mean something.

That's why economists like Stiglitz make a distinction between finance and substantive economies. The substantive economy is the way things get made and circulated—the kind of thing that economic anthropologists usually talk about. Finance is the money-magic part of it, and it may have nothing to do with the substantive part. During the Great Depression of the 1930s, as many as a quarter of Americans were out of work, and everyone was worried. There were no fewer factories. There were no fewer people to buy things. The substantive economy didn't change a bit. But the failure of the money magic was enough to bring down the whole system.

In 1944, the United Nations sponsored an international conference at Breton Woods, New Hampshire. It was toward the end of World War II, and Europe had been pretty well devastated by the fighting. The conference was meant to get the financial side of things started again. The idea was to help even enemies like the Germans and Japanese to try to avoid any more depressions and other conditions that start wars. By then, some economists had figured out that government policies can make a difference in markets.

This group set up the International Bank for Reconstruction and Development, which we now know as the World Bank, to get the development process started. To ensure economic stability, they set up the International Monetary Fund (IMF). A British economist named John Maynard Keynes was there.

Keynes thought that depressions got started when people didn't have enough money to buy things. Without money, they couldn't create demand for the goods that corporations hire workers to make. The solution is to get money into the hands of the people. There are two ways to do this. One is to cut taxes. But it doesn't work to cut taxes for rich people; they already had money. You have to make a big difference in how much money ordinary people have. The second way is to increase government spending. If the government builds roads and airports and schools and parks, it has to hire workers who get wages that they can spend to increase demand.

The IMF's job was to keep an eye on the economies of the world and, when one of them began to slump, help that country create more demand. The IMF would lend the country money so that the country could cut taxes or increase its spending. The idea behind the IMF was that countries would cooperate to solve economic problems in the same way they cooperate in the United Nations to solve political problems. Everyone in the world who pays taxes supports the IMF, but we don't get to vote. The major developed countries have the most power, and the United States has veto power. The creators of the IMF realized that markets don't work very well, and sometimes governments need to do what markets can't.

But then the 1980s brought a big change. That's when Ronald Reagan and Margaret Thatcher were sponsoring the ideology that markets are natural forces, the ideology that justifies corporations, as we saw in chapter 10.

The poor countries of the world were often in such dire straits that they couldn't refuse an IMF loan, no matter how bizarre the terms. We'll see in the next chapter that that can have a very negative impact on the lives of working people just as the Great Depression did in the United States.

At about the same time, there was what Stiglitz calls a purge in the World Bank. Until then, its leaders had been dedicated to eradicating world poverty. In 1981, Reagan put the market fundamentalists in charge. Instead of asking how to help governments solve economic problems, their religion of economics taught them that governments were the problem because they might meddle in the market. They believed, just like a religion, that free markets could solve every problem.

The IMF was supposed to deal with crises, but now the third world was in continuous crisis. Crisis was normal. The World Bank started making what it called "structural adjustment loans" instead of providing money for building projects. But it could only do so if the IMF approved, and the IMF imposed its own conditions.

The IMF was supposed to do the money magic for the whole world and deal with things like a country's rate of inflation, interest rates, balance of payments, and borrowing. The World Bank was supposed to take care of more substantive things like what the government spent money on. Since all of these substantive things could affect the money magic, the IMF thought that everything fell to it. To the market fundamentalists, all countries were the same. The kind of difference we just discussed between Canada and Norway wouldn't even be on their radar.

Both of these Breton Woods institutions are run by the developed countries: the United Kingdom, Italy, France, Canada, Japan, Germany, and the United States. These are known as the G-7. If they add Russia, that makes the G-8.

Stiglitz says, "A half century after its founding, it is clear that the IMF has failed in its mission. It has not done what it was supposed to—provide funds for countries facing an economic downturn, to enable the country to restore itself to close to full employment" (15). And the G-8's religion of market fundamentalism is no better than a G-string at covering up their failures. They've made matters worse. The ideas behind these polices are called the Washington Consensus, which, Stiglitz says, is a consensus of the IMF, the World Bank, and the U.S. Treasury Department about which policies are good policies.

There was a self-intensifying loop in the process of the Depression. Countries closed down on themselves and didn't want to do anything to help other countries. To deal with that problem the Breton Woods conference also suggested a World Trade Organization (WTO) to encourage the free flow of goods and services. It didn't get started for another fifty years, in 1995, and it doesn't make the rules of trade but gives countries a way to negotiate them among themselves.

Stiglitz's big contribution is to point out that all things are not equal. Different countries have different conditions at different times. Sometimes tariffs can be useful. The question is "Useful to whom?" For instance, we discussed the American tariff on sugar that just keeps the price up so that ADM can sell its corn sweeteners. It also helps the Cubans who ran away from Castro and set up new plantations in Florida's Everglades to make money by producing sugar while they destroy the state's environment.

Sometimes it's not good to put a country's money into the international system of money magic, especially if the country doesn't have the institutions to manage it. It can cause the kind of separation from finance and substantive economy that happened in the Great Depression. Stiglitz sums it up this way: "The result for many people has been poverty and for many countries social and political chaos" (18).

Stiglitz says point blank that commercial and financial interests of the wealthiest nations control the Breton Woods institutions for their own interests. (Remember, this guy's an economist. He used to *work* for them.) So corporations like ADM—the guys who make corn sweeteners you see in so many products you eat and drink—are pulling the levers of the world economy. Trade ministers control WTO and speak for their country's trade interests to keep as many subsidies and trade protections as possible to help them. That raises the price of goods to consumers in the country, but that's not the issue. The issue is how to protect those corporations. Nobody asked you whether you were in favor of the sugar tariff.

Finance ministers control the IMF. They are close to financial firms and see the world through the eyes of the money shamans. They impose controls on government spending and cut subsidies in other countries so that prices go up for poor people. They cut health care programs because it's bad for governments to spend money. They tell other countries not to pay for education. And nobody gets to vote on any of this.

Sometimes working people and poor people get pushed to the wall and riot. That's the social chaos part. Or they have nothing to lose and get into an airplane and fly it into the World Trade Center in New York.

Stiglitz sees a parallel between the development of the U.S. economy and the world economy. In the nineteenth century, the United States spread west. The government helped the railroads and telegraph systems with lots of subsidies, and the costs of transportation and communication decreased. Local markets and companies became national. But the government set minimum wages and working conditions and regulated interstate commerce. The government developed and supported the ag colleges and other programs to encourage agriculture that we discussed in chapter 14. The government even gave people land so that a lot of people had a chance to farm.

The difference is that now, when transportation and communication costs are falling and drawing the world closer together, there is no world government to manage things. There's the IMF, the World Bank, the WTO, and neither you nor anyone else gets to vote on who runs them. Democracy?

How could a bunch of highly educated economists with Ph.D.s screw up the world's economy? By looking after the interests of corporations and the ruling class instead of the people of the planet. OK, let's try a little relativism here. Suppose an Inca priest told you that the world would cease functioning if you didn't do what you were told. You'd better believe him because your world would continue functioning and you're not about to test that by questioning the veracity of an Inca priest. The point is that the Inca priest doesn't have to be right any more than these money shamans do. Remember, in hindsight, the Maya kings who kept building temples were wrong.

"But they have to be accountable," you might say.

What happens when the magic doesn't work? One time Paul's neighbor in the Lisu village, Ngwa Pa, the shaman, was possessed by his spirits who told the people of the village that they would see a great thing in the east when the sun came up the next morning. Paul traipsed up to the top of a hill before dawn with a bunch of other villagers to see the wonder that would happen. The sun came up. Everyone went back to work. Nobody knew what went wrong. Sometimes spirits lie. Who knows? Ngwa Pa didn't lose any credibility. When the magic doesn't work, it's someone else's fault.

"But if finance people make mistakes, the market punishes them."

You'd *wish* you were punished like that. We'd all say, "Punish me some more." CEOs from BankAmerica, Citicorp, JPMorgan, Bankers Trust, and the First National Bank of Chicago all made bad loans in Asia. The JPMorgan guy got his remuneration cut by nearly 6 percent, all the way down to $3 million a year. Some guys have to live a *whole year* on that. How do they manage? But it turned out not to be all that bad for the poor guy because of other perks he got that made the total package nearly $9 million. The other guys were punished for their bad behavior with *increases* in remuneration from 8 to 48 percent from around $500,000 a year up to more than $12 million a year. Not bad for a shaman ... who gets it wrong.

How do they get away with it? See if you recognize any of these names:

Heritage Foundation
American Enterprise Institute

Brookings Institution
CATO Institute
Institution for International Economics.

If you listen to NPR or any other news, you'll hear them mentioned for their study or comment about something that's in the news. These are some of the thought controllers we talked about in chapter 10. Their combined budgets were $87.6 million in 1997. The same guys sit on their boards, and the same firms contribute money to them. These are the guys that run the corporations and want you to think that that's the only way to do things.

They want you to be a good consumer and shut up about people who don't have health insurance and work two jobs and are still living under the poverty line. They want you to think that markets make that happen. They want you to be more worried about whether abortions are murder or about your right to have a gun or about terrorists within our borders than you are about what *they* are doing. They try to control the news and spin all the stories their direction. That's a lot of money, a lot of talent, and a lot of contacts that they contribute to making all of us think that what's happening in front of our eyes isn't really happening. They cover up the mistakes. They say that's the way it's supposed to be, the way it has to be. And we're not just talking in the newspapers and on television. A lot of these organizations and corporations have inroads into our public schools. From the time you enter first grade, you're getting lessons about how to follow orders, color within the lines, work hard (on your own) and you'll get ahead and more, as we discussed in the guide to students at the beginning of this book.

Remember that's the same way the corporate cultural revolution that we talked about in chapter 10 came about. It worked then; it's working now. These are institutions that remove the feedback loops between reality and their actions.

Here we have a system that's as dangerous as one that's self-intensifying—one with no feedback loops from reality. It's as if we took that diagram from chapter 5 (shown here as figure 15-1)—and took out the loops to and from "reality." Replace "cultural code" with "genetic code." If we acted that way as a species, we'd be as dead as a bunch of dodos by

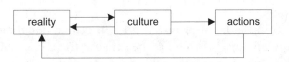

Figure 15-1 Our cultures tell us how to act and our actions change things.

now. Adaptation means there is some kind of feedback between genetic changes and what happens next based on the realities the species has to face. No species can survive the way the IMF does.

Stiglitz is an economist who actually checks in on the substantive world now and then to see what's going on. When he did that, he saw the failures of the religion of market fundamentalism. Anthropologists like ethnography, as we've said a hundred times. If economists more often than not don't see any trees because they can only see forests, sometimes anthropologists miss the forests because we're so busy looking at the trees. But we don't know any anthropologists who can pull down a couple of million bucks a year for being wrong all the time.

Let's take the tree's point of view for a minute. Your government gets caught up in a structural adjustment program and has to pay back loans. Here's how it goes: They have to cut spending so the schools and clinics close and your kids don't have a school to go to. The department of agriculture stops all of its programs to help farmers, so there aren't any subsidies to keep the price of food down. Therefore, you have to pay more for food. You have no access to land, so you can't grow anything, so you look for a job in a factory, and maybe you think that you're lucky to get one that pays enough for you to feed your family one day at a time. You feel so lucky that you don't complain when your supervisor rapes you in the back of the factory during the break. At least you didn't get pregnant; that would get you fired.

The government thinks you're lucky, too. It had to work hard to get that factory here. In fact, it had to tell the corporation that it wouldn't enforce any environmental regulations and would send the police or the army to help the corporation if you and your fellow workers tried to organize a union.

After a while, the water you've been getting from a stream or canal gets a funny color, odor, and taste to it. You first noticed it shortly after the factory started up. One of your kids is wheezing all the time with asthma, but you can't take her to a clinic because there isn't one. That one wheezes herself to death in your arms one night. Your skin is always itchy now. Maybe it has something to do with the water you bathe in. Another kid lives a few years and dies of cancer. Your husband can't find any work, but you keep working. When people talk to you about a union, you remember the people the death squads have killed and ask them to leave you alone.

Your breathing is labored now, and you remember that your mom died coughing up blood with what the nurse at the clinic called TB. One night you start coughing and can't stop. Your husband holds your head in his lap and strokes your hair and the lesions on your skin. You open your eyes for one more look, and the coughing takes over. You can't even tell him that you loved him; you can't thank him for the years with the kids. You feel your lungs turning inside out as you cough your last. You are twenty-eight.

And you've made countless pairs of shoes, stitched countless shirts, woven untold numbers of sweaters, made plastic things you couldn't identify, because that was your job. That was what you could do for your species. You did it the best way you knew how.

Grim? You bet. But, as you're going to see, that's what many anthropologists see around the world. That's globalization from the other end of the telescope. And you don't have to go far to see it. American students might want to spend some time just across their southern border, in Ciudad de Juarez, just across from El Paso, Texas. Americans who live farther north, try South Carolina, Mississippi, Alabama. Europeans can cross the Mediterranean to Libya or any country in Africa or Asia or Latin America.

How does any of this affect us? More than we think.

Wal-Mart is one of the corporations driving this kind of process around the planet, as we saw in chapter 14. It operates lots of factories in China. Communism in the Soviet Union gave us Stalin, and in China it gives us Wal-Mart. Now Wal-Mart's integrating the parts in between the factories in China and the Wal-Mart where you shop. It's getting its own container ships. It's opened its own container facility at the Port of Houston, in Texas. It has its own trucks and drivers. And it is fanatically antiunion.

These are the things that worry Ken Riley, president of Charleston, South Carolina's, longshoremen's union, International Longshoremen's Association Local 1422. Ken and his fellow workers are probably the best-paid black people in South Carolina, the state with the lowest union membership in the country. South Carolina advertises itself that way like the third world country we mentioned earlier ... they aren't going to have any unions. Except maybe the longshoremen, who have been there and been organized longer than the forces that would destroy them. How did that happen? Because they belong to a union that controls the docks all the way up and down the East Coast. Because other organized longshoremen control the docks on the West Coast, in Korea, in Europe. And the moment they relinquish control, it all goes down the drain.

What's the answer? Ken thinks it is for all the transportation workers and unions—the teamsters, the longshoremen, the airline workers, everyone—to get together and make a stronger union.

That's a good plan as long as the government allows it. But in 1999, a Danish shipping company decided to hire a stevedore—the guy who arranges everything at the docks—who was using nonunion labor. The Local 1422 guys picketed whenever one of the Danish ships came to port.

In South Carolina, it's not just a labor thing. It's also a race thing. That same year, the NAACP declared a boycott on South Carolina until the state government agreed to remove the Confederate flag from the state house where it had been flying since ... the Civil War? No—since 1961 when the federal government made its first civil rights laws. It's not about heritage; it's about racism.

Many anthropologists see that racism is a way to keep working-class people of all races so angry at each other that they don't recognize their enemies in the ruling class. So racism is about class.

The longshoremen marched on Columbia, the capital, to reinforce the request to remove the offensive racist symbol from their state house. There were plenty of cops there to be sure that nothing out of the ordinary happened. But on the way, people recognized the marchers as longshoremen and shouted "ILA" as a slogan.

One of the Danish company's ships arrived in Charleston and waited offshore for until the State Ports Authority was sure it could have a lot of cops on call in case they needed them. It had all been planned. More than six hundred of them showed up, and they marched up and down the street just down from the union hall, not far from where the Danish ship was docked. They barricaded streets downtown to keep people away from the docks.

Ken told his guys to let them come. The state was using a lot of money to bring these cops and their helicopters, patrol boats, and dogs to Charleston. Let them come until they use up their budget. The men would not picket. They would not confront. That was a good plan. And it worked until late the night of January 19 when ....

Here you get different stories, and it doesn't really matter who threw the first blow. What matters is that the police had been provoking a confrontation, and they got one. That started a twenty-month-long battle between the longshoremen and the attorney general. The legislature got into the act and passed laws that were even more antiunion. Ken and the longshoremen have learned that if they give an inch, the ruling class will take a mile.

The Charleston longshoremen are as much part of the global system as the third world workers in the factories that make the goods in the containers these men and women load and unload every day.

So how did that system get started? By the 1960s, American corporations were facing competition from other countries. They could either become more efficient, as we explained in chapter 7—that is, use less labor to produce their products—or find some other way to reduce costs. Many focused on a sustained attack on organized labor that started about the same time as the changes in the Breton Woods institutions, with Ronald

Reagan. They thought that if they could bust unions, they would reduce their labor costs and not have to increase productivity.

They also started exporting jobs to third world countries that offered plentiful low-cost female workers for the labor-intensive manufacturing processes, such as making clothes, shoes, toys, and electronics. European countries still had tariffs in place to protect their industries and inexpensive migrant labor coming in from North Africa, Ireland, and the Mediterranean. Japanese corporations revamped their manufacturing methods and increased their productivity with robotics. They also made use of low-cost labor in Taiwan, South Korea, Thailand, and Malaysia.

Some countries tried to become self-sufficient by producing the products that they needed at home and avoiding imports. Remember, this is called **import substitution**, substituting your own products for imports, as we explained in the last chapter. In Latin America, industrial workers organized into unions to demand a share of the fruits of the industrial system. They joined with growing urban middle classes and rural migrants who were coming into cities because they had no other way to make a living. From these coalitions came populist political movements.

These movements and the unions made these countries unattractive to corporations that were looking for places to put factories that would assemble imported components to make a product for export. For instance, Paul once had a Mercury Tracer station wagon. It was identical to a Mazda 323. The parts were made in Japan and sent to Mexico, where workers put them together into Tracers that they sent to North America to be sold. Corporations like GM wanted a labor force that did not expect or could not demand an increasing share of the surplus value they created. Hong Kong, Taiwan, Singapore, and South Korea were authoritarian states that controlled their middle classes and their workers, often with military help from the United States. In helping these governments, the United States was helping corporations get what they needed—cheap and controllable labor.

The policies of different states created different environments. Latin American countries weren't so attractive to corporations; Asian countries were more attractive. The difference was how much they would repress any opposition. We've seen what happens to some small local economies when multinational corporations shift the emphasis from the country itself to the corporation and destroy the links in the economic system.

In chapter 7, we saw the upward spiral of capitalist economic systems. But there's a downside. As they enlarge productive capacity, they produce more than they can sell, so they need to find new markets and reduce costs of production. That leads them to look for new markets and sell their factories where they have to pay higher wages, fire their middle management (like

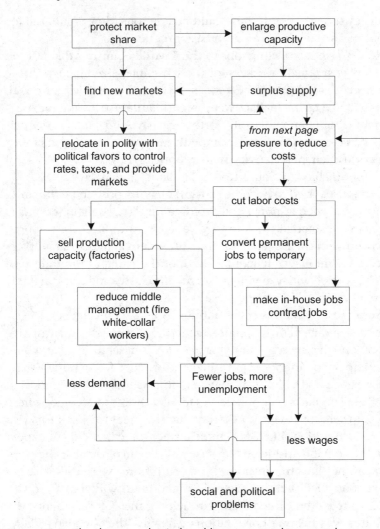

Figure 15-2 The downward spiral and how money shamans take over.

our friend's brother-in-law in the last chapter), try to make full-time jobs into temporary or part-time jobs, and contract out some of the jobs.

The corporations paid lower wages, and that meant less demand. As corporations moved factories and fired white-collar workers, there were fewer jobs and more people looking to social programs for help. With lower wages, the tax money wasn't coming in to support the social programs, and all of this can result in social and political problems.

We can illustrate these relationships with one of our systems diagrams, the mother of all diagrams (figure 15-2). So get ready to work through this one. We'll walk you through it.

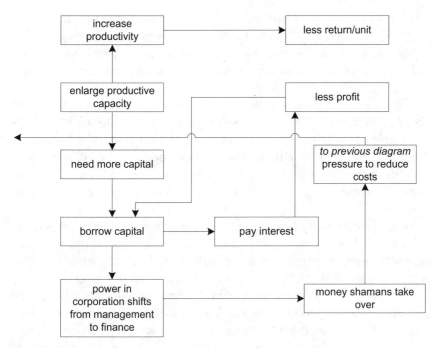

Figure 15-2 Continued.

There's one big self-intensifying loop in this diagram. From "surplus supply" to "pressure to reduce costs" to "cut labor costs" to the four boxes that are ways of cutting labor costs, from selling factories to firing middle management to making permanent jobs temporary and part-time to contracting jobs out—all of these mean fewer jobs, which is another way of saying more unemployment. That means less wages enter the economic system, so people have less money to spend, so there's less demand for goods, and that means that there's more stuff to sell than there are people with money to buy it.

Every loop through that cycle makes the problem of surplus supply greater, which leads to looking for new markets and relocating to different countries with policies that don't make corporations control pollution, that don't make them pay taxes, and that provide markets for their stuff.

At the same time, fewer people are getting wages, and fewer wages in the economy means more people will need public health care, more people will be more annoyed because they can't support their families, and social and political problems will emerge. That is, people will do things that the ruling class sees as "problems." One of those things is to vote, if there's a democracy, for populist candidates, as we discussed earlier.

The pressure to reduce costs also ties into a series of other variables that the second diagram shows. As there is increased productivity, there is less profit per unit of stuff and, finally, less profit overall. That means corporations borrow capital and have to pay interest, and paying interest means less profit. This is a self-intensifying loop, so the process gets faster and faster over time. And less profit means there's pressure to reduce costs. That's where we came in.

There's another process at work as well, what we might call the "politics of production." The state doesn't have anything to do with it, but it's a reorganization of corporations away from the business of producing things to producing wealth. As corporations borrow capital, the power in them shifts from management to finance people. And that means the money shamans take over. And that applies even more pressure to reduce costs.

An alternative to dealing with the causes of the social problems these processes bring is to deal with consequences by closing the lid down tight with repressive police power like the PATRIOT Act authorizes. Who benefits from the fear of terrorism and the subsequent repression?

The speed–of-light communication systems allow for global financial markets. As larger productivity capacity makes for greater productivity, there is less surplus value per unit produced, which means less profit. That situation increases the pressure to reduce costs we just talked about, and it leads corporations to borrow capital or get it on the stock market. But enlarging productivity means that corporations need more capital. So the reduction of profit per unit and the greater productive capacity lead corporations to the stock market or to markets to borrow money. That means they have to pay interest, and that reduces profits and makes for greater pressure to reduce costs. When finance becomes more important than production, the magic of money is more important than the realities of production. With their talk of realism and bottom lines, the money shamans take over corporations.

As corporations spread their manufacturing around the planet, they isolate the process from any local or regional fluctuations; they remove themselves from any local systems and become their own system—just as Wal-Mart is doing. If there is a revolution in Burma, for instance, the corporation can move its factory to Sri Lanka or Israel or Mexico.

Now the corporate economic systems straddle a number of different places and states and are part of none. All the links are inside the corporation. The maquiladora factories of Mexico were isolated from the local economies. They used the labor, paid the wages, and there were no other connections.

We've also seen that interest rates, inflation, government borrowing, balances of trade, and prices of goods are all related. Governments can try to control these variables by policies and institutional arrangements to control interest rates, expenditures for social programs, and taxes. But at the same time, states lose control of their own territorially based economic systems as the links of the systems are all inside corporations or "trade agreements" and not in states or other polities.

Add to this that the IMF controls the conditions for loans, and many governments have very little influence on what happens in their own countries. Those states that can impose conditions on other states gain in power.

Some of the consequences of these processes are that some governments become irrelevant to their economic systems. That makes their political processes irrelevant—it doesn't matter how the leaders are selected because they can't do anything. The local economic systems everywhere are unlinked, disarticulated. As that happens more and more, people have to look for jobs for their subsistence, and it becomes less and less possible to make a living in a household economy. As poor people flood into cities from the country, there is more unemployment and a widening gap between the rich and the poor, a gap we see in the United States when we think of the difference between CEOs and burger flippers.

Some countries, like the Scandinavian ones, have an idea that the government is supposed to help people. This idea that governments are to help people is called a **social contract**. Think of Social Security in the United States. If you work, you pay into it. It's not a pot of money that the government invests. What you pay is used to pay people who can't make a living because they're retired or injured or for some other reason. You pay your part to support those people, and you should be able to bet on everyone else paying their part to support you if you need it. That's called a *social contract.* You do your part, and everyone else does their part, and the government sets up the system and makes sure it runs fairly. This is the redistribution we discussed in chapter 7.

As we write this in the fifth year of the twenty-first century, Americans are talking seriously about changing that system, about doing away with the social contract. Instead of each person who works paying some of the way for those who can't, the idea is that every person should set aside some money to put on the stock market. That's real money magic. That's betting your future with money magic. Nobody benefits, except the companies that buy and sell stocks—and they are the ones that are big supporters of this move and the president who espouses it. Once again we see the state serving the interests of the ruling class.

When states stop funding schools and health care systems because the IMF demands structural adjustments, they are breaking the social contract

they have with their people. People respond with populist political movements, as we discussed in chapter 14; sometimes with revolutions. One
response is localism and identity movements—people no longer take their
identity from their country but from a smaller place, and they participate
in identity politics. We get white separatist movements and Confederate flag movements. There's even a group called Christian Exodus that's
urging its followers to move to South Carolina because it's so backward
and take over the politics of the state, drop out of the United States, and
invite everyone who doesn't agree with them or who is a different color
to leave the state.

The corporations move to places with fewer rules, places where they
can externalize more of their production costs. The local environments
deteriorate.

Finally, money magic is no longer even connected with production
processes. People can talk about the bottom line of a company that doesn't
even produce anything. Finance is no longer linked to the substantive
economy and becomes its own sphere of magic. That makes for strange
and unpredictable movements in global finance markets.

Two economic anthropologists, Monica Lindh de Montoya (2002) and
Miguel Montoya (2002), compared Sweden and Venezuela. Sweden's wealth
is from manufacturing; Venezuela's is from oil. The Swedish government
gets its revenues from taxes; Venezuela gets it from the world oil market.

If a corporation moves a factory from Sweden to the third world for
cheap labor, it hurts the chances of Swedish workers to get jobs and hurts
the Swedish economy. That means less tax income for the state. But what
threatens Venezuela is dips in the world price of oil. Sweden maintains
its social services and the social contract, but Venezuela has had to get
loans and become a victim of the IMF.

There's no upheaval in Sweden. But Venezuelans elected a populist
president, Hugo Chavez. In Sweden, people can save some money and
use it to invest in stocks. In Venezuela, people can't get ahead enough to
think of buying stock. In Sweden, corporations have to let people know
everything they're doing. It's called transparency. People have to be able
to see what you're doing. In Venezuela, there are no such laws. Half the
people in Sweden invest, but only 5 percent of Venezuelans do.

When Volvo threatened to move from Sweden, the stockholders got
together to stop them. In Venezuela, that wouldn't have been possible.
In Sweden, people think about the social contract, and the country has a
tradition of investing only in companies that treat their workers and the
environment well. Nothing like that exists in Venezuela.

The market has spread all over the planet, and some states have become
less important, while others have become more important. The spread of

the market is not inevitable, natural, or an autonomous process. It's a consequence of state policies. But all states are not equal. The only ones that count are the G-8, and the most powerful of those is the United States.

That's a reason for Americans to feel proud, right? Could be, if Americans used that power to do what we discussed at the beginning of this chapter—to provide one share of this planet for every person on it. To the extent that their policies do not do that, Americans must be ashamed, not proud.

The states that establish the rules of globalization serve the interests of corporations. In serving the interests of corporations, these states are unable to serve the interests of their citizens by protecting their environments or ensuring their economic welfare. They break the social contract. In democratic states, those in which citizens elect governments, this causes tensions. There is a tension between the interests of corporations and the interests of the people. That's what we see playing out in the process of globalization as numbers of people gather from around the world to protest wherever international bodies meet to discuss policies of world trade. If we want to understand these movement, and their manifestations from protest to suicide attacks, we must understand the systems that give rise to them.

Nasrudin would go to the market and buy ten eggs for one coin each and then sell ten eggs for the same amount he paid for each single egg. People said, "What kind of trading is this?"

Nasrudin said, "Look at the other traders. And look at me. I don't cheat anyone, and I am surrounded by customers who like me. What could be more satisfying than that?"

Discussion Questions

- Exporting industrial production—what happens when firms have factories all over the globe making different components of products they sell? What are the political and economic causes and consequences? What are the relevant systems?
- Exporting industrial agriculture—what happens to rural economies and communities when industrial production replaces household production?
- Check the zoning ordinances in your hometown, or a nearby city, on the Web. Do those rules apply to all companies and corporations? What's a variance? Who gets them?
- Some laws are local, some state, and some federal. What kind of law do we have for international corporations? What happens if there aren't any?

- Do you know anyone who works for Wal-Mart, McDonald's, Burger King, or Subway? If you do, talk to them. Ask about their wages, benefits, and working conditions. Tell your classmates how it feels to work there. Can you think of any reasons a person might say it was a good job?

Suggested Reading

Beckford, George L. *Persistent Poverty: Underdevelopment in Plantation Economies of the Third World.* New York: Oxford University Press, 1972. (Reissued Kingston: University of West Indies Press, 2000.)

Greider, William. *One World Ready or Not: The Manic Logic of Global Capitalism.* New York: Simon and Schuster, 1998.

Lewellen, Ted. *The Anthropology of Globalization: Cultural Anthropology Enters the 21st Century.* Westport, CT: Bergin and Garvey, 2002.

16

Who decides how much the shrimp boats harvest? *Photo by E. Paul Durrenberger.*

CHAPTER 16

CONNECTING THE PEOPLE TO THE SYSTEM

Did you ever wonder who made your T-shirts, blue jeans, shoes, cars, and other commodities that keep the American and other consumer economies going? When we talked about low-wage factory work fueling the global system, it was just an abstraction. When we talked about young women doing most of the work, it was another abstraction. But anthropologists like to know those people personally.

In the last chapter, you saw how the global system operates, but you didn't see any people in those systems. It's all just arrows and boxes. Ethnography—the details of closely daily observed daily lives—is one leg of the stool that also depends for its balance on comparison and holism. We try to understand whole systems of relationships and then to place them in comparative perspective to draw inferences about the human condition.

But what happens when the stories are not located in any particular place? What do we do when we realize that the causal factors are located at great distance from the places where we do ethnography? What do we do when we find out that no matter how detailed our observations of daily life, no matter how moving our accounts or accurate our methodologies, all of our work is missing the major causes, and we are just describing consequences?

The system, the relations, the holism, the dynamics of the realities escape our worm's-eye view of ethnography. So what was once our great strength—our ability to describe and understand daily life as people live it—becomes one of our great weaknesses as we attempt to understand the reasons, the forces, the determinants of daily life anywhere on the planet. We move with the people. This is and has been our great contribution. We check the assumptions of the great thinkers as we see people living their lives.

Ride with a former International Brotherhood of Electrical Workers union rep as he drives through Chicago pointing out abandoned factory buildings saying, "This plant used to be ours. Gone to Mexico. And this one." Go with Paul to the docks of Biloxi, before Hurricane Katrina destroyed the town, just before the gambling boats arrived, in the late 1980s to hear the shrimpers talking about the threat of imports, the threat of foreign pond-raised shrimp, the problem of too many boats chasing too few shrimp, as they said.

If he just looked at the statistics and worked on the assumptions of economics, Paul would see a tragedy of the commons. That's what economists call it when everyone has free access to a resource like a common pasture. Everyone puts as many sheep or cows on the common ground as they can because they have nothing to lose, and if they don't, someone else will. So pretty soon the commons is overgrazed and useless to anyone. This is usually a story that economists tell to persuade people that everything should be private property. In reality, people aren't that stupid, as lots of ethnography shows.

But Paul found that the shrimpers themselves didn't make any of the important decisions. To focus on the shrimpers left out the processors who made the important decisions. Economists thought it was shrimpers deciding this or that, but it wasn't. As long as Paul focused on the docks or the boats or even the fishing industry, he could only have vague intuitions about the nature of those systems and how they were affecting the shrimpers he was trying to understand.

A couple of sociologists, Bonanno and Constance (1996), chronicled the rise and fall of tuna canneries in California. The joining of nylon nets with power blocks in 1957 revolutionized the tuna fishing industry. American tuna operations expanded their operations from Mexico to Chile. Postwar reconstruction legislation gave the Japanese a distant-water fishing fleet to supply American canneries on American Samoa. As labor costs escalated in the 1970s, the Japanese made use of lower-cost labor and capital from Taiwan, Korea, and Malaysia. Meanwhile the fleets of Taiwan and Korea expanded and offered competition.

In some areas, porpoises swim with tuna, so purse seiners set their nets on schools of porpoises to catch the tuna. The response to the killing of porpoises led to the passage of the Marine Mammal Protection Act of 1972, which set a quota on tuna to control porpoise killing.

Fishers invested in larger boats to maximize their share of the quota before it was filled, so tuna boats grew larger. The American fleet was excluded from its usual tuna grounds in the 1970s when many nations adopted the increasingly common two-hundred-mile exclusive economic zones. At the same time, Latin American countries developed national tuna fisheries, which increased competition for tuna and markets. American fishers began to exploit the western Pacific until the newly emerging nations claimed their exclusive two-hundred-mile economic zones.

During the same decade, processors purchased purse seining boats to integrate vertically to ensure constant supply for their canneries in California and to meet the growing U.S. demand. In the 1980s, the world tuna fleet caught more tuna than the market could absorb, beef and poultry prices were low, and there was an economic recession. In the United States, a major market for world tuna, sales declined.

Costs of fuel, labor, and finance increased, and many U.S. tuna producers left the market. Because the U.S. dollar was strong relative to other currencies, producers of other lands were better able to withstand the cost–price squeeze than U.S. producers. This led to a redistribution of tuna fishing and started the restructuring of the world industry. All but one continental U.S. tuna cannery closed. The same ten multinational corporations catch, process, and trade tuna. As interest rates and the carrying costs of boats increased, vertically integrated corporations sold their tuna boats to shift the risk to operators, imported foreign-caught or processed tuna on the world spot market, and expanded into shipping to supply their plants.

Causes of these shifts include the exclusive economic zones, fluctuations of exchange rates, the world recession, corporate response of seeking lower wages and production costs, policies to attract industry, international financial moves, tax policies, interest rates, and new processing and shipping technologies.

Anthropologists can't see any of these processes with ethnography. If we stay on the docks of Biloxi with Paul, we couldn't see any of the factors that determine the lives of the people who live there.

When Paul's students read Bonnano and Constance's book, they complained that they read through the first half of the book before they ever got to any ethnography, and even then it was pretty thin. It was all theory and tables and accounting stuff. How was that anthropology?

Just before that they had read Mary Beth Mills 1999 ethnography of Thai factory women. Mills discussed the consolidation of the Thai state and its incorporation of the Lao people in the Northeast, but she didn't explain where the factories came from or why they are in Thailand or how they affected the Thai economy. In her ethnography, students saw the workers, but not the system that puts a factory there in the first place. One place those factories came from is the restructuring of the tuna industry.

The Thai Board of Trade favors export-oriented firms. That makes Thailand a favorable locale for tuna canning factories. The fourth largest company in Australia has seven tuna-processing plants in Thailand.

A subsidiary in San Diego purchases frozen tuna on the world market to import to the Thai factories. The same subsidiary distributes Thai tuna products in the United States.

Most of the labor cost of processing tuna is from slicing off the meat. Processors therefore remove the loins where labor is cheap, freeze the loins, and ship them to plants in U.S. territory, such as American Samoa or Puerto Rico, where they can be canned and sold as a product of the United States. U.S. processors have met foreign competition by relying on the world market for tuna loins. In 1990, twenty-two tuna canneries were operating in Thailand.

By 1987, 35 percent of American tuna was imported from Thailand, forcing U.S. processors to move offshore and close their mainland canneries because of high operating costs. They couldn't withstand the foreign competition as the amount of imported tuna tripled, and U.S. companies began to put their labels on imported canned products.

Where is the ethnography? We can't see these processes ethnographically. If we follow the daily lives of factory workers as Mills did or of fishers as Paul did, we lose sight of the causal variables, the factors that determine the conditions of their lives. We study dependent variables and ignore independent variables.

But to concentrate on those systems takes us far away from the docks and the boats, the coffeehouses and bars where we feel more comfortable hanging out with shrimpers and workers. It takes us to corporate reports and archives, to tables of numbers and abstractions that we can't see. It takes us to those nowhere lands where there are no people, the systems that somehow exist in another dimension created by the cultural imagination, places like corporations and nations and agencies. When we find people to talk to, they will be wearing stockings, neckties, jackets. Many anthropologists, accustomed to moving with working people, farmers, and peasants will feel uneasy moving with these "suits."

So we keep doing ethnography. We keep on checking our ideas with what we can observe in everyday life. That's what Josiah McC. Heyman (1991) did in his study of the U.S.–Mexico border region. His meticulously detailed history of the region is based on understanding the dynamics of households while they tried to make their livings under the changing conditions of the border as mines came and went and as people were moved around according to the needs of capital for labor. Here we will just tell part of the complex story that he tells in his book, *Life and Labor on the Border.*

In 1965, Mexico established the legal framework for large export factories or maquiladoras with its Border Industrialization Program. This was like the Thai or, as we'll see later, the Chinese government enticing industry. The program established a zone with special privileges for foreign companies. They wouldn't have to pay tariffs on imports, many of them paid no taxes, and foreigners could own land in the zone. Heyman lived in Agua Prieta, just across the border from Douglas, Arizona. The first factory came there in 1967; by 1986, there were twenty-six of them. Most of the workers in the factories, as in China, Thailand, and Indonesia, are young women. They can provide their families with a regular paycheck.

Young men seek to establish broad networks of relationships that will guarantee them a choice of various alternatives in the future. The short-term cost of this flexible income strategy is that they may be out of work at any given time; the benefit is greater opportunities in the long run. The women deal with this unpredictability by being steadily employed in the factories, even if they don't pay very good wages. The young women coordinate their work with the older women of the households, who do most of the domestic work. In the early 1970s, the workers spent much of their income, about 40 percent of it, in Arizona, but this depended on a stable exchange rate between pesos and dollars.

Then, in 1982, Mexico suffered an economic crisis brought on by many of the forces we discussed in the last chapter. By 1987, the peso was worth one-hundredth of its 1982 value in dollars. What would happen to your budget if all of a sudden a dollar was worth a penny? That's what happened to the folks in Mexico who were buying things in the United States.

Mexico has a huge foreign debt and cannot repay the principal. It struggles just to pay interest. That means it has to increase exports so that they are more than imports—that is, improve their balance of payments to raise money to pay interest. The border factories contribute to increasing the exports to improve the balance of payments, so they're important to the money shamans of Mexico. There are plenty of other places with cheap labor competing for factories. The Mexican government had to reduce the real wages of workers to compete with the Caribbean and East Asia in a race to the bottom.

By one calculation, in 1986, the real wages of Mexican workers was just over half, 60 percent, of what it was in 1982; by another, it was just under a half, at 45 percent. That's drastic either way you figure it. The 1982 minimum wage was $74.64 per week. In 1986, it was $23 per week. That's less than $5 per day. To boost exports, factory sound trucks drove through neighborhoods advertising for workers. Because people were worse off, they worked more to try to keep even as we would understand from the analysis of household economies in chapter 6. Households started sending younger children to work in the factories.

Take a moment and refer back to the last chapter to see what's going on here. This is international capital creating conditions in Mexico to coerce

them into supplying cheap labor via crippling loans on which Mexico has
to pay interest. This is a way to recruit labor into the factories just like
the enclosures in England were. It's another way to deprive people of
livelihood and give them no alternative but factory work.

The minimum wage is so low and household needs are so great that
factory managers can manipulate and control their young women workers
by even small bonuses, awards for overtime, and other privileges.

The official or corporatist unions in Mexico are part of the government. They don't have much to do with the workers. Since low wages
are part of the government's policy, the official unions don't challenge it.
The devaluation of the peso destroyed the cross-border way of life. The
policy of strong exports and low wages meant lives of factory drudgery
for many, and such things as building or owning a house and education
for kids are not possible to attain.

So, in Heyman's ethnography we see the direct consequences of money
magic and the global system for the everyday lives of working people. And
it hasn't been good. So if jobs are leaving the United States to go to Mexico
and it's not doing the Mexicans any good, who is benefiting? Capital.

But that's not the end of the story. These factories are owned by companies from all over the world: Malaysia, Philippines, China, Mexico, the
United States, Spain, Japan, Taiwan, and Korea. In 1998, Mexico hiked
the minimum wage 14 percent, but the price of goods had gone up 18.6
percent. Workers were still losing out. In 1987, it took eight hours and
forty-seven minutes of wage labor at minimum wage to earn enough to
buy the $54 basic subsistence "basket" of goods for two people for a week.
In 1998, it took thirty-four hours. That's just for a couple, not for any kids
or old people. In 1998, the Mexican government removed its subsidy for
tortillas so that their price doubled.

Back to money magic. Between 1998 and 2002, dollars went down
relative to pesos. That means that pesos gained some value relative to
dollars. More dollars per peso. But the dollar strengthened relative to the
money of the Philippines, Sri Lanka, Singapore, Malaysia, and Thailand.
That meant that the same dollar could buy more in those lands at the same
time it bought less in Mexico. So the dollars capital paid for labor in Mexico
went up in Mexico and down in Asia. Since 2002, the dollar has increased
again against pesos. That lowered the cost of business in Mexico. This is
the kind of thing international financiers keep an eye on.

In 1994, the North American Free Trade Agreement (NAFTA) set up new
rules for clothing and textiles. The special breaks in tariffs that Mexico
got under NAFTA let it replace China as the largest supplier of cloth and
clothing to the United States. But then in 2000, the United States gave
the same breaks to the Caribbean, Central America, and China. In 2001,

when China joined the World Trade Organization, the United States gave China other breaks, and China and the Caribbean became the leading suppliers of clothing and cloth to the United States. The question is whether Mexico can drive down living standards and wages even more to keep up its exports to pay the interest on its debts. Each move in this international game of finance and manufacturing, each change of rules and regulations, means a worse life for workers all over the world.

Many of these plants use toxic chemicals, including heavy metals, solvents, and acids. There are no adequate systems of water treatment to control environmental pollution. Letting you work in a poisonous factory that's polluting your air and water so that you can get by until the next day is no favor. Most maquiladora workers are women between sixteen and twenty-eight. It is not only their health at stake but that of their kids as well.

This system plays out in different ways in different countries. Sometimes the women work in factories and bring a paycheck home to help out, as in Mexico and Indonesia. Other times they leave home and move to where the factories are. There, like the earliest industrial workers in the United States in the age of water power, they live in dormitories or crowded urban rooms, as in China and Thailand.

Here's the important lesson. It's one that economists don't understand. The lesson is this: The working people of the world don't have any important decisions to make in this system. Nothing they can do or say or decide or think has anything to do with how it operates. How does a decision to buy one less tortilla because the price doubled affect the laws of NAFTA or the interest that Mexico owes or the fact that their government feels they actually have to pay the interest on such monstrous loans? As long as it's business as usual, working people cannot do anything. To exercise any agency, people must be able to imagine different systems. Then they join the Zapatistas. But that's a different part of Mexico, way south in Chiapas.

When the international banking community demanded a restructuring of the Mexican economy to better pay interest on the loans, the government cut off subsidies to peasants for fertilizers and chemicals and removed price supports for crops. The government wanted to obliterate traditional peasants and replace them with industrial agriculture, as we discussed earlier in Russia and the United States. They wanted them to produce export crops and improve the balance of payments. They wanted to see the communal lands of peasant communities privately owned. These changes went through in 1992.

On January 1, 1994, the first day of NAFTA, the Zapatista Army of National Liberation seized towns in eastern and central Chiapas and proclaimed a revolution. Today the revolution continues. Chiapas is full of anthropologists who know the people and the area up close and personal. They've done and are doing the ethnography. We can't tell the story here, but you can read it in the books by June Nash (2001) and George Collier and Elizabeth Lowery Quaratiello (1994). So extreme conditions make for extreme responses. But there is some sense of agency.

Mills describes how schools and government programs impose nationalism, Thai ethnic identity, and language in the Lao areas of northeastern Thailand. New roads allowed rural people to develop new economic relations with distant markets and moved peasants toward producing cash crops for commodities, as we discussed in chapter 14. Young women from these peasant households do not go to Bangkok and work in factories because they need to support their families. They do it in response to images of modernity from Thai elites in mass media, bureaucracies, and schools. The wages the young women send home do make contributions to poor households, but they're most important to prosperous households that have enough land to make good livings. Here's why: The young women yearn for the modern consuming lifestyle and adventure in the big city, but they have to balance that against their sense of duty. Working in Bangkok goes against the ideal of feminine restraint and virginal purity, but the contributions to the households show they are dutiful daughters supporting their families at home so that they can pay the expenses of farming, educating younger siblings, building new houses, and making donations to the Buddhist temples. These show their morality, while televisions and refrigerators they buy for their parents show their modernity.

But low-wage workers in Bangkok can't live the high life of urban adventure or consumption. The girls use most of their wages for food and crowded living quarters. They have running water, electricity, markets, and some entertainment, but they have to put up with pollution, noise, congestion, crowding, isolation, insecurity, and unhealthy and oppressive working conditions. Managers try to use traditional patron–client roles to control women, but the women don't accept it. However, any slight protest they may make is quickly disciplined. The Thai government has a history of violence against any demonstrations or labor organizing.

It's hard enough for single women, but if they're married and have kids, they have that many more mouths to feed. They get out of their houses and away from their parents, but they don't have any relatives to help them when they need it. If women manage to get a little education, their opportunities in the rural villages are limited. About the only possibility is to go home, get married, raise kids, and become an agricultural worker. Whether they stay in the city or return to the village, these women accommodate rather than challenge economic and political structures. Images of modernity emphasize the goals of individual fulfillment and self-expression and shift the women's attention away from their oppressive conditions that limit their opportunities to actually be the modern people they imagine they might be. The villages raise the kids, provide the factory labor when they grow up, and offer the place to return home to when they're used up by the time they're thirty. In this way the villages subsidize the low wages the firms pay their workers.

Similar things are going on in Indonesia, where Diane Wolf (1992) learned about households whose daughters work in factories. While some anthropologists talk about "household strategies" or plans, in fact, people in poor Indonesian households make decisions experimentally as they go along. They do not have strategies. They don't enjoy the luxury of being able to plan into the future. There may be household coping mechanisms or household practices, but no strategies or planning.

Unlike in Thailand, in Indonesia there is a relationship between the resources available to households and the likelihood that their daughters will work in factories. However, Wolf shows that while households of factory workers are poor in land, women from the poorest families with a high number and ratio of dependents do not work in factories because their presence is needed for the daily work of maintaining the household or to take care of their own children. Corporations have "conveniently" located their factories in rural areas.

The Indonesian factory workers continue to live in their own households with their fathers and mothers and siblings. They don't have to move to the big city and live in cramped rooms like the Thai factory workers. They don't escape the control of their parents, but since they make major contributions to their households, their position in the household changes, and they have a lot more influence than they would if they didn't work.

An anthropologist from Hong Kong, Pun Ngai (2005), used the connections of her family network to help her find a place for seven months at the end of 1995 to the middle of 1996 in a factory that made navigational components for German cars. Hong Kong people owned the electronics factory that was located in an industrial village of the Shenzhen special economic zone in Guangdong Province.

Young rural Chinese women are leaving their villages to work in special industrial zones where the Communist government has allowed and even encouraged international capitalists to build factories to feed the insatiable markets for products. The young Chinese women are caught up in three different systems that sometimes work together and sometimes work against each other:

- the socialist state, with strict restrictions on where people can live;
- global capitalist production with its continual need for disciplined labor and ever increasing consumption;
- the patriarchal Chinese family system, with its oppression of women.

Pun Ngai chronicles women's struggles to form and live their identities; discover the range of choice, how much agency they actually have, among the different pushes and pulls of these systems; and maintain their senses of self in the face of often absurd circumstances that the larger systems determine.

After it made its revolution in China in the name of the urban working class, the Communist Party made the workers or proletarians (*gongren*) a privileged class. These proletarians were workers, neither male nor female, but the status of worker was out of reach of the vast rural peasantry. To ensure geographic stability, the socialist state registered people by their places of birth. A person's birthplace is important for identity and language as well as for getting the official papers that are necessary for travel and many other transactions.

This working class wasn't so much real as it was something necessary for Mao's communism—it was a product of state ideology. But Deng Xiaoping started neoliberal reforms, and his kind of communism imported global factories and denounces any practices or ideologies that might get in the way. One thing that would surely get in the way of these factories would be anything like class struggle. After all, the Communist state is collaborating with global capitalism.

But a product of that is a real working class. A lot of people are working for wages, as we discussed in chapter 6. This working class isn't just something people invented because it fit an ideology. In fact, the state would really rather that nobody noticed they were in the working class. So, in China, as the economic system changed and created a real working class, the state began to deny that there is any working class. Sound familiar? The Communist Party that was supposed to be the leaders of the working class now invites businessmen, managers, and capitalists to join it.

Most of the new workers are rural women who get temporary changes of their residency status so they can live in the growing manufacturing centers. The Chinese term *dagong* means "working for the boss" or "selling labor," and it means that you're selling your labor. If Mao's revolution was meant to free working people, those working people are now selling labor to capitalists with the blessings of the Communist state. The Chinese word *mei* means "younger sister," but it also means young and unmarried. Chinese put the two words together to get *dagongmei,* which means something like "factory girl."

The male counterpart is *dagongzai.* Industrial commodity labor is highly gendered, and the young women are constantly reminded formally and informally that their roles and their work are the roles and work of young women.

These women work long hours at exhausting jobs and live in crowded dormitories because they want to consume the stuff of modernity—they want to be modern women with fashionable clothes and makeup and hair. This consumer desire changes the disciplined and obedient factory girls into shameless sexual women who are seductive and liberated enough to release the lust of the consumer who always wants to buy more stuff. Their desire to be like city dwellers drives dagongmei fantasies of consumption that their wages cannot support. In fact, they are rural women—they walk and talk and act like rural women. No amount of makeup or new clothes can change that. In trying to live up to images of womanly beauty and disguise their rural origins, they just reinforce their class and gender differences.

In Mao's China, everyone was a comrade, neither male nor female, neither high nor low. Reform China replaces the classless, sexless comrade with sexualized consumers and producers in highly gendered workplaces. People seek identity in consumption. The more they try to move themselves away from rural poverty and become modern women, the greater their desire to consume, and the harder they work to get the money to buy the goods. Here is another self-intensifying loop. The more stuff they buy, the more they emphasize their original identity as rural women.

Chinese patriarchy worked as well with Chinese socialism as it does with capitalism. Urban men don't want these working girls as wives. At about the age of twenty-five, most women factory workers return to their villages to be married into the patriarchical households they were trying to escape.

There is no escape for the Arab women who work in Israeli factories. Anthropologist Israel Drori's ethnography (2000) shows how managers use cultural understandings to control women and make them subservient. They expand the local forms of patriarchy beyond the homes into their work lives to manage the women who produce clothing for the international market. He shows the cynical use of knowledge not to understand people or help them but to subordinate them on the job.

Drori documents the daily lives of Druze and Arab seamstresses and supervisors in the Galilee region of northern Israel as they fell in love and were torn from their lovers; as they anticipate establishing their own households; as they get married and are raped by husbands; as they work day in and day out to bring income into their male-dominated households.

Israeli managers act like fathers and brothers to control women as Arab men control daughters and sisters. These roles express closeness within relationships of unequal power. Women gain some autonomy through their work, but the work just puts patriarchy in another form in the factory; it doesn't let the women escape it.

Drori shows the seamstresses negotiating the shared culture of work in these plants by the way they give meaning to their work, negotiate with management, and attempt to redefine concepts of gender, rights, obligations, and autonomy in terms of familiar family values that bridge their home lives and their work lives. By relating to management as patriarchs, workers use the moral feelings and behavior they know from home. But this use of homelike relationships at work contributes to complex, self-contradictory, interlocking activities that can lead to conflict. The reconstruction of patriarchal relationships in the plants creates an organizational culture of control that maintains hierarchal relationships at work.

Management must create a work culture of shared meaning that derives from both local homes and their managerial responsibilities. If the managers want to use the women's labor, they have to do it in terms that are acceptable to the workers' male family and community members and keep the production lines running in the factories.

Drori had to make some hard choices of his own. To make room for his vivid ethnographic treatment of the lives of workers and managers in complex situations, he had to sacrifice discussing larger issues, such as the enduring violence of the area, the subjugation of peoples and their resistance and fight against it, as well as the struggle of labor to organize a collective voice through unions. While most organized labor in Israel belongs to the General Labor Union, the ethnography shows that such a structure is ineffective, perhaps counterproductive, for representing the interests of Arab and Druze women in the Israeli garment industry.

Seamstresses are not subservient, quiet, apathetic, or fatalistic but passionate, active, and determined to seize opportunities to better their lives when they arise. The problem is that such opportunities never arise. All of the passion, activity, noisiness, agency, and determination of these women comes to nothing without institutional structures that could make these women effective at changing rather than adapting to their situations.

This is the world you live in and on. The cell phones, computers, and HDTVs built in these factories across the globe connect all of us in a political economy like we've never experienced in the history of humankind. There is so much to learn, so much to understand of this new global system. The challenge is to never lose sight of the people.

Discussion Questions

- Without getting too personal about it, everyone read a clothing label from your own or someone else's clothing. Make a list of the countries your and your classmates' clothing comes from. What do these countries all have in common?
- See if you can find out whether any of the countries on your list are involved in a "structural readjustment" program.
- What kind of choices do you think the people who made your clothing had? In other words, do you think they really like working in those factories?
- If not, why do you think they are working there? What difference does this make to you? Should it make a difference? Why or why not?
- The next time you go clothes shopping, try to find clothes made in America. What do you think happened when clothing manufacturing moved out of this country? What kinds of jobs did people get after they lost their union textile or other manufacturing jobs?
- According to the federal government, how many jobs were created last year? Pick a sector of the economy, and find out what the average wage and benefits were for those jobs. Then figure out how that compares (adjusted for inflation) with the average wage and benefits of the same sector jobs in 1970. What does the difference do for families who want to buy a home? Let one parent stay at home to raise the children? Put their children through college? Retire early?
- What kind of questions would you ask politicians who promise to bring jobs to your community?

Suggested Reading

Collier, George A., with Elizabeth Lowery Quaratiello. *Basta! Land and the Zapatista Rebellion in Chiapas.* Chicago: Food First Books, 1999.

Drori, Israel. *The Seam Line: Arab Workers and Jewish Managers in the Israeli Textile Industry.* Stanford, CA: Stanford University Press, 2000.

Heyman, Josiah McC. *Life and Labor on the Border: Working People of Northeastern Sonora, Mexico, 1996–1986.* Tucson: University of Arizona Press, 1991.

Mills, Mary Beth. *Thai Women in the Global Labor Force: Consuming Desires, Contested Selves.* New Brunswick, NJ: Rutgers University Press, 1999.

Ngai, Pun. *Made in China: Women Factory Workers in a Global Workplace.* Durham, NC: Duke University Press, 2005.

17

The end is indeed near! *Photo from iStockphoto, © Nick Schlax. Used with permission.*

CHAPTER 17

THE END IS NEAR

You've met some of the characters—they are mostly nameless; they are the people. You won't know them by their celebrity in the news, but you may remember them by the name of the group they belong to—Icelandic fishers, Gulf Coast shrimpers, American blacks—or the part of the world where they live—Trobriand Islands, Truk, Burma, Thailand. You know some of the plot, some of the stage directions. It's a story based on the work of many anthropologists over many years.

There are questions of ethics and values—things like ethnocentrism and sexism and racism. There are questions about where you stand. Anthropologists usually stand with the people whose stories we tell, not with the kings or presidents or priests or rulers. But we do more than tell the stories; we try to understand why the stories are the way they are—the structures the people are living in and how they got to be that way.

We have seen that all things human are interconnected. Anthropology is holistic. There's a lot of complexity, but it's not so complex that you can't understand it. You just have to use your brain and the analytical skills you have learned and not be fooled by appearances.

Tom Robbins (1977) is a novelist, not an anthropologist. The Chink, one of the characters in his book *Even Cowgirls Get the Blues* (and yes, that's his name, politically incorrect though it may be—that's in fact part of the author's point because the character is Japanese), says, "Life isn't simple; it's overwhelmingly complex. The love of simplicity is an escapist drug, like alcohol. It's an antilife attitude. . . . Death is simple but life is rich. I embrace that richness, the more complicated the better" (256). Anthropologists often end books like this with stirring words. We think that's a great custom, so we're going to borrow some stirring words for you.

Charles Hockett (1973) talked about state systems. He called them civil society, meaning societies with cities. This is what he said about three-quarters of the way through the last century:

Not only cities but most aspects of the civil pattern have ceased to have any survival value. Minor tinkering will get us nowhere. Obviously we cannot return to tribalism. We need something totally new—something at the moment unimaginable.

Man's task in the twentieth century is not to kid around with limited political, economic, or religious loyalties. No institution—no family, no city, no church, no nation, no international organization—deserves our respect and support except insofar as it functions to promote the welfare of the entire human species. Man's task in the twentieth century is to disassemble the juggernaut [of civil society] itself, before it shakes to pieces and in the process destroys the precious chrysalis within. That is our only hope.

Can we do this?

Certainly we cannot if we continue to rely on the sorts of political leaders the nations of the world have chosen in recent decades—men with the breadth of perspective and imagination of a bunch of prunes. But it is not clear that other leaders could do any better. Despite our enormous collective ingenuity, it is possible that our problems now exceed our capacities. (670)

What do you call something that rings more true now than when it was written in 1973? Prophetic, maybe.

Anthropology lets us see the juggernaut. All the corporate think tanks and company-paid professors can't hide that. We go behind the simple answers of the thought controllers. We have seen the juggernaut too many times. Nowadays we see it in Afghanistan and Iraq; before we saw it in El Salvador, Guatemala, Nicaragua, the Spanish Civil War, Burma. Can we disassemble it?

Listen to Marvin Harris (1971):

If anthropology has any suggestion to those seeking to participate in the creation of novel varieties of personal and cultural life, it is that to change the world one must first understand it. The importance of this advice varies directly with the odds against the desired personal or sociocultural innovation. When the odds are drastically against a hoped-for outcome, ignorance of the causal factors at work amounts to moral duplicity. In this sense, the study of humanity has the force of a moral obligation; all who are interested in the survival and well being of Homo sapiens must find in it a common purpose. (596)

That's what anthropology does. That's what it is for. We have given you some of the tools of the trade. We've shown you how you can see through, behind, and into political and economic systems and the cultures that go with them. Today it's pretty obvious that all people live in a global system. The hunters of the Amazon use shotguns and sell game. Ecotourists are everywhere You can get to any place on the planet in a day or two. Even the remnant groups that most closely resemble foragers are parts of larger systems.

To understand the global system, we can't rely on the worm's-eye view of ethnography. You can't do classical ethnography where there are no communities—where the people you are trying to understand don't live in one single place but all over the place. Shrimpers in Mississippi, for instance. Or Teamsters in Chicago or longshore workers in Charleston.

So how do we do the ethnography of globalization? We're going to have to count on your collective ingenuity and creativity to do it. You have the foundation. You have strong shoulders to stand on. But you're the ones who are going to have to do the job.

We told you at the beginning that we'd tell you what anthropology knows. Human systems keep changing, and our knowledge of them has to change with them. Sometimes systems even define new rules—for instance, when finance takes over from management, and the money shamans are in control of our economic systems.

We know what economists do: they tell us that their religion is reality because it supports the capitalist system. In this they are very human, just like the Inca priests preaching that the god kings were natural and necessary.

There are a lot of different kinds of sociologists, and we can't go into that here, but one thing they do is take the polls and surveys and tell us how people are reacting to or dealing with the system to provide information to the people in charge so they can keep the system going, suggesting an occasional tweak here or there. Some of them do other things, pretty much as we're advocating here.

Many psychologists and therapists support the system, too. They have the tough work of helping individuals struggling with the constant contradictions of the system and trying not to go crazy or get totally depressed when they do everything they're supposed to do and it doesn't work out the way it's supposed to. Like those white-collar people who get fired and just know they deserve it. Working people who work hard all their lives and are still poor are in a better place than that. They hoped that stuff about hard work paying off was true, but they never experienced it. Psychologists and therapists try to convince folks to fix themselves rather than to mess with the system. The system is too big. It's quixotic to think about fixing that. Get used to it. And if you can't, maybe we can find some drugs that'll help.

Some anthropologists do most of the above, too. Some work for corporations to help them make money. Some work for governments to figure out how to convince people to accept programs that are going to hurt them. Some work for marketers to figure out how to get people to buy more stuff they don't need. Anthropologists can make a lot of money doing that kind of work, by the way.

But some help us to see things as they are—help us to see behind and beyond the mind-fog of state and media mind control to understand how our political economies and cultures work. In showing us those realities, these anthropologists provide alternatives to the system. To be fair here, we have to say that lots of sociologists, a few economists, and some psychologists also do that. And you don't have to be a scientist to see clearly. Lots of journalists, novelists, songwriters, and poets do that even better than we do, especially at getting the word out about what they've discovered.

Anthropologists aren't free of the kind of magic that economists use, either. To be an anthropologist, you pretty much have to go to graduate school and get a magic piece of paper called a Ph.D. Universities are one of the last hold-outs of medievalism. But we won't go into that here. You're experiencing your own brand of it.

You get a Ph.D., and that gives you the tools, some of the vision, and lets you see parts of the system at work. You can use the skills you've learned to tell other people the vision of anthropology—the vision of a single species and how we got to be the way we are and why it's important to make a fair world and not to settle for an unfair one. You can tell people what happens to unsustainable systems.

They'll say, "You don't understand—it's very complicated." They'll say, "But that's the way the market works." They'll say, "Actually, in reality, ..." And so on. But some will hear. Some will listen.

You'll have to get used to being pretty much invisible and having lots of people not paying you much attention. That's OK. They have other things to worry about. If you want to make a difference, if you want to help move toward a more fair system, anthropology is one thing to do. There are others. You may become a novelist or a journalist, a sociologist, or even (gasp) an economist, and you can still use what you've learned here.

The more you understand things clearly, the more choices you have. Understanding also brings responsibility. The greater your understanding, the greater your responsibility to the rest of the species. Shamans may be nuts, but they put that talent to work in the service of their people.

The better your understanding, the more agency you have. One of those choices is the ethical and political choice we mentioned earlier. Whenever it's up to you, be sure that what you do and say moves in the direction of everyone on the planet having one share. Not more and not less. It doesn't matter where you are. You may be a restaurant worker, a computer specialist, a sales "associate," a community organizer, or a businessperson. You will have that choice at times. The important thing is to recognize when it's yours and use it well.

You know the heroes of fiction—people like Zorro, Xena the warrior princess, Wonder Woman, Superman, Don Quixote. They all held justice close to their hearts as all of us learn to when we are kids. We are supposed to outgrow the stories of heroes like these when we give up on justice, when we grow up and accept that we live in an unjust world. These heroes all live in streamlined worlds where everything goes their way and they can overcome any obstacle the bad guys throw at them.

Except Don Quixote. He's nuts. He thinks he's living in a different time or a different reality than the rest of the people. In his eyes, the bar maid becomes the damsel of the castle, but he never despairs in his quest for justice.

The English-speaking world has picked up on the crazy part of his character, and the word *quixotic* means "at least impractical and bumbling, perhaps humorous, maybe nuts." To call someone quixotic is negative—a bad thing to be. Our friends who speak Spanish and Portuguese, however, tell us those folks pick up on the noble part of it and say it's positive—a good thing to be.

Different writers could make any of the legendary heroes of fiction into bumbling idiots disconnected from the realities of life. Since Cervantes, other writers have told stories of quixotic characters. One is in the movie *They Might Be Giants.* George C. Scott plays Justin Playfair, a judge who may think he's Sherlock Holmes. He wears the clothes and talks the talk. Joanne Woodward plays Dr. Mildred Watson, a shrink trying to figure out whether he's crazy. When she tells him that she's Dr. Watson, he says the game's afoot, and he drags her along on a crazy but somehow saner-than-it-looks adventure through New York.

At one point, she says, "You're just like Don Quixote. You think that everything is always something else."

"Well, he had a point," Playfair answers. "Of course, he carried it a bit too far. He thought that every windmill was a giant. That's insane. But, thinking that they might be, well . . . . All the best minds used to think the world was flat. But what if it isn't? It might be round. And bread mold might be medicine. If we never looked at things and thought of what might be, why, we'd all still be out there in the tall grass with the apes."

We know you didn't sign up for a course in comparative literature, but we want to end the book with something hopeful, something that lets you know that you have some choices to make. One of those choices is to keep on saying, "They might be giants," and keep on checking even if it makes you feel out of step, out of balance.

It's OK to be a little unbalanced. Anyone looking behind the curtain of his or her culture is going to feel uncomfortable and unbalanced. Most of our cultures these days tell us to accept unfairness. We're telling you that you don't have to. We're telling you that for the good of our species, none of us should accept it.

We once had the pleasure of hearing the author John Nichols speak. He's the guy who wrote *The Milagro Beanfield War* and other books that we've enjoyed reading because they help us see things clearly. This is what he said:

> You eat right, you exercise, and you still die. Everyone dies, but the point is to enjoy life. The sun goes nova and the history of the planet and the sun is a blink of an eye in time. It's equal to the life of a mosquito. In the final analysis everything is hopeless.
>
> Capitalism and so on. Any hope? You just keep on struggling.

If we keep on telling you how the world sucks, there's not much place for hope. So we're saying, yeah, the world sucks, but make it a better place. Keep on struggling. It's funny that to find so many heroes we have to go to fiction or myth. That's where we started this story. On the edge of the fire with the myth teller.

But we don't always have to resort to fiction. We can point to real-life heroes like Ken Riley or Martin Luther King Jr. or Gandhi, but we also know that to make them heroes is only to tell part of their stories. They were just ordinary people forced to do extraordinary things. You can look inside yourself to that part of you that knows that it should be a fair world and discover the extraordinary thing you will do.

You've learned why the world isn't fair and how it got that way. We're telling you now that it's up to you to make a difference. Most of us live in societies where we can still vote. A lot of Americans are pissed off with the one-party system we have to endure, the Republocrats, but we can still participate in one of its branches and try to get better nominees for offices. What would happen if everyone in the United States voted for their own interests? For the fair thing? It has happened once or twice in American history. During the Great Depression, for example, when the Republocrat bosses were shaking in their boots because it looked like there might be a revolution in the streets, they put up Franklin Delano Roosevelt with his New Deal. But the powers that be have been dismantling the New Deal ever since, hoping we'd all be too busy being good consumers or just trying to stay afloat to notice.

Could Americans do it again? Could we rock the boat enough to make them play fair for a while? This is a question that shook apart the United Farm Workers in the 1980s and shook apart the whole labor movement in the summer of 2005. Shall we use our time and resources on politics and trying to get good folks elected? Or do we organize our power in the workplaces by getting more people into unions and working for their own interests directly at work, and not even play the corporation political game of who buys which politician?

Either way, or any way you can imagine, to change the status quo requires one thing: organizing. If you'd like to learn more about that, go to the Web site for the Organizing Institute of the AFL-CIO. On your computer, you can sign up anywhere in the country. You can go to a seminar for a couple of days to learn what organizers do in the labor movement. If you like what you see and they like what they see, you can learn more and then get a job with a labor union. It'll pay wages and have benefits.

If unions don't trip your trigger, there are many other social action organizations where you can train as an organizer. It's not a job for family people, as Suzan can tell you. She's done it. But it gets you in touch with people. It's all there from the adrenaline rush to the nightmares that invade your dreams. You experience everything from crushing defeat to exhilarating victory. You'll work your ass off. You'll learn more than you ever thought you could. And you'll be doing good work. No matter what, you'll walk away with the skills to change the way things are, and you'll carry with you the insights you've learned from anthropology to help guide your way.

A former head of the Chicago Coalition for the Homeless was talking to Suzan one day. He was exasperated with a new batch of organizers he had hired. They had gone out to the homeless shelters, as organizers are supposed to do in their first few weeks, and had come back to him complaining about the treatment of the homeless people at these shelters. The food wasn't good. The bedding wasn't comfortable. The places weren't safe. He turned to Suzan and those organizers and said, "Our job is not to make the homeless shelters better. Our job is to get rid of the need for homeless shelters."

Answers depend on the questions. The question is not "Isn't a factory job for pennies a day a better alternative for third world people than no job at all?" The question is "Should anyone have to work in a factory? Should anyone have to work for pennies a day?"

This is the kind of view anthropology can give you. This is the difference you can make. We all face situations where we can do one thing or another. We know the right thing to do, and we also know that it's not the thing that pays off best or the thing that we're "supposed" to do. We're telling you it's OK: Do the right thing. Do the fair thing.

So in part, we're appealing to the Zorro, the Wonder Woman, the Xena, and the Superman in all of you. We're appealing to the Don Quixote in you, too. But we're saying be sure to check whether those really are giants. Use all of your knowledge and skill to find out what's really going on. Don't break your lances on windmills, but be willing to see those windmills in a new way. And be willing to call them giants if that's what they turn out to be.

But the problem with hero stories is that one hero always comes to save the day for a group of people. The people never think that they could organize themselves and work together to solve the problem themselves. They don't know the strength of their own numbers and their own intelligence. They wait around to be saved. They look for a hero. And, sure enough, in the stories, the hero comes and saves the day.

The Chink in *Cowgirls* is a weird guy who lives in a cave in the badlands. He has a reputation for being a prophet or holy man. Sometimes people make pilgrimages to see him, hoping that he can reveal something to them. He always refuses to see them because he refuses to be anyone's prophet. He says that by turning them away, he's setting them free before they become disciples. He says:

> All a person can do in this life is to gather about him his integrity, his imagination and his individuality—and with these ever with him, out front and in sharp focus, leap into the dance of experience.
> "Be your own master!
> "Be your own Jesus!
> "Be your own flying saucer! Rescue yourself.
> "Be your own valentine! Free the heart!" (p. 260)

So we say don't wait for some hero to show up. That's fiction. That only happens in stories. And we say you don't have to be that hero, either. Heroes are fictional, but we all have Zorro, Xena, Superman, and Wonder Woman inside us already. You don't have to be a celebrity, either. We don't know who made the first tool. We don't know who walked first on two feet or planted the first crop. They're the ones who started it all. Everyone since then is just a footnote. Einstein? Nothing compared to that first chopping tool. Attila the Hun? Genghis Khan? Alexander the Great? Who figured out a person could ride a horse? It's better if you're remembered by the group you belong to or the place you live, like the people anthropologists study. But organize that group so it can move the world. Make that place known for the hope it gives people who have lost all hope.

That's what it is to be human.

Suggested Reading

Robbins, Tom. *Even Cowgirls Get the Blues*. New York: Bantam, 1977.

GLOSSARY

Acephalous—without a head. A term British anthropologists used to describe egalitarian societies.

Adaptive—biologically speaking, a feature that lets more offspring survive and grow up to reproduce; culturally speaking, a feature that promotes the survival and well-being of most of the people in the system so it can continue.

Agency—the ability to make real choices. Agency depends on the choices systems make available as well as your position and power in the system. More power means more choices. But no matter where you are in any system, you have some choices.

Arbitrary, learned, and traditional—These three things go together. Anything that is arbitrary is not something people can figure out. They have to learn it. Anything we learn is traditional. This is a fact about languages. Their sounds and meanings are not built into the world or into us. There is no relationship between a thing and the word for it (arbitrary), they aren't coded into nature or genes (must be learned), and we learn them from others (traditional).

Archaeology—the field of anthropology that concentrates on gathering and interpreting material evidence we can use to understand the histories of our cultures. The nature of the evidence demands certain techniques, for instance, of excavation, but archaeologists are asking and helping to answer the same questions about cultural processes that cultural anthropologists are asking and answering, so there's a lot of interchange between archaeology and sociocultural anthropology. Many see them as the same thing but using different sources of evidence.

Aspiration—the puff of breath after a consonant—for example, after the *p* in *pit*. We use a superscript *h* to represent this sound.

Balanced reciprocity—People give exactly as much as they receive and receive exactly as much as they give.

Asymmetrical redistribution—redistributive exchange in which the center people do not give away everything received, but keep some of it to support themselves, their relatives, or specialists. See **redistribution**; **rank**.

Biological anthropology—the field of anthropology that focuses on the history of our species, how we came to be the kinds of animals we are, and the role of culture in the process—questions about our biological nature and its relationship to culture.

Bipedal—walking on two feet all the time.

Blaming the victim—when people blame destructive or malicious acts by others on the person on the receiving end. For instance, "If you didn't want to get injured, you shouldn't have gone to Iraq."

Capital—the money that buys the things someone needs to produce exchange values, to produce commodities to sell on markets to get the capital back plus some profit.

Capitalist system—system of production to produce **exchange value** and extract **profit** that is organized by markets.

Classes—groups of people in a political economy defined by their differential access to resources in a stratified system. See **stratification**; **political economy**; **state**.

Cline—what is created when all the points of the same elevation are connected. By extension, the line we create whenever we connect all of the dots in a diagram that are the same—for instance, barometric pressure on a weather map. It shows the distribution of a single value for a variable.

Commodity—something that people can buy and sell on a market.

Comparative—noticing and explaining similarities and differences among many different systems.

Core—the rock left in one's hand after breaking off a flake with a hammerstone to make a pebble tool.

Corporatist state—See **welfare state**.

Cross cousins—the children of ego's parent's siblings of the opposite sexes: father's sister's kids and mother's brother's kids.

Cultural adaptation—the way people solve problems. The solutions don't always work in the long run. The solutions may cause new problems or make old ones worse.

Cultural capital—a misleading metaphor for everything you know that might be of use to you in making a living. This is a misleading metaphor meant to convince people that everyone has some capital and that if you're not rich, it's because you haven't used your capital well. See the definition of *capital*. See also **blaming the victim**; **meritocratic individualism**; **deficit theory**. We say that cultural capital is not capital. It's knowledge.

Cultural codes—emic categories and the way people use them to make sense of their worlds and decide what to do.

Cultural ecology—an approach in anthropology that emphasizes that while all of the elements of a culture are interrelated, the parts that have most to do with the way people make their livings, the cultural core, are the most important and determine the rest.

Cultural relativity—suspending judgments and opinions and being open to understanding other ways of life. We don't ask whether something is good or bad; we ask how the people understand and use it.

Culture core—the social, political, and religious patterns most closely connected to the way people get their livings, central aspects of the culture.

Deep structure—the logical relationships between words to form sentences.

Deficit theory—the theory that if a particular group of people don't do something well, then something is wrong with those people. Often used to justify racism. Akin to **blaming the victim**. "You're experiencing this problem because something's wrong with you."

Dependent variable—a variable that hangs on, or depends on, other variables in the system. It is the thing we want to explain. The other values of the other variables determine the value of the dependent variable.

Descriptive relativism—suspending your natural ethnocentrism so that you can describe another culture from the point of view of the people in it.

Discrete—recognizably different according to some standard.

Displacement—being able to talk about different times, places, and hypothetical situations. Unique to human languages.

Drudgery—how much a person doesn't want to work anymore. The drudgery of labor depends on how important it is to produce whatever the people are working to produce.

Duality of patterning—languages have two different levels, sound and meaning, each with its own system of relationships.

Ecology—the total web of relationships among life forms in an area.

Economic capital—that which corporations convert into profit by using labor. See **capital**.

Economic system—the relationships of consumption, production, and exchange so that if one changes, the others also change.

Egalitarian—a political form in which there are as many positions of prestige as people capable of filling them. All have equal access to resources. See **acephelous**. Associated with reciprocal exchanges.

Emic—the differences that make a difference inside the culture or language. Those features of the world or sounds that cultures or languages define and recognize.

Epistemological relativity—the idea that all ways of knowing things are equally true.

Epistemology—how we know things. Different cultures define different ways of knowing things. A set of assumptions that governs what and how we think and how we see the world and act within it. Cultures are epistemologies.

Ethical relativism—the idea that there are no absolute values of good and bad; ethical judgments depend on the culture.

Ethnocentric—displaying **ethnocentrism**.

Ethnocentrism—thinking that your way of doing things is either the only way or the best way. The opposite of **cultural relativity**.

Ethnographic—basing our ideas of how any given system works on detailed local description and observation. Being with the people we want to understand and seeing things from their point of view.

Ethnography—living with a people and observing everything they do and say. See **ethnographic**.

Etic—all the differences that anyone outside the system can see. People inside the system may not see it the same way, but if we only valued the inside views, we could never compare different systems. The etic stance lets us stand outside any culture to understand them all.

Exchange value—value determined by the amount of labor it takes to produce something. How much you can get for something if you trade it for another thing.

Exponential—every time the value of something is increased on the horizontal axis, the value on the vertical axis gets bigger by doubling or by squaring or by *multiplying* by some value instead of by always *adding* the same amount. So the bigger it gets, the faster it gets bigger.

Federal system—a group of groups in which each member group recognizes a central authority. For instance, each state in the United States recognizes the authority of the U.S. government. But each state retains certain powers and rights.

Feuds—fights between groups of people who are usually related, often started out of vengeance.

Fieldwork—living with the people. See **ethnography**.

Firms—production units of **capitalist** systems.

Flake—the small piece of a rock that breaks off when you strike a core with a **hammerstone**.

Free labor—people who are available to work for wages because they have no alternatives, such as household production, or are not caught up in alternative systems of production, such as slavery.

General reciprocity—giving to or helping others without any specific expectation of return, but with a general expectation that others will help you or give to you when you need it.

Grammar—the theory of a language that an adult speaker of the language develops by growing up around people who speak it. It specifies the relationships between sound and meaning.

Hammerstone—the rock used to hit the core to create a pebble tool.

Hand axes—stone tools that are symmetrical on both sides. People made these according to a plan they had in mind. Much more complex than pebble tools.

Hegemony—when one country rules or controls others. A term often used by anthropologists for when one group has control over another, especially by controlling the way they think. For instance, some say that the rulers have hegemony over the cultural codes of the ruled because the rulers shape the way people think in schools, media, and religious institutions.

Holism—seeing things as connected. Instead of looking at religion, literature, politics, economics, or history as separate spheres of life, anthropologists see them as connected.

Household production—production units based on the balance of need and drudgery.

Ideologies—almost a synonym for **cultural codes** when they are used for political ends. When ideologies are political—conservatism, liberalism—the people select parts of their cultural code to support one political position.

Import substitution—substituting your own products for imports.

Incest prohibition—a prohibition on having sex with certain relatives.

Independent variable—the variable that causes or has something to do with the dependent variable. A change in the value of an independent variable causes a change in dependent ones.

Individual transferable quotas (ITQs)—quotas based on the history of a fisher's catch in the past that can be bought or sold.

Interdependent variables—when an increase or decrease in the value of one variable creates an increase or decrease in another and the second variable, the interdependent one, passes it on to a third.

Kindreds—the group of all relatives within a certain genealogical distance who are related by any link at all—for instance, all first cousins.

Lineages—a group of people all related to a common ancestor through either the link with women or the link with men.

Linguistic anthropology—the field of anthropology that studies the nature of language and how it is related to the rest of culture.

Locomotion—moving around.

Loop—following a series of arrows in a system brings you back to the starting point.

Marginal utility—the usefulness of the next thing compared with the one before.

Market exchange—exchanging things in terms of exchange value. Usually involves money.

Markets—places where things are exchanged; the exchange of things according to **exchange values**.

Matrilineal lineages—a group of people descended from the same ancestor through women.

Matrilocal (also uxorilocal)—residing with the wife's people.

Meritocratic individualism—the belief that we are separate individuals who think for ourselves and that we get rewarded according to our individual merit.

Mind control—See **thought control**.

Mutual grooming—the practice of going through each other's fur looking for things that shouldn't be there and removing them.

Nationalism—when a nation claims to be the best one.

Natural capital—a misleading metaphor for natural resources, like coal and iron ore, that someone has access to. This is a metaphor used to make people think that natural resources are really a kind of capital. Compare with the definition of *capital*.

Natural selection—the process by which those characteristics that allow individuals to have more offspring become more widely spread in the population (selected for) and those that allow individuals to have fewer offspring become more rare (selected against). See **adaptive**.

Necessary labor—the amount of labor to produce necessary value, the value necessary to reproduce the same amount of labor.

Necessary value—the amount of value that necessary labor produces. Capitalist firms pay this amount as wages so that workers can continue to work and reproduce labor.

Negative utility—a metaphor based on the idea of utility as usefulness. Negative usefulness would be something damaging.

Neo-conservatives—people who believe in an ideology that advocates a global market policed and controlled by American arms for American objectives.

Neolocal—residing in a different place from the family of either mate.

Open, openness—a feature of human language that allows us to say new things that have never been said before so that we don't just repeat what we've heard.

Opposable thumbs—being able to move the thumb just opposite fingertips to grasp things between the tips of thumbs and fingers.

Parallel cousins—the children of the parent's siblings of the same sex—father's brothers and mother's sister's kids.

Patrilineal lineages—a group of people of the same ancestor linked through the men.

Patrilocal (also virilocal)—residing with the husband's people.

Pebble tools—large pebbles with a **flake** or two knocked off to make a sharp edge.

Phoneme—each distinct sound that any human language understands as different from other ones. Different languages recognize different sounds. Each language uses between thirteen and forty of them.

Phonemic—as of or pertaining to phonemes. A phonemic system is the set of sounds the native speakers actually hear and distinguish as distinct.

Phonetics—all the sounds people can actually make. People put different phonetic sounds together to make single phonemes, like t^s and t^b and p and p^b in English.

Phonological system—specifies the relationships among sounds in a language.

Political economy—the interacting economic and political systems.

Polymorphic—of many forms.

Price—largely but not exclusively determined by value. May be higher or lower depending on such factors as fashion.

Profit—surplus value that the owners of capital appropriate and may put back into production or into political action or consumption.

Qualitative—something that cannot be counted, quantified; for example, how good the smell of baking bread is when you smell it on an evening walk in the fall.

Quantitative—something that can be counted.; for example, the number of molecules of bread you have to inhale before you can detect the smell of baking bread.

Rank—a political form in which there is equal access to resources but fewer positions of prestige than people capable of filling them. Associated with redistributive exchange.

Reciprocity—giving as much as you get, at least in the long run. There's usually a time delay between the giving and the getting.

Redistribution—based on reciprocity, but instead of people giving things directly to each other, giving things to some central person who then redistributes them to the people who need them.

Redistributive system—a system of exchange based on redistribution.

Regulating mechanism—a part of the system that keeps the values of variables within certain limits.

Reliability—the notion that everybody else who checks the same thing will get the same results.

Residence rule—a pattern of where newly married couples live.

Ruling class—that class in a stratified political economy that has access to resources. See **class**; **political economy**; **stratification**; **state**.

Science—the epistemology that we never accept anything as really true, just as what we *think* we know until we find out differently by checking it over and over again against what we can observe. Science is based on **reliability** and **validity** as well as the assumptions that we base theories on. When valid and reliable observations don't match theories, we change the theories.

Self-help—if someone has done you harm, you harm that person back. See **feud**. This may mean not harming the same individual but harming his or her kinship group, village, or other social group.

Self-intensifying loop—See **loop**. In a system without a regulating mechanism, each trip through the loop makes the values of the variables get greater. See also **exponential**.

Semantic system—all the possible relationships among meanings in a language.

Sexual dimorphism—two forms by sex; the physical differences between sexes.

Shaman—a person spirits can possess.

Social capital—a misleading metaphor for the people someone knows who can help when needed. The idea is that social relations can help people. But the metaphor is misleading because it's meant to convince us that we all have some kind of capital even if we don't because we all have some social relations that can be useful to us. See **capital**; **blaming the victim**; **meritocratic individualism**; **deficit theory**.

Social contract—the idea that people support their governments when the governments actually help the people.

Sociocultural anthropology—the field of anthropology that studies how contemporary cultures and societies work and how they got this way.

State—the institutional structures in stratified political economies that enforce and ensure unequal access to resources. Based on force or **thought control** or both. See **stratification**; **hegemony**; **ruling class**; **subordinate classes**.

Stratification—a political economy in which there is unequal access to resources. See **state**.

Structure—how things are put together with other similar things. Grammatical structure is how elements of language relate to each other so we can connect sounds to meanings. Kinship structure is how different kinds of kin-based groups are organized. Political structure is how different aspects of political systems are organized (see **federal system**; **welfare state**). Economic structure is how parts of economic systems are put together. As a general term, it means how things are organized. See **agency**. Agency is our own sense of control and ability to decide. Structure is outside our immediate control, though we can change it with concerted effort.

Subordinate classes—those classes in stratified political economies that do not have access to resources. See **stratification**; **class**; **political economy**; **state**.

Surface structure—the particular word order in a language.

Surplus labor—the amount of labor people do after they've produced the value necessary for them to work another day and reproduce. To get people to do it, you have to have a system that doesn't allow them any other alternatives, often based on force.

Surplus value—the extra value that **surplus labor** produces, the source of **profit** in capitalist systems.

Sustainable—a system that does not have a **self-intensifying loop** and can continue in operation indefinitely.

Swidden—slash-and-burn fields.

Syntax—the way deep structure and surface structure fit together as two parts of grammar.

System—a set of elements connected such that if you change one of them, you change the others.

Thought control—ruling-class control of cultural codes to make people think their political economy is natural and inevitable, ordained by gods or history as the only possible political economy and to make people think they have little or no agency to use in changing the system. See **classes**; **ruling class**; **subordinate classes**; **state**; **hegemony**; **agency**; **structure**.

Universal grammar—the grammar that all human languages have in common.

Use value—the **qualitative** value of something based on its use. What people use something for.

Validity—means that you're really measuring what you think you are measuring.

Variable—something that can be more or less; it varies.

Wages—the amount that firms pay people for working. It must equal the amount of value it takes to continue to work and reproduce labor (see **necessary value**). Historically, people do not work for wages unless there are no alternatives. In return for allowing the people who get necessary value for wages for their work to work, firms expect workers to produce more than that amount (see **surplus value**), which is the source of profits.

Welfare state (also corporatist state)—a government in which businesses, labor, professionals with technical knowledge and experience, and government officials all negotiate together to make policies that benefit everyone. For instance, farmers, agribusinesses, the department of agriculture, and the people elected officials appoint in a ministry of agriculture would all negotiate together to make agricultural policy. Everyone has a voice through such organizations. The usual examples are Sweden and other Scandinavian countries.

REFERENCES

Apostle, Richard A., Gene Barrett, Peter Holm, Svein Jentoft, Leigh Mazany, Knut Mikalsen, and Bonnie McCay
1998 *Community, State, and Market on the North Atlantic Rim: Challenges to Modernity in the Fisheries.* Toronto: University of Toronto Press.

Bakan, Joel
2004 *The Corporation: The Pathological Pursuit of Profit and Power.* New York: Free Press.

Beckford, George L.
1972 *Persistent Poverty: Underdevelopment in Plantation Economies of the Third World.* New York: Oxford University Press. (Reissued 2000, Kingston: University of West Indies Press.)

Bell, Kirsten
2005 Genital Cutting and Western Discourses on Sexuality. *Medical Anthropology Quarterly* 19, no. 2: 125-148.

Bigelow, Gordon
2005 Let There Be Markets. *Harper's Magazine,* 310, no. 1860, May 2005: 33-38.

Bonanno, Alessandro, and Douglas Constance
1996 *Caught in the Net: The Global Tuna Industry, Environmentalism, and the State.* Lawrence: University Press of Kansas.

Brodkin, Karen
1988 *Caring by the Hour: Women, Work and Organizing at Duke Medical Center.* Urbana: University of Illinois Press.
2000 Global Capitalism: What's Race Got to Do with It? *American Ethnologist* 27, no. 2: 237-256.

Chayanov, A. V.
1986 *The Theory of Peasant Economy.* Madison: University of Wisconsin Press.

Collier, George A., with Elizabeth Lowery Quaratiello
1994 *Basta! Land and the Zapatista Rebellion in Chiapas.* Oakland, CA: Food First Books.

Drori, Israel
2000 *The Seam Line: Arab Workers and Jewish Managers in the Israeli Textile Industry.* Stanford, CA: Stanford University Press.

Doukas, Dimitra
2003 *Worked Over: The Corporate Sabotage of an American Community.* Ithaca, NY: Cornell University Press.

Durrenberger, E. Paul

1989 *Lisu Religion.* DeKalb: Northern Illinois University Center for Southeast Asian Studies.

1992 *The Dynamics of Medieval Iceland: Political Economy and Literature.* Iowa City: University of Iowa Press.

Durrenberger, E. Paul, and Suzan Erem

2005 *Class Acts: An Anthropology of Service Workers and their Union.* Boulder, CO: Paradigm Publishers.

Ehrenreich, Barbara

1990 *Fear of Falling: The Inner Life of the Middle Class.* New York: Perennial.

2001 *Nickel and Dimed: On (Not) Getting by in America.* New York: Metropolitan Books.

2005 *Bait and Switch: The (Futile) Pursuit of the American Dream.* New York: Metropolitan Books.

Ekvall, Robert

1968 *Fields on the Hoof: Nexus of Tibetan Nomadic Pastoralism.* New York: Holt, Rinehart and Winston.

Elliston, Deborah A.

1995 Erotic Anthropology: "Ritualized Homosexuality" in Melanesia and Beyond. *American Ethnologist* 22, no. 4: 848–867.

Emihovich, Catherine.

2005 Fire and Ice: Activist Ethnography in the Culture of Power. *Anthropology and Education Quarterly* 36, no. 4: 305–314.

Erem, Suzan

2001 *Labor Pains: Inside America's New Union Movement.* New York: Monthly Review Press.

Fink, Deborah

1998 *Cutting into the Meatpacking Line: Workers and Change in the Rural Midwest.* Chapel Hill: University of North Carolina Press.

Frank, Thomas

2004 *What's the Matter with Kansas? How Conservatives Won the Heart of America.* New York: Metropolitan Books.

Galbraith, John Kenneth

1992 *The Culture of Contentment.* Boston: Houghton Mifflin.

Goldschmidt, Walter

2006 *The Bridge to Humanity: How Affect Hunger Trumps the Selfish Gene.* New York: Oxford University Press.

Goodenough, Ward H.

1956 Residence Rules. *Southwestern Journal of Anthropology* 12, no. 1: 22–37.

Hanks, Lucien

1972 *Rice and Man: Agricultural Ecology in Southeast Asia.* Chicago: Aldine-Atherton.

Harris, Marvin

1971 *Culture, Man, and Nature: An Introduction to General Anthropology.* New York: Crowell.

1974 *Cows, Pigs, Wars, and Witches: The Riddles of Culture.* New York: Random House.

Henry, Jules

1963 *Culture against Man.* New York: Random House.

Heyman, Josiah McC.
1991 *Life and Labor on the Border: Working People of Northeastern Sonora, Mexico, 1996-1986.* Tucson: University of Arizona Press.

Hockett, Charles
1973 *Man's Place in Nature.* New York: McGraw-Hill.

Jolly, Alison
1972 *The Evolution of Primate Behavior. New York: Macmillan.*

Lapham, Lewis H.
2004 Tentacles of Rage: The Republican Propaganda mill, A Brief History. *Harper's* 309 (September).

Lave, Jean
1988 *Cognition in Practice: Mind, Mathematics and Culture in Everyday Life.* New York: Cambridge University Press.

Leach, Edmund
1954 *Political Systems of Highland Burma.* Boston: Beacon.

Lowie, Robert H.
1948 *Primitive Religion.* New York: Liveright.

Malinowski, Bronislaw
1922 *Argonauts of the Western Pacific: An Account of Native Enterprise and Adventure in the Archipelagoes of Melanesian New Guinea.* Long Grove, IL: Waveland Press (reprinted).

Mead, Margaret
1950 *Sex and Temperament in Three Primitive Societies.* New York: Mentor.

Mills, Mary Beth
1999 *Thai Women in the Global Labor Force: Consuming Desires, Contested Selves.* New Brunswick, NJ: Rutgers University Press.

Montoya, Miguel
2002 Emerging Markets, Globalization, and the Small Investor: The Case of Venezuela. In *Economic Development: An Anthropological Approach* edited by J. H. Cohen and N. Dannhaeuser. Walnut Creek, CA: AltaMira. Pages 265-289.

Montoya, Monica Lindh de
2002 Looking into the Future: Anthropology and Financial Markets. In *Economic Development: An Anthropological Approach* edited by J. H. Cohen and N. Dannhaeuser. Walnut Creek, CA: AltaMira. Pages 241-264.

Nash, June
2001 *Mayan Visions: The Quest for Autonomy in an Age of Globalization.* New York: Routledge.

Newman, Katherine
1993 *Declining Fortunes: The Withering of the American Dream. New York: Basic Books.*
1999 *No Shame in My Game: The Working Poor in the Inner City.* New York: Knopf

Ngai, Pun
2005 *Made in China: Women Factory Workers in a Global Workplace.* Durham, NC: Duke University Press.

Nichols, John
1974 *The Milagro Beanfield War.* New York: Holt, Rinehart and Winston.

Orwell, George

1952 *Homage to Catalonia.* New York: Harcourt, Brace. (Originally published in 1938 by Secker and Warburg, London.)

Pálsson, Gísli

1989 Language and Society: The Ethnolingiuistics of Icelanders. In *The Anthropology of Iceland* edited by E. Paul Durrenberger and Gísli Pálsson. Iowa City: University of Iowa Press. Pages 121-139.

Rappaport, Roy

1967 *Pigs for the Ancestors: Ritual in the Ecology of a New Guinea People.* New Haven, CT: Yale University Press.

Reed, Adolph

2001 *Class Notes: Posing as Politics and Other Thoughts on the American Scene.* New York: New Press.

Richardson, Miles

1975 Anthropologist—The Myth Teller. *American Ethnologist* 2, no. 3: 517-533.

Robbins, Tom

1977 *Even Cowgirls Get the Blues. New York: Bantam.*

Sahlins, Marshall

1968 Culture and Environment: The Study of Cultural Ecology. In *Theory in Anthropology: A Sourcebook* edited by Robert A. Manners and David Kaplan. Chicago, Aldine. Pages 367-373.

1989 *Social Stratification in Polynesia.* American Ethnological Society Monographs No. 29. Brooklyn: AMS Press.

Schlosser, Eric

2002 *Fast Food Nation: The Dark Side of the All-American Meal.* New York: Harper.

Scott, James

1985 *Weapons of the Weak: Everyday Forms of Peasant Resistance.* New Haven, CT: Yale University Press.

Spiro, Melford

1966 Religion: Problems of Definition and Explanation. In *Anthropological Approaches to the Study of Religion* edited by Michael Banton. New York: Tavistock. Pages 85-126.

1991 *Anthropological Other or Burmese Brother? Studies in Cultural Analysis.* Somerset, NJ: Transaction.

1996 *Burmese Supernaturalism.* New Brunswick, NJ: Transaction. (This is a reissue of the expanded edition published in 1978 by the Institute for the Study of Human Issues, which was based on the original 1967 edition from Prentice Hall.)

Steward, Julian

1955 *Theory of Culture Change: The Methodology of Multilinear Evolution.* Urbana: University of Illinois Press.

Stiglitz, Joseph

2003 *Globalization and Its Discontents.* New York: Norton.

Tattersall, Ian

2004 Innovation in Human Evolution. In *The Epic of Evolution: Science and Religion in Dialogue* edited by James B. Miller. Upper Saddle River, NJ: Pearson. Pages 91-98.

Wallace, Anthony
1956 Revitalization Movements. *American Anthropologist* 58, no. 2: 264–281.
White, Curtis
2004 *The Middle Mind: Why Americans Don't Think for Themselves.* New York: Harper.
Williams, Brett
2004 *Debt for Sale: A Social History of the Credit Trap.* Philadelphia: University of Pennsylvania Press.
Wolf, Diane
1992 *Factory Daughters: Gender, Household Dynamics, and Rural Industrialization in Java.* Berkeley: University of California Press.
Yates, Michael D.
2003 *Naming the System: Inequality and Work in the Global Economy.* New York: Monthly Review Press.
Zinn, Howard
2003 *A People's History of the United States: 1492–Present.* New York: HarperCollins.

Sources for Nasrudin and Sufi Stories

Ornstein, Robert
1972 *The Psychology of Consciousness.* New York: Viking.Shah, Idries
1968 *The Way of the Sufi.* London: Jonathan Cape.
1973 *The Subtleties of the Inimitable Mulla Nasrudin.* London: Jonathan Cape
1977 *Pleasantries of the Incredible Mulla Nasrudin.* Therford, Norfolk, UK: Lowe & Brydone.

INDEX

absurdity, 134
accountability: lack of in the global system, 228
adaptation, 14-21; lack of in the global system, 229-230
affect hunger, 16
agency, xvii, xviii, 16, 140, 201; and awareness, 139, 171, 194; and choice, 161, 167; and class, 171, 198; and action, 194; illusion of, 198; lack of, 249; of Arab women, 254
aggression, 17, 18, 33
agriculture: Tsembaga, 72-76; Lisu, 86, 87; Shan, 102, 111; Medieval Iceland, 118-127; commercial, 205-218; industrial, 205-218
America: not attractive to medieval Icelanders, 125, 126; spin doctors, 130; equality, 131, 132
anthropology, xiii, xv, xxi; main question of, 5; four fields of, 5; biological, 5 (*see also* biological anthropology), sociocultural, 5 (*see also* sociocultural anthropology); basic assumptions of, 5; job of, 40; beyond academic, 194
archaeology, 5
Archer Daniels Midland, 76, 227
Apostle, Richard, 222
attorneys and class, 200
Aztec, 6, 223, 224

Bakan, Joel, 136
Beckford, George, 223
belief, 9, 150-158; in state religions, 139
Bell, Kirsten, 38, 39
biological anthropology, 5, 11, 31
bipedalism, 12-21
blaming the victim, 51
Bonanno, Alessandro, 244
Brodkin, Karen, 201
Buddhism, 131-132, 150-151; Shan sermons, 155; as a state religion, 156
bureaucrats: mealy-mouthed language of, 48
Burma, 206; real name of, 102; military dictator of, 102; religions of, 150, 151

Canada, 222-224
capital, 91, 193; kinds of, 194; metaphoric, as thought control, 194, 195; and race in the United States, 201; and agriculture, 207-218
capitalism, 91-105, 135, 156, 193; development of, 104-105, 165; maintained by policy, 105, 165; and agriculture, 205-214; in Russia, 213-214; conditions for, 213; globalization and, 221-239; in China, 251-253; any hope? 262
cars, xvi, xviii, 194, 196, 223
causality, xviii, 206, 243, 246
Chandler, Raymond, 185
change: possibility of, 179, 260; collective action and, 180-181, 193; and understanding, 194, 260; requires organizing, 263
Chavez, Hugo, 238
Chayanov, A.V., 95, 96, 211-216
chieftain, 109, 110-112; Icelandic, 113, 117-127, 143, 187, 224
China: revolution in, 213; KMT, 102; and Wal-Mart, 231; women factory workers in, 251-253
choice(s), xvii, 16, 66-68, 161; understanding and, 260; structure of, 105, 118, 166, 167; and force, 112, 198; illusion of, 137, 179, 180, 196; defined by political economics, 166, 249; as part of culture, 180; women's in China, 252-253; and fairness, 261
Chomsky, Noam, 50
class, ix, 30, 40, 52, 185-202; Shan, 103; stratification and, 110; states and, 129-142, 187, 221; evolution of, 141; and agency, 171, 179; in the United States, 188, 196; politics of, 191, 221; importance of for anthropology, 196; academics make invisible, 198
collective action, 179-180, 193, 198, 231; and cooperatives, 209; and heroes, 264
Collier, George, 250
container shipping, 222, 231
color, skin, 27-33, 40
commodity, 84, 89, 156, 166, 193

ABOUT THE AUTHORS

Paul Durrenberger received a PhD in anthropology from the University of Illinois at Urbana in 1971. He has taught at Antioch College, Eastern New Mexico University, the University of South Alabama, the University of Iceland, the University of Iowa, and is now a professor of anthropology at Penn State University. His many years of teaching introductory courses in anthropology are one foundation for this book. The other is his years of fieldwork among Lisu tribal people of the Thai highlands, Shan peasants in the lowlands of northwest Thailand, in Iceland, and in the United States. In the United States he has done ethnographic work with fishermen in Mississippi and Alabama, farmers in Iowa, and union members in Chicago and Pennsylvania. He has published numerous academic articles and books on these subjects. He is active in the American Anthropological Association, the Society for Applied Anthropology, and the Society for Economic Anthropology. He collaborates with archaeologists John Steinberg and Doug Bolender in archaeological investigations of medieval Iceland. His webpage's address is: *http://www.personal.psu.edu/faculty/e/p/epd2/* and his e-mail address is epd2@psu.edu.

Suzan Erem earned her Journalism and English degrees from the University of Iowa in 1985 and then spent more than a dozen years working in the labor movement before becoming a freelance writer. As an undergraduate, she was frustrated with anthropology that seemed confusing and irrelevant, but she saw its potential for making sense of the modern world. She is author of *Labor Pains: Inside America's New Union Movement* (Monthly Review Press 2001) and coauthor with Diana Dell of *Do I Want to be a Mom? A Woman's Guide to the Decision of a Lifetime.* A long-time member of the National Writers Union, UAW Local 1981, Suzan's client list has included the American Federation of State, County and Municipal Employees (AFSCME), International Brotherhood of Teamsters, Service Employees International Union (SEIU), Leukemia & Lymphoma Society of Illinois, Infant Welfare Society, AIDSCare, Healthcare Alternative Systems and others. She can be reached through her Website: www.lastdraft.com.

Paul and Suzan coauthored *Class Acts: An Anthropology of Service Workers and Their Union* (Paradigm 2005), and collaborated on a National Science Foundation study of unions in Chicago and Pennsylvania. They are currently coauthoring a book on a 2000–2001 battle between Charleston longshoremen and the South Carolina attorney general. They are married and live in State College, Pennsylvania.